Praise for The Theology

"This is a book to be savoured like a beautiful meal. Its understanding of the Eucharist springs from both a profound study of the Scriptures and the traditions of the Church, and also a sensuous delight in that most intimate and sustaining of human activities, cooking and eating. This nourishing theological work also challenges us to build a society in which all of humanity shares at the common table of God".
Timothy Radcliffe, OP, Blackfriars – Oxford University

"This book deserves to be widely read and, if you will forgive the metaphor, digested."
Christian Century

"Montoya's book is a delight to read, and is a significant contribution to the effort to apply theological thinking to the everyday realities of embodied life."
Modern Theology

"For all its erudition, this book is more complex and valuable than a simple examination of Christian consumption. It offers rich reflection on the prophetic and generous ways in which Christianity might still disciple consumers who desire the superabundant grace made material in the flesh of Jesus Christ."
Theological Book Review

"This much-needed book takes seriously the Churches' unique contribution to understanding the importance of food."
Church Times

"A thought provoking and engaging work on the role of the Eucharist in Christian life."
CHOICE

Illuminations: Theory and Religion

Series editors: Catherine Pickstock, John Milbank, and Graham Ward

Religion has a growing visibility in the world at large. Throughout the humanities there is a mounting realization that religion and culture lie so closely together that religion is an unavoidable and fundamental human reality. Consequently, the examination of religion and theology now stands at the centre of any questioning of our western identity, including the question of whether there is such a thing as "truth."

ILLUMINATIONS aims both to reflect the diverse elements of these developments and, from them, to produce creative new syntheses. It is unique in exploring the new interaction between theology, philosophy, religious studies, political theory and cultural studies. Despite the theoretical convergence of certain trends they often in practice do not come together. The aim of ILLUMINATIONS is to make this happen, and advance contemporary theoretical discussion.

The Theology of Food: Eating and the Eucharist

Angel F. Méndez-Montoya

WILEY-BLACKWELL

A John Wiley & Sons, Ltd., Publication

This paperback edition first published 2012
© 2012 Angel F. Méndez-Montoya

Edition history: Blackwell Publishing Ltd (hardback, 2009)

Blackwell Publishing was acquired by John Wiley & Sons in February 2007. Blackwell's
publishing program has been merged with Wiley's global Scientific, Technical, and Medical
business to form Wiley-Blackwell.

Registered Office
John Wiley & Sons, Ltd, The Atrium, Southern Gate, Chichester, West Sussex, PO19 8SQ, UK

Editorial Offices
350 Main Street, Malden, MA 02148-5020, USA
9600 Garsington Road, Oxford, OX4 2DQ, UK
The Atrium, Southern Gate, Chichester, West Sussex, PO19 8SQ, UK

For details of our global editorial offices, for customer services, and for information about
how to apply for permission to reuse the copyright material in this book please see our
website at www.wiley.com/wiley-blackwell.

The right of Angel F. Méndez-Montoya to be identified as the author of this work has been
asserted in accordance with the UK Copyright, Designs and Patents Act 1988.

Library of Congress Cataloging-in-Publication Data

Méndez-Montoya, Angel F.
    Theology of food : eating and the Eucharist / Angel F. Méndez-Montoya.
      p.   cm. – (Illuminations)
    Includes bibliographical references and index.
    ISBN 978-1-4051-8967-5 (hardcover : alk. paper) – ISBN 978-0-470-67498-7
    (pbk. : alk. paper)
  1. Lord's Supper–Catholic Church.   2. Food–Religious aspects–Catholic Church.
  3. Catholic Church–Doctrines.   I. Title.
    BX2215.3.M463 2009
    234′.163–dc22
                                                      2008047633

A catalogue record for this book is available from the British Library.

Set in 10.5/12pt Sabon by SPi Publisher Services, Pondicherry, India

1   2012

Contents

Foreword

When the World Began

In the beginning was the Word. It was only when human beings appeared that the Word became food on a table. We know that language allows us to understand each other and to express what we think and feel. We humans, however, are more than language. We humans are *cookingage*, i.e., that which allows us to prepare the food with which we can nourish not only our body, but also our spirit. It was when we started to cook our first meals and when we started to conjugate the incarnate Word that we noticed that we were human. Both table and Word humanize us. No wonder it is essential that the table on which our meals are served be conjoined with good conversation: at the table, the word is essential.

Although plants must have been the main ingredient of primitive diets, through a series of leaps forward – from when people began hunting to the agriculture of the Mesopotamian lands with their spices and seasonings – we arrived at the delicious dishes served at feasts, with their exotic fruits and roast meats. Thus food came to be not only our physical sustenance, but also part of the customs and rites of the peoples of the world.

Today, I face the marvelous challenge of inviting readers to journey through the pages of this book, which Angel Méndez, a Dominican friar and doctor in philosophical theology, sets before us. Page by page, it leads us along a pathway that is deeply committed to history and to our ancestors' way of life: those who filled our lives with flavor, from the primitive gatherings round cooking fires to the dinner-party table, turning each meal into a celebratory rite.

Friar Méndez, with his profound knowledge of alimentary theology, will make us re-create the fact that *mole* may well act as a pathway to love. This link, out of which the spirit of love gradually emerged – a spirit that must be present whenever we sit down to eat – means that in eating we satiate not only the hunger of our stomach, but also the hunger of our spirit in the very act of sharing. It's true, however, that the presence of love is often lacking at the table, even though the abundant dishes laid on it are excessive. The amalgamation of food and love, manifested in the act of sharing and celebrating a eucharistic meal, is becoming less and less common.

I cherish the hope that we will be able to make each one of the ingredients that Friar Angel shows us and teaches us about grow in shared love, and that we may thus offer them to the Almighty Maker, without keeping them to ourselves in our insecurity – as the ancient Israelites tried to do with manna. The deep commitment, of body and soul that Friar Angel thus has to the perfect culmination of a holy day in his delectable contemplation of the Eucharist will help us achieve that state of ecstasy which engages all our humanity – physical and spiritual.

Dearest reader, you are welcome to wander along the marvelous, winding path that takes the form of sentences, history, and the exposition of ways of life and faith. With love and mastery, Friar Angel Méndez introduces us to a gastronomic experience that takes us to the very roots of the holy everlasting supper.

Our table is a table of hope and charity – or caritas, as Friar Méndez notes. Wherever hope is great, caritas should be even greater. The more we love what we trust, the more we love what we hope for. Just as our bodily eyes see through the sunlit air, so caritas makes spiritual use of its qualities through hope, and hope through charity.

A wise man once said, "Goodness and gluttony are opposites within the individual in which they exist because goodness preserves the self whereas gluttony destroys and corrupts it. They nevertheless exist in the same individual. If goodness, a virtue, and gluttony, a vice, therefore coincide within the same individual, how much more convenient that goodness be something within which there is no vice, something that cannot be vice." The Supreme Maker did not distance Himself from our brothers, our friends, ourselves, not even when each one of us – we who have turned the holy moment of our meals into the mere pleasure of gluttony – renounced the wholeness of spirit and the communion of a whole people.

It is a great joy for me to enter into the spirit and customs of what used to be called New Spain. It is from here, however, that is, from the Old World, from the very entrails of the dust-ridden lands of the Manchegan gentleman Don Quixote of La Mancha, that I – like Don Quixote riding the run-down Rocinante – with great interest and deep pleasure am attempting to delve into the realm of *mole*. However, all the dishes at Camacho's wedding would have little worth if we did not fill them with the love and rites of the Holy Supper. Let us, then, accompany Friar Méndez through these pages, close to *mole* sauces, turkeys, partridges and lamb, with some castrated cockerel, and on feast days some beef from our larder, and, like good old Sancho Panza, some stigmas of saffron and some chunks of onion for a better burp. May they trigger love and dialogue at the table, in good spirits and unending company, like that of our armed knight. In each corner of our selves such feasting touches our deepest feelings, sustaining not only the body but also the soul, and thus, step by step, in perfect harmony, achieving communion in wholeness just like the holy universal supper.

I would once again like to express my gratitude to Angel Méndez for such a marvelous work that will constantly sprout, generation after generation, like grains of wheat or kernels of maize. It is my deepest hope that these lines will nourish us with charity and hope and that this compendium will fill our saddlebags as we walk towards the plenitude of the Holy Table with our brother and theologian, Angel Méndez.

Joaquín Racionero Page
On the Day of St. Fermin, the Year of Our Lord 2008, Madrid
Translated by Leslie Pascoe Chalke

Preface

In general terms, food matters. It displays a complex interrelation between self and other; object and subject; appetite and digestion; aesthetics, ethics, and politics; nature and culture; and creation and divinity. In particular, this reading of food can cast light on what it means to practice theology, and why it so relevant for theology to be attentive to matters regarding food, and also the lack thereof. For, from a Catholic perspective, this book envisions God both as superabundance and intra-Trinitarian self-sharing of a nurturing Love, Truth, Goodness, and Beauty. God's gift is further shared with creation and humanity. Creation is a cosmic banquet and interdependent network of edible signs that participates in God's nurturing sharing. The Incarnation is a continuation of God's kenotic sharing, that, at the eucharistic banquet, performs a more radical form of self-giving by becoming food itself with the purpose of incorporating humanity into Christ's body, which already participates in the life of the cosmos and of the Trinitarian community. Because food matters, theology's vocation is thus to become "alimentary," reorienting the interdependency between human communities, humanity with the ecology, and all creation with God.

By looking at some cultural and material practices and food narratives this book creates a dialogue that constructs a multifaceted eucharistic discourse, arguing that food is not "just food." At the end, however, since this book envisions God as the ultimate source that nurtures all theological practice, and since this same God exists as surplus of meaning, the book situates itself within a milieu of mystery. For this reason it is only a prolegomenon to a eucharistic discourse: perpetually open to yet more elaboration, and responsive to the touching, tasting, and nourishment of God's superabundant self-giving.

Acknowledgments

For me, writing this book was an experience of true communal table fellowship. There are many people whom I want to thank for their support and encouragement, suggestions, inspiration, and prayers, all of which kept me moving forward. I cannot take full credit for what I hope might be a good end-product, but only for any errors that may remain.

An earlier version of this book appeared in the form of a doctoral dissertation in philosophical theology at the University of Virginia, but the actual process of writing took place in three different locations. Besides Virginia, I also wrote some of the book in Mexico City, while the last stage of writing took place in Cambridge, UK, where I was scholar in residence at the university there. Thus, I first want to express my gratitude to the Dominican community of Charlottesville, Virginia, that hosted me while I was studying for my doctoral degree. I then lived for six months in Mexico City, where I mainly concentrated on researching the Mexican dish called *molli*. I am very grateful to my Dominican brothers at the Comunidad de Santa Rosa de Lima, in Mexico City, who hosted me during this research period. Finally, I want to thank my brothers at Blackfriars in Cambridge, who very generously hosted me in their community, where I did most of my writing until the book's completion. Writing this book in the midst of fraternal communities provided me with an environment of daily prayer and eucharistic practices, as well as enabling me to share communal meals, all of which became true food for thought in my writing on food and theology.

I also want to thank the several benefactors who so generously supported me during the process of studying, researching, and writing. First, the brothers from my own Dominican province, the Province of St. Martin de Porres (Southern Dominican Province, USA), for their support and trust. The Dominican community of Austin, under the leadership of Father James McDonough, OP, was also tirelessly generous and supportive, and I am forever grateful to them. Also, I could neither have started nor finished my doctoral work without the generous support of two scholarships: the Arts and Sciences Doctoral Scholarship from the University of Virginia, and the Hispanic Theological Initiative, sponsored by the Pew Charitable Trust. I also want to thank Delores Hoyt and Mary Hults for their generous support and continual prayers.

Several people also became key participants in helping me shape my thoughts. I first want to thank Professor John Milbank for always giving me direction, support, and helpful criticism. I enjoyed meeting with him, his wife Alison, and their children at their lovely home in England, usually around delicious meals prepared by Alison. There were also key readers of my drafts to whom I want to express my profound gratitude for their comments and wise suggestions. These wonderful table fellows are Catherine Pickstock, Larry Bouchard, Peter and Vanessa Ochs, Eugene Rogers, James Alison, Joel Marie Cabrita (the main proof-reader of earlier versions of this book), Aaron Riches, Anthony Baker, Mayra Rivera, and Roberto Goizueta.

When I was writing this book at Cambridge I was truly nourished by the participants in a series of Bible discussion groups I directed at Fisher's House Catholic Centre at the university there. Their fresh ideas and suggestions regarding the sacred Scriptures and the issues surrounding food were often discussed in these enjoyable sessions. I am thankful to each one of them for providing material that nurtured my research.

Since this book is mainly about food, eating, and cooking, I made an effort to improve my culinary skills. I want to thank those mentors who are excellent cooks and taught me the delights of cuisine and self-sharing. They are also very close friends who exemplify hospitality and nourishing love: Rodney Adams, Israel Ramirez, Raúl Parrao, Carlos Marquez Peralta, and Benito Rodriguez.

My dissertation has become a book thanks to the encouragement of Rebecca Harkin at Blackwell Publishing. I am very grateful to Rebecca and her staff – particularly to Janet Moth, the project manager – for approving its publication and helping produce a more polished version of my work.

Finally, I want to express my most profound gratitude to the primary providers and source of inspiration of my work. They are my father, Vicente Méndez Dominguez, and my mother, Ofelia Montoya de Méndez. Although they did not live to see its publication, they were always somehow present in the shaping of this book, for they were great cooks and a great example of love and hospitality. My earliest experience of the joy of cooking for others, which for me is a form of theological rejoicing, was learned from the example of my parents. I dedicate this book to them.

Introduction
Food Talk: Overlapping Matters

"Comer: nada más vital, nada más íntimo." There is nothing more vital and intimate than eating, Claude Fischler tells us in *L'Homnivore*.[1] Eating is vital, for without food we perish. In one way or another, all living organisms need to eat or ingest a substance for their growth and survival. To eat – in its many forms and fashions, including drinking, absorbing a substance, and the like – is a way of being incorporated into the micro and macro organic cycle of life. Eating is a primal mark and act of life that evokes the cosmos as a great cosmic banquet. While being so vital, eating is also an experience of extreme nearness, even intimacy, as Fischler puts it. When we eat, we are literally "intimate" with food by physically bringing it near the body, lips, and mouth. The ingested substance breaks the conventional boundaries of inside and outside, oneself and alterity, and infiltrates the body with a variety of scents, textures, flavors, and substances, until the ingested food is incorporated into the body through a complex metabolizing process that transforms – transfigures – its initial consistency into calories, vitamins, proteins, and so forth. Deane W. Curtin rightly remarks that "our bodies literally are food transformed into flesh, tendon, blood, and bone."[2]

Eating transforms food so that it becomes a vital part of our bodies, and, simultaneously, the embodied individual is also transformed by the act of eating. The body can become strong and healthy, weak or ill, by eating or abstaining from food. Eating can vitalize the body, but it can also make it sick and even bring about death. But eating not only brings about

---

[1] Claude Fischler, *El (H)omnívoro: El Gusto, la Cocina y el Cuerpo*, trans. into Spanish from the French original by Mario Merlino (Barcelona: Editorial Anagrama, 1995), 11.

[2] Deane W. Curtin, "Food/Body/Person," in Deane W. Curtin and Lisa M. Heldke (eds.), *Cooking, Eating, Thinking: Transformative Philosophies of Food* (Indianapolis: Indiana University Press, 1992), 3–22: 11.

physiological or biological change; it is also a means of psychological, affective, and even spiritual transformation. Eating and drinking certain products and substances triggers particular moods, enkindles various degrees of emotion, and awakens memories. A dish or a beverage can bring memories of family, home, a country, or a particular experience from the past. In some communities there are foods for celebrating special occasions, such as those prepared for wedding banquets or birth-day parties. There are also foods that some cultures only serve at funerals because of their cultural associations with mourning and lamentation.

Eating can also be thought to enact erotic passions and desires. In *Aphrodite: A Memoir of the Senses*, Isabel Allende tells us that food can literally awaken the most profound eroticism and passionate feelings.[3] Not only can food be thought of as a fuel of eros, it can also be envisioned as a means of the highest spiritual experience of God's love and of human love responding to God's love or God's will. To the observant Jew, the practices of both the prescriptive and the proscriptive dietary laws are analogous to the transformative reality of the Sabbath: what is to be eaten or not eaten contributes to a sense of living in awareness of the time and space of the Torah, of God's law as law to be loved. Analogous relations between eating and awareness of God's love or will may be seen in Islam, as in the Ramadan fast and the feasting that follows.[4] To Christians, food can be thought of as an expression of agape. Eating can be the means not only of physical and emotional change, but also of spiritual transformation; the Eucharist is the paradigmatic example, but it extends to the whole calendar of feast days. We will see how, for these traditions, and especially for Catholic and Orthodox (Eastern rite) Christians, the story of the eating of the forbidden fruit in the book of Genesis narrates the origin of a tremendous transformation that propels humanity into a postlapsarian era, a life outside Eden; while, for some Christian communities, the act of partaking in the eucharistic banquet is believed to be an enactment of redemption, fellowship, and even deification via ingesting Christ's resurrected body – God made flesh.

This book addresses the fact that food matters, and that matters related to food, such as eating and drinking, table fellowship, culinary traditions, the relationship between savoring and knowing, the aesthetic, ethical, and political dimensions of food, and the relation between humanity and divinity through the medium of food, are indeed vital and

---

[3] Isabel Allende, *Aphrodite: A Memoir of the Senses* (London: Flamingo, 1998).
[4] I am grateful to Professors Larry Bouchard and Peter and Vanessa Ochs for their apposite comments regarding food and non-Christian religions.

intimate, displaying complex interrelations that develop over time and amongst multiple localities. Food can be considered as a *locus theologicus*. According to the thesis of this book, these interrelated issues around food cast light on what it means to envision a theological practice that involves "alimentation," satiating a hunger for God who, according to the Christian narratives, offers a material and spiritual source of nourishment to creation. From a Christian – and mainly Catholic – perspective, food matters, so much so that God becomes food, our daily bread.

This book envisions God both as superabundance and intra-Trinitarian self-sharing of nurturing Love, Truth, Goodness, and Beauty. It also intimates God's gift as being generously shared with creation and humanity. In this vision, creation is a cosmic banquet – an interdependent network of edible signs – that participates in God's nurturing sharing. Following from the logic of God's self-emptying love or kenotic sharing, the Incarnation can be seen as a material continuation of this cosmic, eucharistic banquet. That is, God initiates a radical self-giving by becoming food itself, incorporating – and thus transfiguring – humanity into Christ's body. And further, through this self-giving, humanity is brought into the divine, Trinitarian community. Because food matters, theology's vocation is to become alimentation: a theology not only concerned *about* food matters, but also a theology envisioned *as* food. I call this twofold practice *alimentary theology*. In becoming "alimentary," theology can deepen our awareness of matters regarding food while reorienting the dimension of interdependence between human communities, humanity with ecology, and all creation with God. "To share bread is to share God." Such is the message proclaimed by the many inter-faith voices forming the "Zero Hunger" project, and it is also the main theological message of this book.

Moreover, if Ludwig Feuerbach's assertion that "we are what we eat" is correct, a theologian may wonder what exactly the relationship between ontology and alimentation is. With regard to investigating this, Donato Alarcón Segovia makes a helpful distinction between the notions of nutrition and alimentation. He explains that, although these two terms are interdependent, nutrition "refers both to the processes of incorporation of food's nutritional content and to what is considered to be the proper amount and proportion of such nutrients for the function of an organism through time."[5] Alarcón Segovia points out that, as distinct from nutrition,

[5] "La nutrición se refiere tanto a los procesos por los que se incorporan los nutrientes contenidos en los alimentos como a lo adecuado de éstos tanto cuantitativa como proporcionalmente para la función de un organismo a través del tiempo" (my translation). Donato Alarcón Segovia and Héctor Bourges Rodríguez (eds.), *La Alimentación de los*

"alimentation refers to voluntary and conscious acts that not only depend on instinct but also on geographical, economic, and physiological factors."[6] He adds that social, cultural, and religious views also construct the notion of alimentation. The notion of alimentation, which will be used throughout this book, connotes a transformation that takes place both in food and in those who eat it. Alimentation already implies transformation, a certain aspect of construction or creativity; like creating a piece of art, or any creative act in which the imagination plays an essential role. It implies both preserving traditions and experimentation and creativity. But, above all, to be nourished implies being in the care of the cosmos, the earth, family, loved ones, and – according to some religious traditions – in divine care. We *are* what we eat. This speaks of the ontological reality of "being nourished." In dialogue with Thomas Aquinas, Sergei Bulgakov, Alexander Schmemann, William Desmond, and others I will propose an understanding of ontology as the co-arrival of superabundance and sharing, neither absolutizing nor demanding total ownership. Writing from a Christian and Catholic perspective, this "alimentary ontology" also implies a universal divine sharing, wherein caritas is envisioned as the main source of individual and communal sustenance. And, again from a Christian perspective, this is a profoundly theological matter. At the core of any ontology there is a sense of God's excessiveness nourishing all that "is" with the alimentary vitality "to be." Henceforth, I hope to persuade the reader that one of the main tasks facing contemporary theological discourse is to be that which it eats; that is to say, to be nourished by divine caritas in the making of theology – a "culinary art" – and thus become a form of alimentation to others.

When we think about nourishment we are confronted with great complexity. Such thinking reveals our individual and group conceptions of, for instance, what is or is not edible; when one must eat and when avoidance of food is recommended or even mandatory; what are the principles for labeling food as healthy or unhealthy. Alimentation involves individual and communal discernment regarding food, and this

---

Mexicanos (Mexico City: El Colegio Nacional, 2002), 5. Although nutrition is a territory more or less dominated by scientific research, I wonder what might be the method for categorizing proper or improper food. Another question regards what methods we use to measure the "adequacy" (or lack of it) of categories such as quantity and proportionality. And finally, a further question concerns the agents of such categorization: that is to say, who are the "ideal" agents to undertake it? This further shows how interconnected nutrition is with anthropology, sociology, cultural theory, and so forth.

[6] "La alimentación … es un acto volitivo y consciente que en el hombre no solo depende del instinto sino también de factores geográficos, económicos y fisiológicos. También los hay sociales, religiosos y culturales." Ibid., 5.

entails some degree of societal negotiation. There is a relationship between people's "foodways" (to use Carole M. Counihan's term[7]) and people's understanding of self and other: an understanding that is historical, contextual, and diachronic all at the same time. Thus, while alimentation is an experience of extreme immediacy, it is also true that it is a mediating act. For it mediates between self and other, the inner and the outer self, the sign, the signifier, and the signified.

This mediation that takes place in nourishment is closely related to the dynamics of the construction of meaning, which also provide an analogy with the studies of linguistics and semiotics. In line with the approach of Claude Lévi-Strauss and Roland Barthes, this book examines food as a system of signification and communication. For these thinkers, speaking about food requires looking at it as a network and system of significations. Food, Barthes tells us, is "not only a collection of products that can be used for statistical or nutritional studies. It is also, and at the same time, a system of communication, a body of images, a protocol of usages, situations and behaviors."[8] Food itself already presents a complex grammar, "a rich symbolic alphabet through its diversity of color, texture, smell, and taste; its ability to be elaborated and combined in infinite ways; and its immersion in norms of manners and cuisine."[9] When speaking about cuisine, for instance, Massimo Montari also suggests a close analogy with language. Montari explains that cuisine, like language, contains a "vocabulary (the products, the ingredients) that is organized according to grammatical rules (recipes that give meaning to the ingredients and transforms them in dishes), a syntax (the menus, that is, the order of dishes), and rhetoric (social protocols)."[10]

Likewise, for Lévi-Strauss, ultimately to learn who we are we could look at food and cooking patterns, for they tell us something about the basic structure of our systems of signification; just as an analysis of language

---

[7] Counihan defines foodways as "the beliefs and behavior surrounding the production, distribution, and consumption of food." *The Anthropology of Food and Body: Gender, Meaning, and Power* (London: Routledge, 1999), 2.

[8] Roland Barthes, "Toward a Psychosociology of Contemporary Food Consumption," in Carole Counihan and Penny Van Esterik (eds.), *Food and Culture: A Reader* (London: Routledge, 1997), 20–7.

[9] From the introduction to Counihan and Van Esterik (eds.), *Food and Culture*, 2.

[10] "[la cocina, como el lenguage] posee vocablos (los productos, los ingredients) que se organizan según reglas gramaticales (las recetas, que dan sentido a los ingredientes transformándolos en platos), sintácticas (los menus, o sea, el orden de los platos) y retóricas (los comportamientos sociales)." My own translation from the Spanish version of Massimo Montari (ed.), *El Mundo en la Cocina: Historia, Identidad, Intercambios*, trans. Yolanda Daffunchio (Buenos Aires: Paidós, 2003), 11.

reveals a basic structure of meaning, which – according to Lévi-Strauss – ultimately tells us something about the structure of the human mind.[11] However, and echoing post-structuralist concerns, it is a question whether Lévi-Strauss's structuralist approach really does reveal a "universal" structure that applies to every particularity and locality across every context and time. Beyond this discussion and beyond any attempt to universalize, this book holds as a basic principle that food and nourishment express complex systems of signification. Again, this is a sort of mediation that is analogous to that of language, yet not necessarily applicable or observable in all contexts. And if it signifies, I prefer to consider it more as a mobile signifier that even exceeds the thing signified. I argue that such is the case for eucharistic signs. Perhaps the analogy of dialogue and discourse works better here for articulating how food matters. Following Graham Ward, dialogue and discourse are here understood as expressive acts, not exclusively founded upon spoken or written expressions, but on other forms of composed communication similar to "music, painting, architecture, liturgy, gesture, dance, in fact any social action."[12] And of course, with regard to my present thesis one must add alimentation to this list. Thus as a discourse and as an expressive act, alimentation is inseparable from concrete material and cultural practices, narratives, and symbols.

Our foodways could be seen as narrative performances of how societies construct notions of self and community, and their relationship with the world; and these may also include a belief in spiritual, invisible, and transcendent entities or realities. The cultural anthropologist Mary Douglas is right in pointing out that our ways of categorizing food should not be looked at in isolation, apart from other categories, because all categories somehow reflect other preceding or already mixed ones.[13] When one talks about food, one encounters a reality of overlapping categories and notions. Douglas is particularly interested in the symbols that are reflected in foodways and which are like a microcosm of society at large. What goes on during a family meal, for instance, reflects multiple interacting discourses and narratives such as food preparation and presentation, eating patterns, protocols and rules, social and gender roles, religious beliefs, and so forth. For her, the family reflects and

---

[11] See e.g. his essay "The Culinary Triangle," in Counihan and Van Esterik (eds.), *Food and Culture*, 28–35. See also *The Raw and the Cooked: Mythologiques*, vol. 1, trans. from the French by John and Doreen Weightman (Chicago: University of Chicago Press, 1969).

[12] Graham Ward, *Cultural Transformation and Religious Practice* (Cambridge: Cambridge University Press, 2005), 6.

[13] In this sense, Douglas attempts to move beyond the universalism of Lévi-Strauss by pointing out not the synchronic aspects of food, but rather the diachronic ones.

performs microcosmically the values of the larger culture and society. Douglas explores the instances of society's taboos that, for her, display this sort of complex network of codification and control, and that often are closely related to other regulations regarding the body – such as food, sexual, and excretory conventions.[14]

Echoing Douglas's findings, this book also suggests that, when we talk about matters regarding food, we inevitably encounter interrelating and overlapping categories and notions. If we look at particular foodways and their relationship with categories such as "nature" and "culture," for instance, we soon find that looking at each category in isolation only offers a very minimal understanding of how these categories are represented and practiced. In fact, this form of categorizing in such distinctive groupings – while useful for heuristic purposes – may also impede our recognition of how categories can be mutually constitutive. We encounter both categories of nature and culture as directly related to some dimension of somatic performance. The experience and conception of the body and the framing of somatic experiences are also implicit in categories such as nature and culture, yet not exclusive to just these two categories. Indeed, this somatic dimension also relates to society's categorization of notions such as sexuality and gender, as well as aspects such as age and geographic location. Moreover, these latter issues could also imply conceptions of race, ethnicity, and national or group identity, which further entail issues of power, social class, and wealth distribution. Additionally, many of these issues may directly or indirectly imply some religious belief and faith tradition. When we talk about food, we are, then, in the midst of a rich and complex mosaic of languages, grammars, narratives, discourses, and traditions, all of which are tightly intermeshed. In this binding, they overlap and even "contradict" each other.

I have made the deliberate choice of discussing overlapping themes and notions with the principal purpose of displaying the complexity of food matters. But this overlapping of themes will also serve as a heuristic device for reflecting on theology from a variety of perspectives and contexts. I hope that this consistent overlapping of themes will generate different "alchemic" results, depending on the context in which they appear in a given chapter. The effect that I am looking for with this approach could be compared to the use of certain spices in a salad, which create a different flavor if those same spices are used in the same quantity

---

[14] See especially Mary Douglas, *Purity and Danger: An Analysis of Concept of Pollution and Taboo* (1st pub. 1966; London: Routledge, 2001); and "Deciphering a Meal," *Daedalus* (Winter 1972), 69–70.

in a soup or a stew. I attempt to introduce this particular concept in my first chapter, in which I explore a traditional Mexican dish – called *molli*, from its pre-Colombian roots – which is paradigmatic of this overlapping of themes and categories within food. I will, furthermore, argue that *molli* can become a model for the art of *making* theology. Taken as a whole, my aim in this book is to stimulate in the reader an experience analogous to that of tasting and eating an extravagant *molli*.

Just as the subject of food involves various and overlapping ingredients, both material and thematic, so this book speaks to a varied readership. A principal intention of my research has been to interact with a variety of communal discourses, practices, and disciplines. Taking my lead from its emphasis on the Eucharist, my first engagement is with Catholic theology and a Catholic readership. I explore ways to both preserve tradition and to rehearse new modes of articulating doctrinal theology, persistently adhering to a process of *metanoia* – a transformation of the heart expressed in the daily practices of caritas (first from within a Catholic tradition). My hope is that this book may resonate with other faith traditions both within and outside Christianity. And because food is such an elemental matter, it is also my hope that this book may communicate to readers who do not belong to any particular faith. I speak variously to my readers as table fellows: first as *a cook to other cooks* (that is, to fellow theologians within or close to my own tradition, and also in other traditions, who may be encouraged to design different sorts of alimentary theologies); then as *a cook to the partakers of this feast* (that is, to readers of this alimentary theology, whether or not they participate in the Catholic tradition); and finally as *a host to his guests* (that is, as a teacher and Dominican friar offering this alimentary theology to those who may receive and enjoy it together in a kind of eucharistic fellowship, wherein my role mutates from being a student or even a teacher to being a brother eating at the same table). That is to say, it is my hope and desire to consistently envision the process of doing theology as a breaking of bread together, as an interdisciplinary discourse that brings about nourishment.

I also realize that this rhetoric of overlapping may be a product of my own particular theological and cultural location. As a Mexican born in a border town in Baja, California, who has lived for some years in both the USA and the UK, my theology is a hybrid of various cultural backgrounds. As a Latino, I inherit similar concerns to those of some North American Latino and Latina theologians who – following some aspects of Latin American liberation theology – accentuate the dimension of immanent practice and search for new ways of bringing about individual and social transformation. At the same time, my theological work reflects the influence of John Milbank's discussions on transcendence. Included here are some of the voices within the "Radical Orthodoxy" platform, which seeks to recover the richness of doctrinal themes that shapes the already mixed subject of philosophical theology. It is a deliberate choice to thus mix "extravagantly," as a hybridized *molli*. For, in a manner that aims neither to antagonize nor to assert victory over other approaches, this book explores creative ways of evoking the in-betweenness of transcendence and immanence. The reader may rightly observe that it does not focus on a particular theologian, or on an individual theological school of thought. Instead, by hybridizing a variety of theologians and theological approaches, its main focus is food and the Eucharist. With this hybrid I hope to demonstrate that matters of food reflect something about a divine transcendental sharing that does not annul but, rather, intensifies immanence. Moreover, this overlapping of theological angles is also reflective of my being a Dominican friar. As a member of the Order of Preachers, my work presents a hybrid of contemplation and practice, such that both intellectual and pastoral concerns constitute and challenge one another. The reader will also observe that this book mixes various texts in philosophical theology with a deep engagement with the sacred Scriptures – a hermeneutic and homiletic tradition that is at the heart of the Order of Preachers. After Aquinas, I echo the Dominican tradition, whereby faith and reason, theory and practice, are mutually nurturing.

As a general methodology I start each chapter with an exploration of concrete practices and narratives regarding food, which I then allow to guide a philosophical-theological reflection. In chapter 1, I use the Mexican *molli* as a paradigm for the rich complexities of the art of making theology, comparable to a culinary art. In chapter 2, I begin with the erotic narrative of Laura Esquivel's *Like Water for Chocolate*, and explore ways in which this novel evokes the relationship between knowing and savoring; a relationship that tells us something about a dimension of participation in the known. Since one of the most important ingredients of practicing alimentary theology is becoming aware of the union between divine and human desires, in chapter 3 I provide a taste of a counter-ontology of alimentation that echoes a previous "sophianic" and eucharistic culinary gesture, which one could intimate both from reading the Genesis narrative of eating the forbidden fruit and from a portrait of Sophia hosting a banquet and becoming food itself as it is presented in some sapiential narratives within the Scriptures (for example in Psalms, Proverbs, the Song of Songs, or the book of Wisdom). Finally, in chapter 4 I argue that envisioning a sharing in the Body of Christ tells us something about the intrinsic political dimension of God's nurturing manna; a divine gift akin to Isak Dinesen's *Babette's Feast*. All the chapters lead to and evoke a reflection on the Eucharist, but in addition a eucharistic discourse consistently revisits these concrete practices to provide them with theological "nurturing." In other words, cultural and material practices and food narratives will create a dialogue that constructs a multifaceted eucharistic discourse.

Because of all the complexities of alimentation, I shall argue that food is not "just food." This, I hope, will become more apparent when we reflect on how food can provide a greater awareness of partaking of the eucharistic banquet, while a eucharistic, "alimentary theology" can provide discipline and guidance for our daily food practices, which, in turn, challenge us to better nurture one another. At the end, however, since this book envisions God as the ultimate source that nurtures all theological practice, and this same God exists as surplus of meaning, the book situates itself within a milieu of mystery. For this reason the following is only a prolegomenon to a eucharistic discourse: perpetually open to yet more elaboration, and responsive to the touching, tasting, and nourishment of God's superabundant self-giving.

The Making of Mexican *Molli* and Alimentary Theology in the Making

Doña Soledad's recipe for *mole poblano* – a traditional Mexican dish – contains a total of 33 ingredients. After they have been prepared these ingredients are ground until they are a refined powder (similar to ground coffee) which can then be stored in the freezer for a long time. In fact, similar to a good red wine, the older the *mole*, the better is its taste. It was Doña Soledad herself, a 60-year-old mother and grandmother living in Mexico City, who taught me how to prepare this complex dish. Her son, who is a professional chef, also became my mentor in teaching me how to make this Mexican recipe. Besides learning how to make *mole*, I also wanted to share it with my friends in a big fiesta, or feast. We were initially planning to make it for about 20 people. However, we ended up preparing *mole* for 100 people, and decided to divide the ground *mole* into equal parts to store it and use it for future dinner parties.

Doña Soledad learnt this recipe from her mother, who in turn learnt it from her mother – and this chain goes back many generations. In fact, and as we shall see in this chapter, one of the origins of this dish goes back as far as pre-Colombian times. Making this ancient recipe took us about 12 hours from buying the ingredients to the final product. After a long day's work, we put all the prepared ingredients into a local industrial mill, to make a refined powder. We then put this powder to "rest" in the freezer. Two weeks later, Doña Soledad's recipe was first shared amongst my friends in a farewell dinner before my departure for Cambridge, England. The remaining *mole* powder was later made up into the final dish in England, among the Dominican friars of my community at Blackfriars in Cambridge, and then, six months later, among a community of Dominicans in Berlin. The more I cooked *mole*, the more I learned how to refine my touch in finding the perfect balance, allowing all the ingredients to interact and create true gastronomic pleasure. Through this experience of preparing and sharing *mole* among friends I became aware of an analogy that could be suggested between the making and sharing of this dish and the art of doing (or making) theology – which is also a sort of co-crafting (involving both God and humanity), a "culinary product."

By taking the Mexican *mole* as a metaphor, and a cultural, material, and concrete practice, the main purpose of this first chapter is to explore what it means to practice theology in general, and to partake of the eucharistic banquet in particular, in that both are eccentric alimentary hybrids that feed our hunger. The chapter will build the foundations for the main argument of this book: theology's vocation is to become a form of nourishment to people, and in doing so imitate God's nurturing gesture of sharing. Thus, here I will look at the preparation of food (in this case, Mexican *mole*) as a paradigm for engaging in the crafting of theology, and I will discuss theology in terms of food to be shared.

These interrelated and mutually constitutive elements of nourishment and theology I will call "alimentary theology." I will speak from my experience as a Catholic, and as one who is increasingly becoming "tricultural" (Mexican, American, and English). I hope that my particular angle may provide some food for thought to people from diverse religious and cultural practices, and to those who think about how religious beliefs may become transformative and nourishing.

Of course *mole* and theology are not identical, and so this comparison might sound contrived. My intention is not to collapse the differences and clear distinctions that exist between them. I only desire to stretch the theological imagination regarding thinking and talking about God as well as practicing the Eucharist, which I firmly believe is not only something concerned with reason, faith, and doctrine, but is also the bringing together of complex ingredients – such as the body and the senses, materiality and the Spirit, culture and the construction of meaning, and a divine–human blending of desires.

1 Doña Soledad's Mole

Ingredients

100 g. garlic, chopped
150 g. onion, chopped
250 g. almonds
250 g. hazelnuts
125 g. pine nuts
125 g. pistachios

250 g. shelled peanuts
250 g. cashew nuts
250 g. fresh plums, stoned and chopped
250 g. raw pumpkin, peeled and chopped
250 g. raisins
8 tablespoons anise
50 g. ground cinnamon
500 g. sesame seeds
2 tablespoons cloves
4 tablespoons cumin powder
250 g. coriander seeds
2 tablespoons whole black peppercorns
2 tablespoons ground black pepper
50 g. fresh ginger, peeled and chopped
500 g. wide chilies (a dry poblano pepper with a reddish hue)
1.25 kg. *mulato* chilies
1.25 kg. *pasilla* chilies (both *mulato* and *pasilla* are varieties of *capsicum annuum*; *mulato* is a dry poblano pepper, but with a darker hue than wide chilies)
80 g. seeds from the three sorts of chili
50 g. avocado leaves
20 g. bay leaf
20 g. marjoram
50 g. fresh horseradish
180 g. dark chocolate, chopped
200 g. brown sugar
20 g. fresh chopped thyme leaves
100 g. breadcrumbs
100 g. tortilla corn
sunflower or maize oil for cooking
salt to taste

Preparing the *mole* powder
Remove the veins and as many seeds as possible from the chilies.
Put the chilies in a tray, drizzle with oil, and put them in the oven for 10 minutes at 150°C.
Put the hazelnuts, peanuts, cashews, and the seeds from the chilies in a tray, drizzle a small amount of oil on them, and roast them in the oven for ten minutes to release their flavors.
Using a small amount of oil, fry the spices (anise, cinnamon, sesame seeds, cloves, coriander, black pepper, and ginger) with the chopped garlic and onion until golden.

Once these ingredients have been roasted and fried, put them into a manual or industrial mill together with all the remaining ingredients and salt to taste, and grind until you have a fine, well-mixed powder.

Cooking the *mole*
Enough for 10 people.

400 g. *mole* as prepared above
250 g. red tomatoes, skinned and chopped
2.5 liters chicken broth
140 g. dark chocolate, broken into pieces
salt, pepper, and brown sugar to taste
oil for frying

Sauté the tomatoes in a frying pan, then add some of the chicken broth. Bring to the boil and simmer for 5 minutes (or until the acidity of the tomatoes disappears).

Add the remaining broth, and then add the *mole* bit by bit, very slowly, until it has all dissolved. Add the chocolate, and finally add salt, pepper, and sugar to taste. It should have the consistency of a thick sauce.

For a better taste, cook the *mole* a day before serving it so that it can be rested to allow the flavor to develop.

To serve, bring the *mole* to boiling point and serve warm over cooked chicken, pasta, rice, or vegetables.

It was very early on a Friday morning, about 6 a.m., when I met with Israel (Doña Soledad's youngest son, and a professional chef) in hectic Mexico City – a city of about 20 million people. We drove towards the periphery of the city to La Central de Abastos (the Central Supply Station), which is a 304-hectare outlet with all sorts of wholesales supplies, including food products, furniture, clothing, plants, and so on.[1] Most businesses in Mexico City and from neighboring towns obtain their products there for a significantly reduced price. Israel was very focused on finding the very best ingredients for the *mole*. It took us nearly two hours to collect everything we needed and then carry it to the car. Since we had decided to make enough *mole* for about 100 people (since it improves with storage), some of the bags we carried were very large and heavy.

---

[1] For more information on the Central de Abastos, see the weblink: <www.ficeda. com.mx>.

But nothing was as arduous as having to open and remove all the veins and seeds from each of the three kinds of chili (the first step of the preparation). There were hundreds of them. To do this, we needed to put on plastic gloves in order to protect our skin from their spice and acidity. There were four of us doing the job: Doña Soledad, Israel, Rodney – a visiting friend from the US who offered his help – and me. Just getting the chilies ready took us about two hours. Once we finished, we moved on to the second step of the recipe (frying, roasting, and seasoning the ingredients). In performing this second step it is fascinating to observe the change of texture and color of the ingredients: some become darker, while others acquire a pale color, some become smoother while others become rough. This step is also "choreographical": the ingredients dance to a kind of music while being fried and roasted. But even more fascinating is realizing how, little by little, the sense of smell intensifies when the many spices and ingredients start releasing their aroma. The smell that spread in the house became too intense, almost unbearable. When we put the chilies in the oven we had to open all windows and doors, and at times step outside, for the scent of hundreds of roasted chilies not only penetrated our nostrils, but was felt on the skin and in the eyes as well.

Once they were ready we put all the prepared ingredients (which we previously put into large saucepans) in the mill. Israel insisted on achieving a very refined powder in order to obtain a good mixture, so we ground and reground the products seven times. It was nearly 7 p.m. when we finally obtained our precious *mole* powder, which we then put in plastic bags in the freezer to let it rest and allow the flavors to mingle. And a good rest was what I was truly longing for at this point.

Two weeks later, the *mole* was ready to cook for the first time. Israel was also my guide in moving on to this third step. We met a day before the fiesta to prepare the *mole* sauce and let it rest for one day before serving. The most exhausting task at this point was dissolving the ground powder into the boiling liquid chicken broth (previously mixed with the tomatoes and seasoning). One has to pour in the powder very slowly, until it is entirely dissolved in the liquid, which, little by little, starts to acquire a dark brown-red color. As the pouring in and stirring of the mixture progresses, the *mole* sauce becomes thicker and darker. As the sauce is heated, the scent of all the spices and ingredients permeates first the kitchen, and then the entire house. Performing this step was a corporeal, mantra-like experience: constantly pouring in the *mole* powder, letting it dissolve, and stirring the sauce. I also included a repetitive prayer – similar to praying the rosary – to Pascual Bailón (I shall say more about him later) to ask for his spiritual assistance in making this *mole* truly exquisite. After completing enough sauce for 20 people, the *mole* sauce was finally ready, and had a glorious smell. We then turned the heat off, and after letting it cool for a few hours we put it in the fridge.

The following day we prepared the farewell fiesta at a friend's house. Several friends arrived early in the afternoon to help. Israel and I cooked chicken thighs and legs. Once these were ready, we put the cooked chicken into the *mole* sauce, and allowed it to heat very slowly. We had also prepared a mushroom soup for our first course. The *mole* was the second and main course, and we planned to serve it with white rice and home-made corn tortillas. For dessert, we served vanilla ice cream with mint Irish cream on top (as we shall see later, serving *mole* allows you to play with syncretism, so including Irish cream for dessert offered a bit of international flavor to our dinner). We also decided to serve very good tequila for the dinner drink, which we served in small glasses.

Everything was ready when the guests started to arrive around 7 p.m. The table (large and with space for 20 people) was set with flowers and candles. Since the weather was lovely – it was the middle of spring – we decided to place the table in the garden. We sat at the table around 8.30 p.m., so as to allow our guests time to arrive, socialize, and have drinks before dinner. Since all the guests were close friends of mine – most of them professional dancers and choreographers from my younger years of being a professional dancer in Mexico City, and some whom I had not seen in years – the crowd was friendly, relaxed, and happy to meet other friends. When we were gathered at the table, a friend proposed a toast and recited a prayer, particularly asking for blessings upon me, as I was to move to England and undertake the task of writing my doctoral dissertation. We then began to dine.

To quote Isak Dinesen's *Babette's Feast*, I would say of what happened during our meal that "nothing definite can here be stated."[2] I can only say that the diners became more and more delighted in their eating and drinking, and most intensely so while tasting the *mole* dish, which was truly exquisite in its harmonious balance of flavors. I say this with some degree of both pride and modesty. Making *mole* is a laborious task that requires much energy and time. But the excellent outcome was not only due to my own work, for I was blessed by having both Doña Soledad herself and her son Israel guiding me through the making of this complex dish. Nonetheless, it filled me with joy to see the pleasure (expressed in both gestures and sounds) of the dinner guests as we ate Doña Soledad's *mole* recipe and breathed in its aroma.

[2] Isak Dinesen, *Babette's Feast*, in *Anecdotes of Destiny and Ehrengard* (New York: Vintage Books, 1993), 53. I shall say more about *Babette's Feast* in chapter 4.

One could even say that this experience of eating *mole* among friends was "religious" or "divine." Although this may sound exaggerated, there is a deep truth in it. After all, many cultures and traditions throughout the ages have expressed the connection between eating, drinking, and an experience of the sacred.[3] And, in particular, Mexican *mole* has a long tradition of being associated with divine and otherworldly forces. I shall now turn to this exploration of the many layers of the "divine," as well as the human, in preparing and creating Mexican *mole*.

2 A Gastronomic Miracle

Sor (Sister) Andrea de la Asunción is in a great hurry. She is a Dominican nun living in the Dominican convent of St. Rose of Lima. It is near the end of the seventeenth century (around 1680) in Puebla de los Angeles, Mexico (then known as the New Spain, La Nueva España). Sor Andrea de la Asunción is hurrying and feels anxious because, as the assigned cook for the convent, she has been given the difficult task of preparing a lavish banquet for the arrival of "don Tomás Antonio de la Cerda y Aragón, marques [marquis] de la Laguna y conde [count] de Paredes, virrey [viceroy] de México y esposo [husband] de doña María Luisa Manrique de Lara, novia espiritual [spiritual girlfriend] de sor Juana Inés de la Cruz."[4] In her haste and anxiety in having to host such a distinguished figure, Sor Andrea receives a gastronomic vision: to mix up all sorts of ingredients and spices, even contrasting elements such as various chilies (Mexican peppers) and chocolate, and create a lavish, extravagant sauce that she will then cook with turkey – *guajolote*. The result of Sor Andrea's providential and eccentric culinary creation was baptized *mole* because, the story goes, Sor Andrea spent many hours *muele y muele* (grinding and grinding) various spices in order to achieve the dish's final consistency, thus creating true gastronomic ecstasy for all her guests, and all people thereafter.

[3] On the subject of religion and food, see especially Perry Schmidt-Leukel (ed.), *Die Religionen und das Essen* (Munich: Heinrich Hugendubel, 2000); Charles B. Heiser, Jr., *Seed to Civilization: The Story of Food*, 2nd edn. (San Francisco: W. H. Freeman, 1981); Mary Douglas, *Purity and Danger: An Analysis of Concept of Pollution and Taboo* (1st pub. 1966; London: Routledge, 2001), and *Food in the Social Order: Studies of Food and Festivities in Three American Communities* (New York: Russell Sage Foundation, 1984); Claude Lévi-Strauss, *The Raw and the Cooked: Mythologies*, vol. 1, trans. John Weightman and Doreen Weightman (Chicago: University of Chicago Press, 1983); and Stewart Lee Allen, *In the Devil's Garden: A Sinful History of Forbidden Food* (Edinburgh: Canongate, 2002).
[4] Paco Ignacio Taibo I, *El Libro de Todos los Moles* (Mexico City: Ediciones B, 2003), 51.

Paco Ignacio Taibo I points out that the origins of this story lie in folklore, the creation of popular narrative.[5] And there is yet another popular story. In this story we are also immersed in the monastic world of colonial baroque Mexico, and in Puebla de los Angeles as well. Like Sor Andrea, Fray (Brother) Pascual Bailón is also the principal cook in his convent.[6] Fray Pascual is also in a hurry. He is anxious because a very important archbishop is visiting his monastery. And monasteries (of which there were many, particularly in Puebla) were quite famous in colonial Mexico for their sophisticated cuisine and gastronomic inventions – a sort of *nouvelle cuisine* of the so-called "New World." Preparing banquets and eating was, as in most Mexican fiestas, the central event. The success or failure of a feast depended upon how gastronomically impressive (or not) the food served at the gathering was. It goes without saying that our friar cook had a massive responsibility upon his shoulders.

The story goes that, while Fray Pascual was preparing the main dish, in his anxiety and haste he accidentally dropped a huge piece of soap in the cooking pot, and irreversibly ruined the meal. He became furious with himself for such a catastrophic distraction. In his fury he started throwing into another pot – where he was cooking a turkey – all sorts of ingredients and spices, including chocolate and various chilies. But immediately after his attack of fury, a feeling of repentance suddenly overcame him. He dropped to his knees, and with all his heart he begged for God's forgiveness and help. The story relates that the miracle was granted him. This miracle gave birth to the *mole poblano*, an extravagant stew/sauce concocted of a symphony of flavors that not only delighted the honorable guest for that day at the convent, but which also – as the legend goes – became one of the most glorious culinary achievements in Puebla, across Mexico, and throughout the entire world. Such was his success that Fray Pascual was beatified by the church, and is now known as the patron saint of cooks: a saint not to be found in the clouds of highest heaven, but in the pots, the fire, the spices, the smells, and the flavors of the kitchen. When it is time to cook, many people in Mexico (myself included) still pray to the saint-chef for a successful outcome with these words: "Pascualito muy querido / mi santo Pascual Bailón / yo te ofrezco mi guisito / y tu pones la sazón"[7] (Very dear little

[5]   Ibid.

[6]   Both stories of the baroque *mole* created by Sor Andrea and Fray Pascual are oral stories that have been transmitted throughout the centuries. I am here primarily taking a version from Taibo I, *El Libro de Todos los Moles*.

[7]   The word *sazón* is difficult to translate into English. It is more than "seasoning." *Tener sazón* means to posses a natural gift for cooking delicious food. It is a special culinary touch that makes a dish something extraordinary.

Pascual, my holy Pascual Bailón, I offer you my dish, and may you offer your distinctive "culinary touch").[8]

One of the "origins" of the *mole* is, then, the popular imagination: allegorical stories that were passed orally between communities. These stories were also recipes that were part of the culinary tradition of religious communities, families, towns, geographical regions, which were then further transformed by others, each bringing their individual touch to the *mole*. The number of ingredients in the *mole* varies according to region and personal taste. Some may have as few as five ingredients, while others have more than 30 – as in Doña Soledad's recipe. There are an infinite number of *moles*, for *mole* itself is a hybrid that changes, transforms, and adapts itself according to the particular tradition, taste, and fancy of the cook. Some people like it more spicy; others prefer to taste the sweetness of chocolate and cinnamon or anise; others may be inclined to intensify the taste of almonds, walnuts, pistachios, and so on. Nevertheless, the hybridity of *mole* is not the mere result of spices and ingredients, plus an added personal touch. It is also a cultural hybrid, a mixture of multiple culinary world-views and cosmovisions.

3 *Molli*: Food of the Gods

Many recent historical and anthropological researchers point to the fact that *mole* was already an important part of pre-Colombian cuisine.[9] For the purpose of this chapter I am concentrating on the food and cooking traditions within the region of Mesoamerica.[10] As far as the term "cuisine" goes, I use it here in a broad sense: as a development of cooking

[8] Regarding references to Pascual Bailón, see, in addition to Taibo I, the essay by Herón Pérez Martínez, "La Comida en el Refranero Mexicano: Un Estudio Contrastivo," in Janet Long (ed.), *Conquista y Comida: Consecuencias del Encuentro de Dos Mundos* (Mexico City: UNAM, 2003), 505–28.

[9] Most of my historical and anthropological research on food in both the pre-Colombian and colonial times in Mexico is taken from Long (ed.), *Conquista y Comida*, a book that resulted from an international and interdisciplinary symposium entitled "1492: El Encuentro de Dos Comidas," which took place in Puebla, Mexico, in July 1992. See also Gustavo Esteva and Catherine Marielle (eds.), *Sin Maíz no Hay País* (Mexico City: Dirección General de Culturas Populares e Indígenas, 2003); Jeffrey M. Pilcher, *Vivan los Tamales! La Comida y la Construcción de la Identidad Mexicana* (Mexico City: Ediciones de la Reina Roja, S.A. de C.V., 2001); and Maximiliano Salinas Campos, *Gracias a Dios que Comí: El Cristianismo en Iberoamérica y el Caribe, Siglos XV–XIX* (Mexico City: Ediciones Dabar, 2000).

[10] Davíd Carrasco explains that the term Mesoamerica is "given by scholars to designate a geographical and cultural area covering the southern two-thirds of mainland Mexico, Guatemala, Belize, El Salvador, and parts of Honduras, Nicaragua, and Costa Rica."

techniques, the combination of food products and ingredients, a series of traditions and practices that relate to food and eating and that differ from one region to another, a sense of taste, social construction shaped around food, ritual practices centered on food, and so forth. Cuisine is a category that relates to what Carole M. Counihan calls "foodways," which she defines as "the beliefs and behavior surrounding the production, distribution, and consumption of food."[11] In other words, cuisine is understood as a sort of alimentary linguistic/discursive and symbolic form of communication, one that shapes communities and cultures, as well as changing according to place and time.

The Mesoamerican system of food production was indeed complex. Héctor Bourges Rodríguez argues that Mesoamerican cuisine enjoyed a high reputation as a result of its "long development, complexity and wisdom, for it had deep roots in history."[12] He also suggests that Mesoamerican cuisine had an "exceptional aesthetic sensibility and a fine nutritional balance suggesting specialized nutritional knowledge."[13] Bourges Rodríguez disagrees with the common portrayal of Mesoamerican nutritional practices as lacking in balance, and particularly as lacking in animal proteins. He shows that pre-Colombian Mexican cuisine was indeed rich in both animal and non-animal proteins, which were mainly collected by hunting animals and birds and fishing, as well as from gathering a variety of insects, reptiles, beans, and seeds. Besides proteins, the diet of Mesoamerican people was "largely based on vegetables, fruit, an abundance of fibers, a small amount of fat and large amounts of energy."[14]

Cooking techniques were also important in the acquisition of a proper nutritional balance. These included grinding, boiling, smoking, grilling,

---

For further analysis on Mesoamerica in pre-Colombian times, see David Carrasco, *Religions of Mesoamerica: Cosmovision and Ceremonial Centers* (San Francisco: Harper, 1990), 1. For other sources on Mesoamerica, particularly regarding religious views, see Miguel León-Portilla, *Native Mesoamerican Spirituality* (New York: Paulist Press, 1963); Alfredo López Austin, *Hombre-Dios: Religion y Politica en el Mundo Náhuatl* (Mexico City: Universidad Autonoma de Mexico, 1973); and Diego Duran, *Book of Gods and the Rites and the Ancient Calendar*, trans. and ed. Fernando Horcasitas and Doris Heyden (Norman, OK: University of Oklahoma Press, 1970).

[11]   Carole M. Counihan, *The Anthropology of Food and Body: Gender, Meaning, and Power* (London: Routledge, 1999), 2.

[12]   Héctor Bourges Rodríguez, "Alimentos Obsequio de México al Mundo," in Donato Alarcón Segovia and Héctor Bourges Rodríguez (eds.), *La Alimentación de los Mexicanos* (Mexico City: El Colegio Nacional, 2002), 97–134: 124; all citations from this essay are my own translation from the Spanish original.

[13]   Ibid., 125.

[14]   Ibid.

and cooking food over charcoal or in holes made in the ground. Frying did not exist, for this was a later import brought by the Spaniards. Perhaps one of the most innovative cooking techniques used in Mesoamerica was the use of *tenéxtli* or *cal* (lime) which allowed the preparation of *nixtamal* – the cooking of corn in water with *cal*. This technique created a texture in the cooked corn that enabled the making of tortillas, to be used "simultaneously as a plate, wrap, spoon, and food."[15] Bourges Rodríguez points out that this technique allowed for more effective absorption of nutrients, particularly niacin and calcium, while also preserving the corn fibers.[16] Reflecting a rich sense of aesthetic variety, the banquets prepared for the Aztec emperor Moctezuma were a telling example of Mesoamerican cuisine.[17] Early Spanish historians reported with awe that for Moctezuma's banquets there was prepared every day a lavish presentation of about 300 different dishes that he could choose from.[18] Beauty, variety, and nutritional balance were the elements that constituted this time-honored cuisine.

Foodways in Mesoamerica had a profound religious significance as well. In his book *Gracias a Dios que Comí*, Maximiliano Salinas Campos analyzes this centrality of food in pre-Colombian traditions, and shows how these traditions were linked with religious symbols and rituals. Life and death, communal relationships, and the people's relationship with its deities were deeply embedded within food practices and alimentary symbols.[19] Following the same line of thought, Davíd Carrasco argues that Mesoamerican cosmology – particularly within the Aztec world – was deeply rooted in the symbolism of food and eating. Carrasco remarks:

[The Aztecs] developed a sophisticated cosmology of eating in which gods ate gods, humans ate gods, gods ate humans and the sexual sins of humans, children in the underworld suckled from divine trees, gods in the underworld ate the remains of humans, and adults in the underworld ate rotten tamales! It is also important

---

[15] Ibid., 112.
[16] Ibid.
[17] For more information on the Aztec culture and Moctezuma's empire, see Carrasco, *Religions of Mesoamerica*. See also Carrasco, *City of Sacrifice: The Aztec Empire and the Role of Violence in Civilization* (Boston: Beacon Press, 1999).
[18] This historical testimony is mainly taken from Bernal Díaz del Castillo, who wrote a book entitled *Historia verdadera de la Conquista de Nueva España*. This version is taken from Bourges Rodríguez, "Alimentos Obsequio de México al Mundo," 124.
[19] See Salinas Campos, *Gracias a Dios que Comí*, 7–19.

to note that at certain points in their sacred history, the Aztecs conceived of beings in their sky as a devouring mouth and the earth as a gaping jaw.[20]

According to Carrasco, the Aztec cosmic world-view considered eating an important part of a sacred economy that transformed everything into food, and that such a transformation was a means of cosmic and human divinization.[21] In this particular Aztec cosmovision, both the earth and the human body were conceived of as food; as one of their mythical songs read: "we eat the earth and the earth eats us."[22] The earth was depicted as a large mouth and a sacred digestive system for the cosmos. Humanity was first created out of corn by the gods, and, at the moment of death, humans nurtured the gods. Death was not viewed as final, but as a transformation into a source of cosmic energy, to the extent of becoming nourishment to feed divine hunger. The human heart and its blood were the most important sources of fuel in the recycling of cosmic energy. In this context, human sacrifice – and its dramatics of excision of the heart – was not conceived as mere cruelty, but rather as a highly honored ritual and liturgical act that contributed to the recycling of energy and the preservation of the cosmos.[23]

Mexican *mole* became an archetype of this cosmic-divine nourishment. *Mole* was not first created, as has commonly been understood, as part of the seventeenth century's convent cuisine tradition, borrowed from Spain (an already hybrid mix of cultures and cuisine traditions, as

[20]   Carrasco, *City of Sacrifice*, 168.
[21]   Not all of the Aztec cosmovision was based on food and eating symbols and practices. However, for the purposes of this book I am concentrating on this particular symbolic aspect, and hope to provide some explanation of why food in general, and *molli* in particular, were important to the practices of Mesoamerican culture. I am grateful to Professor Vanessa Ochs for suggesting this important clarification.
[22]   Carrasco, *City of Sacrifice*, 172.
[23]   This is the main argument in David Carrasco's *City of Sacrifice*, particularly ch. 6, "Cosmic Jaws: We Eat the Gods and the Gods Eat Us," 164–87. For a similar argument, see Christian Duverger, "The Meaning of Sacrifice," in Ramona Michel, Nadia Naddaff, and Feher Tazi (eds.), *Fragments for a History of the Human Body*, 3 vols. (New York: Zone Books, 1990), 3: 367–85. Regarding the Aztecs' notions of the human body as part of "a cosmic banquet" or an "eating landscape," see Alfredo López Austin, *The Human Body and Ideology: Concepts Among the Ancient Nahuas* (Salt Lake City: University of Utah Press, 1988). Finally, for an analysis of Mesoamerican notions of the body, particularly regarding the body as nourishment, see Sergio Raúl Arroyo, "In Praise of the Body," *Artes de México*, 69 (*In Praise of the Meosamerican Body*) (2004), 75–7.

we shall see later). The invention of *mole* goes far back, toward the Aztec world: the cuisine of the so-called *mexicas* of Tenochtitlán (located in central Mexico).[24] In fact, the word *mole* comes from the Náhuatl *molli*, meaning sauce, mixture, or stew.[25] Or at least this is what the early conquistadors from Spain thought the word meant. Yet, prior to that meaning, which is not totally unrelated to the Spanish understanding, *molli* actually means *alimento*: alimentation or nourishment.[26] The *molli* of the *mexicas* was a thick sauce made of a great variety of chilies and spices, plus chocolate, to which was most commonly added different sorts of meat, particularly *huexolotl*, what we now know in Spanish as *guajolote* or *pavo* (turkey).[27] Chilies and chocolate (in the form of cacao) were highly valued, for they were, like the *huexolotl*, Aztec deities. So, to eat *molli* that was made out of several deities was a way of eating the gods, who in turn would eat humans – as Carrasco points out – at their moment of death.

As one of the most popular dishes in pre-Colombian civilization, *molli* was mainly served at important festivals and consumed during religious rituals. It was also a gastronomic delicacy at the banquets of the Emperor Moctezuma and social and religious leaders of Tenochtitlán. The *mexicas* preferred to serve *molli* with *frijoles* (beans) and *tortillas de maíz* (corn tortillas). Again, beans and corn were also highly valued because they were viewed as different representations of Aztec gods that symbolized divine sustenance. This is particularly the case with corn, which was highly revered as one of the most important deities within the Olmec, Mayan, and Aztec mythologies, and which was also considered as the essential matter for the creation of humanity.[28] Because of its main ingredients of chilies and chocolate, plus the elements of corn and beans, and

---

[24]   For a further analysis of *mexicas*, and Tenochtitlán, see Carrasco, *Religions of Mesoamerica*, and the additional sources listed in n. 10.

[25]   Náhuatl was the official language, or the "true *lingua franca*" as Miguel León Portilla puts it, of Mesoamerican culture. For a further analysis of Náhuatl language, culture, and cosmovision, see Miguel León Portilla, *La Filosofía Náhuatl*, 9th edn. (Mexico City: UNAM, 2001).

[26]   Taibo I, *El Libro de Todos los Moles*, 108. From this point I will use the term *molli* rather than the baroque *mole* in order to emphasize its original cultural and etymological roots.

[27]   In the *mexica* mythology the *huexolotl* was revered as a deity, and was also considered a symbol of great nobility (hence, the use of its feathers for the emperor's crown). See Doris Heyden and Ana María L. Velasco, "Aves Van, Aves Vienen: El Guajolote, la Gallina y el Pato," in Long (ed.), *Conquista y Comida*, 237–53.

[28]   See e.g. Esteva and Marielle (eds.), *Sin Maíz no Hay País*, esp. 29–55.

the additional cooking with turkey, the Aztec *molli* was not just an ordinary dish; rather, it was a food of the gods, a divine alimentation.[29]

4 Alimentary Hybridization, or the Craving for Spice

Because of the deep religious, social, and cultural significance of *molli*, it is not surprising to find that it survived the systematic extermination of the European *encubrimiento* ("covering up") of America – to use Enrique Dussel's term.[30] In fact, one of the socio-religious and cultural practices that the Spanish conquistadors had most difficulty wiping out was the dietary customs of the mistakenly named "Indians."[31] But during colonial times the exchange and transformation of dietary customs were inevitable, and this transformation occurred in both directions (in the New as much as in the Old World). What is so interesting about the colonial baroque period in Mexico is the resulting hybrid or *mestizaje* not only of races, but also of inherited cultural, social, political, and religious practices. The culinary constructions of the original inhabitants of the American continent, as well as of Europe, were not an exception to this hybridization of (often) clashing world-views. From the perspective of alimentation, this complex mixture was what José N. Iturriaga calls "hibridación alimentaria." This "alimentary hybridization" was the way in which all the continents and cultures "mixed up their foods" ("mestizaron sus comidas").[32] And we must not forget that, in addition to this *mestizaje*, there was also an alimentary *mulataje* that resulted from the African presence in the Americas, as in the Caribbean.

---

[29] For more detailed information on the historical roots and religious symbolism of chilies see Patricia Van Rhijn (ed.), *La Cocina del Chile* (Mexico City: Planeta, 2003). For chocolate, see Martín Gozáles de la Vera, "Orígen y Virtudes del Chocolate," in Long (ed.), *Conquista y Comida*, 291–308. For beans see Lawrence Kaplan and Lucille N. Kaplan, "Leguminosas Alimenticias del Grano: Su Origen en el Nuevo Mundo, Su Adopción en el Viejo," in Long (ed.), *Conquista y Comida*, 183–98. For corn see Esteva and Marielle (eds.), *Sin Maíz no Hay País*, and Pilcher, *Vivan los Tamales!*
[30] Enrique Dussel argues that what actually took place on the arrival of the conquistadores on the American continent was not a "dis-covery," as has been commonly understood, but rather a "covering up," because of the systematic obliteration of the inhabitants' customs, belief systems, and lives. See Enrique Dussel, *The Invention of the Americas: Eclipse of "The Other" and the Myth of Modernity*, trans. Michael Barber (New York: Continuum, 1995).
[31] The first European explorers that came to the American continent mistakenly thought they were in Asian-Indian lands, and thus gave the name "Indians" to the inhabitants.
[32] José N. Iturriaga, "Los Alimentos Cotidianos del Mexicano o de Tacos, Tamales y Tortas: Mestizaje y Recreación," in Long (ed.), *Conquista y Comida*, 397–407: 399; my translation from the original Spanish text.

If we examine this closely, it is permissible to say, as Iturriaga does, that the alimentary *mestizaje* of the Mexican colonial period somehow included *all* continents. Prior to the arrival of the Spanish people on the American continent, medieval Spanish cuisine already enjoyed an impressive international culinary tradition. Spain's cosmopolitan culinary expressions were a product of Christian Roman and Muslim Arabic influences. Xavier Domingo explains that both Christian and Muslim culinary world-views craved a rich variety of spices and aromas.[33] This excess of spice constituted what Domingo calls "the medieval flavor" ("el sabor de la Edad Media").[34] The Islamic occupation of Spain from the eighth to the fifteenth centuries intensified this syncretistic culinary tradition, and its receptivity to food and gastronomic pleasure.[35] It was indeed syncretistic and hybridized, for the Christian Roman and Muslim Arabic culinary traditions resulted from prior historical explorations and exchanges with both the Asian and African continents.

Therefore, complex elaborations of food, and a taste for spice, were central aspects of Spanish cuisine before the Spaniards' arrival on the American continent. In fact, as interdisciplinary research shows, one of the main reasons for Christopher Columbus's explorations – which eventually took him into the American continent – was this European craving for "exotic" spices.[36] George Armelagos also shows that "the

---

[33] Xavier Domingo, "La Cocina Precolombina en España," in Long (ed.), *Conquista y Comida*, 17–28.

[34] Xavier Domingo mentions the following products and spices that made up this medieval flavor: "la albahaca, la canela, el cardamomo, el culandro, el clavo de olor, el comino, el tomillo, el hinojo, la galanga, el jengibe, el hisopo, el perejil, la hierba luisa, el romero, la menta, la mostaza, la nuez moscada, el oregano, la pimienta negra y la blanca, la ruda, el azafrán y la salvia." Ibid., 25.

[35] For a further analysis of the Islamic culinary influence on Spanish cuisine, see Antonio Riera-Melis, "El Mediterráneo, Crisol de Tradiciones Alimentarias: El Legado Islámico en la Cocina Medieval Catalana," in Massimo Montari (ed.), *El Mundo en la Cocina: Historia, Identidad, Intercambios*, trans. Yolanda Daffunchio (Barcelona: Paidós, 2003), 19–50. Riera-Melis analyses five main products that were brought to Spain by the Arabs: sugar (from canes), rice, a variety of citrus, eggplants, and spinach. These ingredients were later on imported into America, and also influenced the dietary customs of the New World, from which Mexican cuisine grew. On the influence of Islamic culinary traditions on Spanish cuisine, see also Salinas Campos, *Gracias a Dios que Comí*, esp. 86–117.

[36] "Este gusto por las especias exóticas, uno de los motivos del viaje de Colón, se prolongó durante muchos años y caracterizó la cocina española del tiempo de la Casa de los Austria. Eran sabores que costaban mucho dinero y abaratar su precio, importando las especias por rutas más cortas y al mismo tiempo acabar con la dependencia de los

Europeans had an insatiable desire for spices, and this was a great impulse for [trans-Atlantic] exploration." This craving, he argues, was "even greater than their greed for gold."[37] And they did find in America a true paradise of gastronomic delights, particularly with products such as chilies, chocolate, corn, tomatoes, potatoes, beans, and so forth. America's export of its products to the Old World further influenced the latter's cuisine and dietary customs.[38]

5 Subversive *Molli*

It is thus significant to find "early" stories of the creation of *molli* located in the kitchen space of convents and monasteries. Of course, these narratives often assumed a colonizing form, obliterating the entire history of pre-Colombian cultures and belief systems, including dietary and gastronomic indigenous traditions. From the baroque period to the present, the narrative that most Mexicans know of *molli*'s origin is the one constructed during the colonial period; the earlier pre-Colombian origin has been obliterated from people's memories and knowledge. Yet, in a subversive manner, dietary and eating traditions from the original inhabitants persisted. The ancestors' culinary traditions stubbornly became practices of resistance to colonization.[39] So, while there is a process of transgression and transformation within the practice of making *molli*, there is also a powerful sense of continuation and determination despite subjugation. In the religious communities, encounter

---

comerciantes de las ciudades-repúblicas italianas, de los turcos y de los portugueses, entró en línea de cuenta, sin duda, a la hora de financiar el viaje de Cristobal Colón." ("This taste for exotic spices, which was one of the reasons for Columbus's explorations, was prolonged for many years and became a characteristic of Spanish cuisine in the time of the House of Austria. These were expensive spices, and lowering their price – by importing them via commercial short-cuts, as well as by ending the dependence on traders from Italy, Turkey, and Portugal – doubtless became an important factor at the time when the decision was taken to finance Christopher Columbus's expedition.") Xavier Domingo, "La Cocina Precolombina en España" (my translation). Domingo's argument echoes the main line of reasoning of Long (ed.), *Conquista y Comida*.

[37] George Armelagos, "Cultura y Contacto: El Choque de Dos Cocinas Mundiales," in Long (ed.), *Conquista y Comida*, 105–29: 108; my translation from the Spanish original.

[38] For an analysis and an index of food products that traveled from the American continent into the rest of the world, see Héctor Bourges Rodríguez, "Alimentos Obsequio de México al Mundo." Long (ed.), *Conquista y Comida*, contains a series of essays exploring this aspect of native food products and their influence on world cuisine.

[39] For a study of the history of Mexican resistance to colonization through food and dietary customs, see esp. Esteva and Marielle (eds.), *Sin Maíz no Hay Paíz*, Pilcher, *Vivan los Tamales!*, and Salinas Campos, *Gracias a Dios que Comí*.

and clash, subjugation and subversion, took their most extravagant shape during this process of reinvention of this gastronomic hybrid. For, in the *molli*, not only do a plurality of cultures and culinary traditions, spices, and food elements come together (often conflictingly so), but gods and goddesses as well. If in pre-Colombian times *molli* was a material expression of divine alimentation, in the colonial and post-colonial periods it intensified its divinizing presence in a more eccentric fashion. Somehow the *molli* managed to continue being, throughout the centuries, a "spiritual alimentation," but more stridently so, and in an even more highly flavored, spicy manner.

During the baroque period in Mexico, most culinary inventions were created by women, with a very few exceptions, such as Fray Pascual Bailón. In a male-dominated society where women were not allowed to assume roles of leadership in public spaces, female attempts at empowerment and self-expression often arose in the kitchen (both in the convents and homes).[40] In colonial times, space (both geographical and architectural) was delimited and manipulated by a strong sense of hierarchy, including class, race, and gender control.[41] In a patriarchal colonial world such as that of Mexico, the kitchen and the refectory were virtually the only spaces where women were able to express themselves.[42]

Such was the case, for instance, with the famous erudite Mexican nun Sor Juana Inéz de la Cruz (1651–95).[43] From her early childhood (at about 3 years of age) Sor Juana learned to read and write.[44] Then, during

---

[40] For a study of the historical development of the kitchen in Mexico see Margarita de Orellana, *Los Espacios de la Cocina Mexicana*, *Artes de México*, 36 (1997).

[41] On the issue of the control of space by means of colonial power, see e.g. Walter D. Mignolo, *The Darker Side of the Renaissance: Literacy, Territoriality, and Colonization*, 2nd edn. (Ann Arbor: University of Michigan Press, 2003).

[42] This patriarchal control of space and restriction of women to the kitchen was well established in the history of Christianity. For example, Caroline Walker Bynum argues that during Middle Ages women (particularly religious women) had a complex relationship with food and at times displayed eccentric eating behavior. Many of their mystical experiences were intensely somatic and closely related to food and the Eucharist. Walker Bynum explains that this somatic relationship with food (feasting and fasting) was indeed a form of empowerment in the midst of marginalization. See *Holy Feast and Holy Fast: The Religious Significance of Food to Medieval Women* (Berkeley: University of California Press, 1987).

[43] Most of this reflection on Sor Juana Inés de la Cruz and her relationship with cuisine and the kitchen in a patriarchal society is taken from Angelo Morino, *El Libro de Cocina de Sor Juana Inés de la Cruz*, trans. Juan Pablo Roa (Mexico City: Editorial Norma, 2001).

[44] For biographical and textual analysis on Sor Juana, see Sandra Lorenzano (ed.), *Aproximaciones a Sor Juana* (Mexico City: Fondo de Cultura Económica, 2005).

her childhood and early adolescence she managed to "trick" the male-dominated system of her time by dressing as a boy and sneaking into school in order to obtain an education that was exclusively designed by and for men. When she was 18 years old she entered the convent of San Jerónimo in Mexico and had a prolific writing career, but not without controversy and even public scandal. The ecclesiastical hierarchy eventually forbade her to write or to visit her beloved library and lecture halls, and subsequently she was sent – as a punishment – to the kitchen, where women "were supposed to be."

But, somehow, Sor Juana survived, and transformed the kitchen into a space of creativity and liberation. There is a book of Mexican recipes attributed to her. Sor Juana even considered the culinary arts to be a higher form of knowledge and wisdom than that provided by traditional philosophy and theology. She once remarked that if Aristotle had cooked, he would have written a good deal more.[45] In her *Libro de Cocina* Sor Juana included her own recipe for a *molli* named *clemole de Oaxaca*. Sor Juana's perception of the correspondence between food and knowledge suggests that – as we shall see in the next chapter – there is a relationship between *sabor* and *saber* (savoring and knowing). Perhaps the kitchen and the library are in fact united by one and the same splendid desire: the desire to both savor and know. Sor Juana truly incarnates what Roberto Goizueta describes as the religious world-view of the Mexican baroque era: an experience that is "sensually rich," an experience of divine nearness as being deeply embodied.[46] In this organic and symbolic world both the intellect and affectivity, the rational and the sensual, the human and the divine are intimately connected. Moreover, Ada María Isasi-Díaz is right in pointing out that women's empowerment in the midst of disempowerment has been possible because of their "turning the confinement/spaces to which [women] are assigned

---

[45] "Qué podemos saber las mujeres sino filosofías de cocina? Bien dijo Lupercio Leonardo, que bien se puede filosofar y aderezar la cena. Y yo suelo decir viendo estas cosillas: si Aritóteles hubiera guisado, mucho más hubiera escrito." ("What could we women possibly know if not philosophies of cuisine? Lupercio Leonardo said it so well: that it is certainly possible to both philosophize and season a supper. And I also always say when I see this sort of thing: had Aristotle cooked, he would have written a good deal more.") Sor Juana Inés de la Cruz, *Obras Completas* (Mexico City: Porrúa, 1997), 838–9 (my translation). For an English version, see Sor Juana Inés de la Cruz, *The Answer/La Respuesta*, ed. and trans. Electa Arenal and Amanda Powell (New York: Feminist Press, 1994), 75.

[46] Roberto Goizueta, "The Symbolic Realism of U.S. Latino/a Popular Catholicism," *Theological Studies*, 65/2 (June 2004), 225–74.

into creative/liberating spaces."[47] Thus, this illustration of Sor Juana demonstrates how in the *molli* we find not only a harmony that suggests a festive reality, but also a struggle and subversion. It is hot, spicy, *picante*! Thanks to women, the culinary art that is the Mexican *molli* has been preserved and re-created, but not without pain and struggle.

6 Making *Molli* and Alimentary Theology in the Making

As we have seen in the previous sections, the Mexican *molli* displays and brings attention to multiple interactions of ingredients, narratives, and traditions that coexist in one and the same dish. In using *molli* as a paradigm, I would like to coin the phrase *alimentary theology*, a theology that is more attentive to and welcoming of the multiple layers contained and implied in the making of theology. This is a theology that not only pays closer attention to matters related to food and nourishment, and the many ways they can relate, inspire, and inform theological reflection. Most importantly, it is an envisioning of theology *as* nourishment: food as theology and theology as food. Alimentary theology is envisioned as food for thought; it addresses some of the spiritual and physical hungers of the world, and seeks ways of bringing about nourishment.

For the same reason, alimentary theology envisions theology as a culinary art that is not only aesthetic, but, further, points to the necessity of integrating an ethics and politics that question our systems of global exchange. Theology as food for thought is not a disembodied abstraction, but a performance that increases awareness of the body, allowing corporeal and material experience to become a primary source of reflection.

---

[47] Ada María Isasi-Díaz, "*Burlando al Opresor.* Mocking/Tricking the Oppressor: Dreams and Hopes of Hispanas/Latinas and *Mujeristas*," *Theological Studies*, 65/2 (June 2004), 340–63: 346. There is of course, the possibility of reading too much of liberation and empowerment into the events of Sor Juana's life. As Vanessa Ochs has pointed out to me, it could have been quite otherwise. There are, however, elements in her life of what Isasi-Díaz calls "mocking/tricking the oppressor" which could be interpreted as a reaction to marginalization: she dresses as a man to get into school, she writes on matters related to food and has high regard for cuisine, and so on. To what extent were Sor Juana's actions instances of empowerment? My guess is that this is a question that can be answered from different angles. I am inclined toward a more positive reading since foodways manage to survive despite colonization (here as the obliteration of culture and values), as was the case with pre-Colombian cuisine. Such a reading I propose, following Isasi-Díaz, does not undermine the aspect of suffering and struggle either in Sor Juana's life or in the survival of *molli*.

This embodied alimentary theology is rooted in a multi-dimensional vision of the body, incorporating individual, social, political, human, ecological, cosmic, and divine bodies. As one ultimately learns how to make a good *molli* after hours, days, and years of preparation and practice, so it is with theology practiced as a culinary art that is only learned in the actual making, a constant process of refining. Like cooking, alimentary theology is a theology in the making: a performance that involves both contemplation and action. However, alimentary theology, like a good *molli*, is not just about the skillful crafting (*poiesis*) of a gift. *Molli* and alimentary theology are gifts to be shared in the form of nourishment among concrete communities. Like making an intricate dish, this alimentary theology can be said to be a complex "culinary art": a theological vocation that is simultaneously gift and reception, preparation and sharing, contemplation and consumption, materiality and transcendence, human and divine.

In what follows, both here and in the rest of this book, I shall explore the meaning of alimentary theology, its constitutive ingredients, the implications it calls attention to, and why I consider Mexican *molli* to be paradigmatic for envisioning theology as alimentation.

As I have already noted, Mexican *molli* is the result of many ingredients, elements, and realities coming together. If theology is seen as a culinary art, one can also become aware of its analogy to the culinary extravagance of *molli*. Theology envisioned as nourishment brings greater attention to the many converging ingredients and processes involved in the making of theology: revelation, tradition, faith, history, cultural background, popular devotional practices, and so forth. In addition, and similar to the way in which *molli* is made, this understanding of alimentary theology is also aware of the inherent situatedness or locality (locus) that contributes to the making of theology; or, to be more precise, alimentary theology is aware of the many situations and different localities that play a significant role in the making of theology.

However, while there might be many ingredients in the making of both *molli* and theology, there are some ingredients that predominate over others. In the making of both *molli* and alimentary theology not just "anything" goes. In *molli*, for instance, the chilies and the chocolate are indispensable. Speaking from a Catholic viewpoint, my particular articulation of this alimentary theology contains two indispensable elements: the element of God's desire to share divinity with humanity (through the Creation, time and space, the Incarnation, the cross and resurrection, the Eucharist, the gift of the Holy Spirit, and so on), and the believer's desire to unite with God in and through communal relationships.[48] These two desires (divine and human) coming together play an important role in the making of alimentary theology: they are the "chilies and chocolate" of theological practice. This blending of desires, as in the *molli*, does not create mere homogeneity, but rather constructs a milieu of heterogeneous unity. And this unity creates the love between God and humanity, wherein – in the words of Pope Benedict XVI – both "remain themselves and yet become fully one."[49]

Just as *molli* is a point of contact between different elements, I argue that alimentary theology communicates this reality of in-betweenness, a hybrid discourse of a divine–human encounter. It is discursive because it is an act of communication between God and creation, and the communication expressed between people. Yet I agree with Graham Ward, who remarks that "discursivity" means more than verbal (written and spoken) expression. Paraphrasing Ward's reflection on the discursive dimension of theology, this alimentary theology that I articulate is a hybrid discourse that also includes a great variety of expressions (expressive acts) that communicate, for example, "music, painting, architecture, liturgy, gesture, dance, in fact any social action."[50] And, certainly, one must include food, cooking, and digestion in these diverse forms of communication. As in *molli*, the multiple elements in these expressive acts may reflect a struggle more than a harmonious ensemble or fusion. What exactly is this desire between God and humanity about? Whose voice is it? Whose authority are we talking about? Who is included or excluded in this hybrid discourse? Rather than offering facile solutions, this understanding of theology may instead open further questions and critiques, a space of unfinished and unresolved conflicting discourses. Alimentary theology exposes us to a space of indeterminacy, fragmentation, and ambiguity. These unresolved issues often create an experience

---

[48] Because this view is partial and limited I assume that not all Catholics or other Christians will agree with my prioritization of elements in this particular religious tradition. If this is the case with those who belong to the Catholic or wider Christian tradition, I imagine that disagreement with my viewpoint might be even greater among those from other religious traditions. Again, this is only my personal experience and viewpoint, and not a generalization. This same applies to what I say about (alimentary) theology in the rest of this book.

[49] Benedict XVI, *Deus Caritas Est*, taken from the web: <www.vatican.va/holy_father/benedict_xvi/encyclicals/documents/hf_ben-xvi_enc_20051225_deus-caritas-est_en.html>.

[50] Ward goes on to describe discourse as "that expressive act that intends or means and is therefore immediately caught up in the receptive processes of translation and interpretation. Discourse as *expressive act* becomes inseparable from practices, and practices from hermeneutics" (emphasis in original). Graham Ward, *Cultural Transformation and Religious Practice* (Cambridge: Cambridge University Press, 2005), 6.

of frustration. For me, this experience of irresolution in theology usually brings about a sense of perplexity, similar to that of tasting *molli* when one is uncertain as to what ingredient is being tasted. What do we "taste" in a theological work? Like eating *molli*, this experience of taste in theology is often plural, a complex network of ingredients interacting without a final semiotic resting-place.

Because of the enormous complexity of *molli*, it is difficult neatly to categorize it. Is it a dish, an intercultural expression, a mixture of world-views, an inter-religious cacophony, or a gastronomic manifestation of a power struggle based on race, gender, and class? Even at the level of flavor and taste, it never completely rests with one particular palate's identification of a specific ingredient. As soon as one is able to taste one ingredient, suddenly another taste arises, and then another, and so on. Without arriving at a final synthesis, there is always still more to taste, still more flavors to discover and experience. It is as if the *molli* acts as a mobile signifier moving beyond the signified. A system of continuously displaced signs, for they point to other signs without final semiotic stasis. In *molli* there is an experience not so much of the "either/or" type, but rather the realm of the "both/and." Better yet, in *molli* there is a dynamic sense of in-betweenness at a multiplicity of levels. In its continuous re-creation, *molli* becomes a paradigmatic example of José N. Iturriaga's term "alimentary hybridization." Such gastronomic eccentricity (of even mythical dimensions) is what makes *molli* so amazingly playful, so per-plexing and pleasurable.

When talking of God it seems we must inevitably arrive at this experi-ence of perplexity, for God is ultimately excess. God exceeds any dis-course, including "official" ones. Signification falls short of its signified signs, for God perpetually and dynamically displaces God-self from any sign. Like the non-static semiotics of *molli*, God's significations are like-wise excessive, and extravagant. However, this does not mean that God's signification is a perpetual deferral of meaning that ultimately leaves us dissatisfied, or famished. God's signs are nourished by God's plenitude and superabundant gifts.[51] Here – and particularly from the scope of

---

[51] This book will look at three main aspects of God's nurturing signs. Chapter 2 will explore the aspect of phenomenology and knowledge constructions whereby God and humanity co-create signs. Chapter 3 will explore an ontological dimension of God's nur-turing of signs, particularly the perplexing sign of Being. Chapter 4 will look at how God's nurturing of signs (such as manna) shapes a political body. For a further study of theology's dependence on God's nurturing signs which provides an alternative to post-modern nihilistic theories of meaning and signification, see Catherine Pickstock, *After Writing: On the Liturgical Consummation of Philosophy* (Oxford: Blackwell, 1998).

both the Incarnation and the Eucharist – sign and body dynamically co-arise in a gesture that brings about alimentation.

At the same time, *molli* is a product of human creativity, and a dish whose main purpose is not to be fetishized, but to nourish and to be shared in communal meals. Theology in general, and alimentary theology in particular, is also incarnational, human-made, and as such it attempts not to be a fetish that would make of God a static idol, but rather the result of a human dynamic quest for God, a human response to God's initial desire to become closer to humanity. Theology as alimentation is a discourse that expresses, and hopefully feeds, humanity's hunger for God's goodness, truth, justice, and beauty. This form of theologizing also highlights a communal dimension, for it initiates a complex communal *tropos*, and it is to be shared in the public space – always avoiding the temptation of too exclusive and individualistic purposes.

Both apophatic and cataphatic discourses are thus necessary for a theological feast that expresses God's own excess (a divine ineffability that exceeds both apophasis and cataphasis). While, on the one hand, God's excessiveness can never be reduced to language, symbols, concepts, and so forth, on the other hand God is also incarnational, and encountered in loving relations as well as in language, liturgy, and everyday practices – despite the limits and partialities that we always inevitably encounter. Both Silence and Word nourish the theological vocation.[52] Simply talking about *molli* does not amount to the actual experience of eating it. Talking about God from a safe distance for the sake of preserving God's "purity" because of God's being "beyond" situatedness, leaves us empty and malnourished. God is also personal, loving, and sharing, and walks with humanity the pilgrimage of history, what faith believes and hopes to be God's orientation toward an eschatological future. Theology's extravagance is to become alimentation – alimentary theology. It must feed human hungers, both physical and spiritual. For this reason, alimentary theology is also intimately concerned with the concreteness of everyday life as well as analogical mediations, language, the body, materiality, and so on. Yet this situatedness is not the whole story. Without ever transcending situatedness, and yet because of its participation in the excess of divine desire, alimentary theology is also perpetually opened and unfinished. There is still more to taste, more flavors yet to discover.

Making *molli* is not an easy task, and I ask the reader to recall the description of this laborious process that I offered at the beginning of this chapter. It takes time, discipline, and personal engagement. It is

---

[52] See e.g. Oliver Davies and Denys Turner (eds.), *Silence and the Word: Negative Theology and Incarnation* (Cambridge: Cambridge University Press, 2002).

more than merely following a recipe – although recipes are very helpful in providing guidance and for preserving traditions. But, more than a recipe, it is a meticulous crafting that could be compared to an art form, a culinary art.[53] Like making art, making *molli* involves a self-sharing: much of the cook's person is put into the *molli*, which is then further shared in the communal banqueting. Likewise, alimentary theology takes time and effort, and often great discipline and sacrifice.[54] While, on the one hand, alimentary theology is attentive to preserving traditions and institutions (and here there is a certain analogue to recipes); on the other hand it is also open to being transformed by fresh ingredients (different forms of feedback), such as inter-religious and interdisciplinary dialogue, for instance. Moreover, like the experience of preparing *molli*, alimentary theology requires self-involvement, and there is a sense of

---

[53] "Crafting" and "creation" are distinct notions. In general terms one could say that, while the former requires technical skill and is often understood as mechanical production, the latter implies a greater sense of personal involvement and is usually closely related to aesthetics and – in the Christian tradition – to divine making. Graham Ward points out that both crafting and creating are founded on a notion of *poiesis*, a creative action, that Christianity also understands as "a power to create anew, to transform; it announces a production not a mindless reproduction" (Ward, *Cultural Transformation and Religious Practice*, 8). Ward follows Robert Miner's preference for a Christian understanding of *poiesis* as "creating," rather than "crafting." A principal reason for this preference has to do with a theological account of creativity which is analogous to divine creation, while crafting is thought to relate to a technical, mechanical, and even "mindless" making. Speaking from a Mexican viewpoint, I have a more positive understanding of "crafting" than Ward and Miner. In Spanish the word for crafting is *artesanía*, and it is closely related to art-making. Since pre-Colombian times Mexican *artesanos* (craftspeople) have been greatly respected because of their highly developed gift for creating objects that are a reflection of their personal involvement and deep sensibility, even passion. This is less a Western understanding of crafting (like that of Ward or Miner) and more a syncretistic European understanding that inherits a pre-Colombian view of craftsmanship as an organic cosmic (and thus implicitly sacred) knowledge, and which is intrinsically corporeal. For an investigation of the related subjects of the body, craftsmanship, and cosmovision, see Alberto Ruy Sánchez, *In Praise of the Mesoamerican Body*, *Artes de México*, 69 (2004).

[54] For instance, those who have undergone the process of preparing for doctoral studies may know how painful at times this enterprise is (particularly those doctoral students who are married and have children). For a Dominican friar, becoming a theologian is never seen as mere individual achievement, but rather as a communal task, and for the purpose of serving the church and the wider world. Some theologians may suffer harsh criticism, imprisonment, torture, and even death because of the political and social implications of their theological statements (Bishop Romero in Central America, who was eventually killed for the political implications of his preaching, comes to mind). And in a mostly male-dominated academy of theology, women theologians can speak of this ostracizing experience.

self-fulfillment. There is a joy (at least in my own experience) of sharing the product. This is a "kenotic delight," a non-possessive rejoicing in the feeding of the concrete – not abstract – Other.

7 Body and Flesh: Incarnation and Alimentation

Earlier it was proposed that theology is a hybrid discourse of divine and human desires. While this blending of desires activates the intellect and spirit, it is nevertheless, like cooking and eating, a deeply embodied experience and practice.

Growing, cooking, and eating food are intense somatic or bodily experiences that bring about knowledge. Lisa M. Heldke argues that this somatic knowledge, unlike modern epistemological categories that set the mind over and against the body, actually constitutes a broader and non-dualistic "bodily knowledge" that takes place within food practices.[55] I hope that this reflection on *molli* may increase awareness of the need for theology to become more attentive to the reality of the body, both at the individual and communal levels.[56] The body is constitutive of our being. We are in the world as embodied beings. The fact of embodiment is an important element that underlines our experience of our inner and outer selves. We are never totally divorced from the reality of embodiment, as George Lakoff and Mark Johnson rightly argue.[57]

[55] "For theories like Descartes' [which] conceive of my body as an external appendage to my mind, and see its role in inquiry as merely to provide a set of (fairly reliable) sensory data on which my reasoning faculty then operates to produce objects of knowledge. But growing and cooking food are important counterexamples to this view; they are activities in which bodily perceptions are more than meter reading which must be scrutinized by reason. The knowing involved in making a cake is 'contained' not simply 'in my head' but in my hands, my wrists, my eyes and nose as well. The phrase 'bodily knowledge' is not a metaphor. It is an acknowledgment of the fact that I *know* things literally with my body, that I, 'as' my hands, know when the bread dough is sufficiently kneaded, and I 'as' my nose know when the pie is done." Lisa M. Heldke, "Foodmaking as a Thoughtful Practice," in Deane W. Curtin and Lisa M. Heldke (eds.), *Cooking, Eating, Thinking: Transformative Philosophies of Food* (Bloomington: Indiana University Press, 1992), 203–29: 218.
[56] In the next chapter I will explore how the senses, particularly those closest to the act of eating such as smell, touch, and taste, display this complex reality of embodiment and connectivity with the world. For a an analysis of the senses in general and the sense of taste in particular, see Carolyn Korsmeyer, *Making Sense of Taste: Food and Philosophy* (Ithaca, NY: Cornell University Press, 1999). Chapter 4 will also reflect on the political dimension of the body.
[57] George Lakoff and Mark Johnson, *Philosophy in the Flesh: The Embodied Mind and its Challenge to Western Thought* (New York: Basic Books, 1999).

Without the body it is impossible to experience anything at all, and no thought process take place in a bodiless mind.

But what exactly does it mean to be a body? Are we all ontologically similar because of this reality of embodiment? The body is not a mere pre-social or absolutely determined biological entity, but – like the *molli* – is constructed, shaped, and even "invented" by society. The body is "socialized" by a series of social constructions such as gender, race, class, age, and so forth. We behave bodily according to these social constructions, which are relative to particular localities, and thus the body does not have a universal or essential character. As a social construction, the body could be also seen as a *symbol* of society; it acts as a microcosm of society. Particular communities and social groups construct symbols and concepts that are explicitly concerned with the body: notions such as male/female, sacred/profane, nature/culture, healthy/disabled, and so on. Thus, to theologize in light of a notion of alimentation means to speak from within this complex reality of the body: I embody my own theology, and theology also shapes my own body.

In Christian theology, this already complex reality of the body is linked with a notion of the "flesh," such as is found in John 1:14, which proclaims that *the Word became flesh*. This is both at the core of John's theology and the foundation of Christian theology. Flesh is the most primary sense of embodiment. It lies within the realm of the experience of extreme proximity with humanity's *pathos* that, as Michel Henry describes it, is "pure affectivity, pure impressionness, that which is radically immanent auto-affection."[58] God's incarnation takes this human flesh at its primordial materiality in order to divinize it, from within and not from without. In this act, the God–human conjoins what appears to be a mutually exclusive ontology of divinity and humanity, and maximizes a new ontology that is non-dualistic but participatory and reciprocally related. This is a new ontology revealed as *relationality*.[59] As a living organism, the flesh performs in the body a sharing with Life itself – which is already divinized, but in a way that does not do violence to or transcend its own human condition, but which rather intensifies and celebrates its humanity. This reality of human flesh delighting in a divine embrace posits difference not as in-difference, but as sharing and return.

---

[58] My own translation from the Spanish version by Michel Henry, *Encarnación: Una Filosofía de la Carne*, trans. from the French original, *Incarnation: Une philosophie de la chair*, by Javier Teira, Gorka Fernández, and Roberto Ranz (Salamanca: Ediciones Sígueme, 2001), 159.

[59] In chapter 3 I will further explore this relational ontology and its intimate connection with nourishment.

Moreover, from a Christian perspective one could make the conjecture that, because of Christ's flesh as non-indifference to flesh as such, this divine embrace (the Incarnation) allows us to envision a dimension of *affectivity* and *affinity* as being prior to sheer difference.

Christ's flesh aligns itself with human flesh. In the flesh, Christ blends God's desires with the desires of humanity. Like *molli*, Christ's flesh displays a dimension of a divine–human *mestizaje*, and one which is profoundly encultured. He is born, grows up, experiences hunger and thirst, he loves and cries, becomes tired, suffers, and dies – within the reality of human flesh and within a particular cultural symbolic world-view.[60] God is not indifferent, but shares divinity within and at the core of the human flesh. From within, God continuously walks humanity's historical *pathos* and further transforms it into a present and future story of resurrection and deification. By virtue of Christ's incarnation, flesh is perpetually in flux; it is the in-betweenness of the divine–human relationality. In this vision, humanity is invited to become co-creator of this human–divine *poiesis* (a making that is also performing, a creative practice).[61]

The aesthetic dimension of the flesh brings about an ethical demand, for it depicts the beautiful as the good (that which is beloved and desired). It is all-inclusive. Yet the painful fact is that in human society (and Catholic and Christian social groups are not an exception to this reality) some bodies are rejected and cast out because their embodiment is depicted by those in power as "imperfect" and/or "impure": black and brown bodies, female bodies, disabled bodies. and so on.[62] In spite of this human rejection, Christ identifies with the excluded one (Matthew 25): the one who is desired, and embraced with love by God – not rejected. Christ transforms a social cycle of violence, and reveals self and other as mutually constitutive by virtue of divine kenosis. Christ's

---

[60] This analysis of the relationship between flesh and culture is inspired by Graham Ward's notion of "culture," which articulates it as "a symbolic world-view, embedded, reproduced and modified through specific social practices." Although Ward does not address here the particular issue of the relationship between flesh and culture, I believe that one does not exist in isolation from the other. Hence, the aspect of syncretism or *mestizaje* that they share, for both – like *molli* – are not monolithic, but "polyphonic, hybrid, and fragmentary, always being composed and recomposed." Ward, *Cultural Transformation and Religious Practice*, 5, 6.

[61] I will say more about *poiesis* in the next chapter.

[62] For a reflection on how in fact this violent politics of exclusion of the "imperfect bodies" echoes a colonial Christian missionary agenda, see Sharon Betcher, "Monstrosities, Miracles, and Mission: Religion and the Politics of Disablement," in, Catherine Keller, Michael Nausner, and Mayra Rivera (eds.), *Postcolonial Theologies: Divinity and Empire* (St. Louis, MO: Chalice Press, 2004). I am grateful to Mayra Rivera, who generously gave me a copy of this book.

reversal speaks of peace and reconciliation in a world of violence, exclusion, and destruction.

The Catholic narrative proclaims that in Christ's "in-fleshing" the world reaches its climax and is enacted in the Eucharist wherein God becomes food and drink in and through materiality. As we shall explore in the next chapter, in eating this divine food, sensuality – particularly the senses of touch and taste – is intensified in a way that nothing material is surpassed. Catholic theology envisions the Eucharist as the body of Christ that, in its act of self-sharing offered up as alimentation, transforms the partakers into Christ's own body, and calls us to feed both physical and spiritual hungers.

The Eucharist, like *molli*, is an alimentary hybrid, a complex interplay of multiple narratives.[63] The eucharistic body (the hybrid of humanity and God, materiality and divinity) displays its own corporeality as a sharing of differences whereby difference is not eliminated but celebrated: peoples of all races, classes, genders, and sexual orientations, the healthy and the sick – all are united by the one and excessive divine perpetual love that nourishes body and soul.[64] I said earlier that one drop of *molli* contains the entire world, for it brings together different nations, cultures, races, and so on. Likewise, the eucharistic body nourishes in its act of sharing and celebrating difference. The catholicity of the body celebrates a corporeal reality bringing together both the local and universal bodies that coincide in the one body of Christ. Under this eucharistic construction, the "alien other" is no long rejected but included. Still more challenging, the other is alien no longer. In the Eucharist, self and other are not juxtaposed, nor do they collapse into one another, but difference is preserved in a stage of mutual constitution. That is the challenge that the Eucharist presents – particularly to those who belong to the Catholic church. I painfully realize that there is still much to learn in this.

---

[63] See e.g. Dennis E. Smith, *From Symposium to Eucharist: The Banquet in the Early Christian World* (Minneapolis: Fortress Press, 2003). Smith rightly argues that the Eucharist does not exist in its own "purity," but it is rather a syncretism, a hybrid constructed by many traditions and narratives (such as Jewish, Greco-Roman, and, later, patristic, medieval, and so forth). And I must add: the Eucharist continues to be reshaped by history, cultures, and communities; simultaneously, the dynamism of the Eucharist also continuous to shape or "make" the Church. See also Paul McPartlan, *The Eucharist Makes the Church: Henri de Lubac and John Zizioulas in Dialogue* (Edinburgh: T&T Clark, 1993).

[64] There is not space here to discuss the soul–body relationship. In the Catholic tradition, this non-dualistic relationship is very important: it actually serves as a re-intensification and celebration of the body, the material, and thus can become a solid foundation for sacramental theology.

8 Daily Bread and Daily Hunger

In word and deed, Jesus Christ – the one who enjoys eating and drinking with the excluded ones – teaches about a God who nourishes and who celebrates love and solidarity with humanity in the midst of a shared table.[65] He teaches us to tenderly call God *Abba*, and as God's children to ask the loving Father for our daily communal bread, *el pan para todos* (bread for everyone).[66] Jesus Christ (the God-human) is the "master of desire," who incarnates God's own desire to feed all hungers, and who promises that the kingdom of heaven will be a lavish banquet, a big fiesta.[67] Yet this feasting will not wait until that eschatological promised day. The Christian narrative proclaims that, after Jesus' ascension into heaven, God sends the Holy Spirit as *donum*, the procession of a divine gift that is a desire to practice reciprocity within an all-inclusive communal feasting (a practice already anticipated within the intra-Trinitarian community). In and with the Holy Spirit, Christianity learns that *imitatio Dei* is in fact *imitatio Trinitatis*. In and with the Holy Spirit, community already takes place here on earth, at the locus of a collective table that offers solidarity to all, particularly to those who physically and spiritually most hunger in the world.

Theology in general, and alimentary theology in particular, cannot be indifferent to the question of why there are so many people in the world who are malnourished, and indeed starving. Frei Betto rightly insists on reminding us of the great number of human bodies dying of hunger and malnutrition. And this horrific fact reflects people's indifference and selfishness:

> According to the FAO, 831 million people are now living in a chronic state of malnutrition. Every day, 24,000 die of hunger, including a child under five years of age every minute. Why is it that there are so many campaigns around other causes of premature

---

[65] For a New Testament analysis of table-sharing see Rafael Aguirre, *La Mesa Compartida: Estudios del NT desde las Ciencias Sociales* (Bilbao: Sal Terrae, 1994), and also Xabier Pikaza, *Pan, Casa, Palabra: La Iglesia en Marcos* (Salamanca: Sígueme, 1998).

[66] See Ricardo López, and Daniel Landgrave (eds.), *Pan Para Todos: Estudios en Torno a la Eucaristía* (Mexico City: Universidad Pontificia de México, 2004). See also Ricardo R. López, *Comer, Beber, Alegrarse: Estudios Bíblicos en Honor a Raúl Duarte Castillo* (Mexico City: Universidad Pontificia de México, 2004).

[67] See Éloi Leclerc, *El Maestro del Deseo: Una Lectura del Evangelio de Juan*, trans. from the French *Le Maître du désir* by Javier Sánchez (Madrid: PPC Editorial y Distribudora SA, 1997).

death, such as cancer, accidents, war and terrorism, without the same being true of hunger, which produces many more victims than these? I can think of only one explanation, and that is a cynical one: that, unlike those other causes, hunger is a respecter of class. It is as though we, the well fed, were saying, "Let the wretched die of hunger; it doesn't affect us."[68]

Hunger has a physical and existential as well as an ethical-political dimension, as we will explore further in chapter 4. Humans are hungry beings, for without eating we die of starvation. But hunger is also a reflection of ethics and politics, for it involves power relations, and the sharing (or the lack of sharing) of God's gift.

From this ethical-political dimension, hunger reflects society's practice of the disempowerment of certain groups and their lack of communal vision, virtue, and caritas.[69] Why is it that hunger is predominantly related to issues of ethnicity, race, gender, sexuality, and social class? Patricia Hill Collins advocates paying greater attention to Black feminist thought as an example that does not ignore these co-related factors. Hill Collins also argues that Black feminist thought contributes to the development of what she calls a "politics of empowerment," precisely because it challenges thinking – to develop an epistemology – from the perspective of just and unjust power relations.[70] This challenge must also move beyond mere epistemology; it must integrate a theological vision of nourishment and communal sharing as the locus of divine self-expression.

Bread, and the lack thereof, has to do with the power of sharing and the potential refusal to do just that. It is therefore a profoundly theological issue, for it has to do ultimately with God's gift and the sharing

---

[68] Frei Betto, "Zero Hunger: An Ethical-Political Project," *Concilium*, 2 (2005), 11–23: 12.

[69] I agree with Frei Betto that alleviating hunger is not just about giving food to people, or making donations, but requires a more holistic approach that targets structural change: see ibid., 13.

[70] "First, Black feminist thought fosters a fundamental paradigmatic shift in how we think about unjust power relations. By embracing a paradigm of intersecting oppressions of race, class, gender, sexuality, and nation, as well as Black women's individual and collective agency within them, Black feminist thought reconceptualizes the social relations of domination and resistance. Second, Black feminist thought addresses ongoing epistemological debates concerning the power dynamics that underlie what counts as knowledge. Offering U.S. Black women new knowledge about our own experiences can be empowering. But activating epistemologies that criticize prevailing knowledge and that enable us to define our own realities *on our own terms* has far greater implications." Patricia Hill Collins, *Black Feminist Thought: Knowledge, Consciousness, and the Politics of Empowerment*, 2nd edn. (New York: Routledge, 2000), 273–4 (emphasis in original).

(or refusal to share) of this gift with one another. That is why the "Zero Hunger" project was an act of commitment that expressed the voice of dozens of religious denominations (Christian and non-Christian) in the shared conviction that "hunger results from injustice and represents an offense against the Creator, since life is the greatest gift of God." They also expressed their belief that "to share bread is to share God."[71] For, as we shall see in more detail in chapter 3, creation is not devoid of God's sharing. This implies that, without God, the possibility of overcoming hunger does not exist. Intrinsic – not extrinsic – to creation there *is* God whose sharing (enacted in concrete human communities) brings about nourishment. This is also another reason why alimentary theology could be a counter-secular practice in the midst of a starving world, devoid of God.

Moreover, as the Mexican *molli* is composed of the personal touch of numerous individuals, communities, and traditions, so alimentary theology invites us to bring our own selves into it, to add our own "spices," and so make it more spicy. Theologians should offer their own particular situatedness, gender, sexual orientation, race, ethnicity, culture, and social class. The making of this theological *molli* shall also include people's own stories of hope, suffering, and struggle. Spiciness is a kind of subversion: its sharpness is *picante*, it stirs our tongues and mouths and awakens us. That which is spicy makes us alert, attentive, responsive – responsible. Thus, to bring our own spice into the theological *molli* also implies the acquisition of a *piquant*, or prophetic voice. This prophetic, "spicy" theology urges us to speak up about the concrete instances when communities fail to feed people's hungers, when there is a refusal to welcome otherness (both human and divine) to the communal feasting table.

Making *molli* and the making of alimentary theology is not an attempt to collapse all differences and boundaries into a homogenizing category of *nouvelle cuisine*.[72] In *molli*, and in the making of alimentary theology, harmonious difference is welcomed and celebrated. This notion of harmonious difference is akin to John Milbank's argument in favor of the construction of a "gothic complex space," which allows the intersecting

---

[71] Cited in Betto, "Zero Hunger," 11.

[72] The warning in this statement regards homogenization more than the notion of *nouvelle cuisine* as such. Undoubtedly, *molli* was and is continually being re-created. So is theology. In this sense, both *molli* and theology are always open to newness. Thus, the notion of *nouvelle cuisine* could well apply to both. I am not arguing in favor of a return to a lost "origin." I want to suggest that alimentary theology, like *molli*, is not about homogenizing, or becoming a monolithic entity, but is instead about being polyphonic, heterogeneous: allowing difference and contrasts, ambiguity and perplexity.

and even overlapping of bonds, ways of life, and identities.[73] In addition to complex space, alimentary theology integrates Talal Asad's notion of heterogeneous time, which includes:

> embodied practices rooted in multiple traditions, of the differences between horizons of expectation and spaces of experience – differences that continually dislocate the present from the past, the world experienced from the world anticipated, and call for their revision and reconnection. These simultaneous temporalities embrace both individuals and groups in complexities that imply more than a simple process of secular time.[74]

But rather than constructing a milieu of sheer difference with a tendency or potential to develop into total indifference, extreme antagonism, or even violence, a Christian-Catholic perspective envisions the eucharistic ecclesial body as a concrete communal locus for this interaction of complex space and time, and which allows differences to coexist in peace and continuous harmony (just as the ingredients in the *molli* interact). As we shall see in the chapters that follow (particularly chapters 3 and 4), the eucharistic body envisions all human beings and creation not as autonomous items existing in isolation – and even in antagonism to – from one another, but rather, as being different expressions of one cosmic, heterogeneous divine banquet.

This notion of heterogeneous space and time does not imply that alimentary theology is a new sort of religion made up of all religions. Neither is it a theology made up of all theologies cooked together in one single pot. It is instead an attempt to think about the complexity of food and its lack in the world. And food is not "just food," but an expression of multiple connections within our bodies, the earth, local and global economies, and finally God. Food is also a construction of people's identities: national, political, economic, social, cultural, religious, somatic, sexual, and so on. Thus, alimentary theology envisions theology as food and food as theology: for both theology and food exemplify the need for a communal practice of delight and sharing.[75] Not surprisingly – as

---

[73] See John Milbank, "Against the Resignations of the Age," in Francis P. McHugh and Samuel M. Natale (eds.), *Things Old and New: Catholic Social Teaching Revisited* (Lanham, MD: University Press of America, 1993).

[74] Talal Asad, *Formations of the Secular: Christianity, Islam, Modernity* (Stanford: Stanford University Press, 2003), 179.

[75] In very general terms, this is the main thesis throughout L. Shannon Jung, *Food for Life: The Spirituality and Ethics of Eating* (Minneapolis: Fortress Press, 2004).

I have pointed out – food has been one of the most paradigmatic symbols in many ancient (the case of *molli*, the Aztecs, for instance) as well
as current religious practices.[76] Most importantly, alimentary theology is
an invitation to bring together people's desire to eradicate spiritual and
material malnutrition, which again have to do with bodies – individual,
communal, ecological.

This is an issue deeply rooted in the daily practices of sharing and
refusal to share. Being attentive and caring not only requires us to reflect
upon relationality and reciprocity among individuals and societies; it
also requires us to become aware of humanity's relationship with animals, plants, and the planet's resources in general.[77] Alimentary theology
is critical of any form of power that is exercised as the violent subordina-
tion of others, but also of the ecological power whereby humanity
exploits the rest of the created order. In saying this I do not mean to
imply that humanity does not enjoy a special place in creation, including
over the angels, as the biblical narratives and Christian tradition teach.
Rather, in saying this I want to denounce the exercise of power as coer-
cion and annihilation, and thus as the betrayal of humanity's vocation to
be good stewards of creation and to promote harmonious and peaceful
relations, including ecological ones. Humanity must be part of the larger
ecological body, for it is not an "other" to us. I am aware that this coercive power has often been exercised by Catholics and Christians throughout history.[78] Because of this reality, alimentary theology insists on
metanoia, a continuous process of conversion incarnated in daily practices of caritas that must start from within.

I envision alimentary theology as a practice of power that is non-
coercive, but communal, rooted in nurturing, loving care for one another,
and imitating God's own radical gesture of love. I hope this will move us
beyond a social practice of mere mutual "tolerance" and instead welcome
an effort to a simultaneously local and global ecological embodiment of
communion expressed as hospitality and mutual nurturance. Nurturing
embodies caritas for every*body*. The making of alimentary theology may
hopefully become a true sharing of food for thought, soul, and body –
the human delight in God's self-sharing.

---

[76] See e.g. *Las Religiones y la Comida*, ed. Perry Schmidt-Leukel, trans. Lluís Miralles
de Imperial Llobet (Barcelona: Editorial Ariel, 2002).

[77] For a further reading on ecology, religion, and genre, see Ivone Gebara, *Intuiciones
Ecofeministas: Ensayo para Repensar el Conocimiento y la Religión* (Madrid: Editorial
Trotta, 2000).

[78] See e.g. Catherine Keller's arguments in her essay, "The Love of Postcolonialism:
Theology and the Interstices of Empire," in Keller, Nausner, and Rivera (eds.), *Postcolonial
Theologies*.

Like the Mexican *molli*, the making of alimentary theology requires faith, creativity, imagination, and God's inspiration, just as Sor Andrea and Fray Pascual Bailón were inspired in making the baroque *mole*. Alimentary theology integrates God's gift that surpasses calculation, and is forever open to transcendence – God's actuality in surplus. Alimentary theology, like cooking a delicious *molli*, is not at all passive, but an active engagement and openness to divine inspiration. It is also interesting to note that both Sor Andrea and Pascual Bailón came up with the idea of the *molli* in the midst of pressure and anxiety, even chaos. Likewise, alimentary theology often results from uncalculated actions, a sudden "event" that arises from a divine donor (God's plenitudinous sharing); and sometimes even from chaotic contexts, as church historians remind us. With the reception of divine inspiration we do not know the full implication of what has been inspired. But this, of course, requires deep discernment in faith, and also a continuous practice of charity, situated within the landscape of hope.

In the making of Doña Soledad's *mole*, nothing was more satisfying than the moment when it was finally shared among friends in a big, convivial fiesta. As was discovered by many of the dinner guests at my farewell party, the experience of savoring this ancient dish was truly ecstatic. I would like to add that, for me in particular, this experience of preparing, sharing, and eating *molli* increased my awareness of a communal sense of ecstasy, for it truly opened a horizon of new ways of understanding self and other.

From a perspective of alimentary theology I would like to explore this notion of understanding further, and argue that there is a special connection between savoring and cognition, and that this is a connection that becomes more evident through eating. If this is so, one could also argue that knowledge displays a dimension of participation in the known via the senses – most particularly by touch and taste at the moment of eating and drinking. And what of growing in understanding of God? Could one also say that knowing God implies a dimension of "savoring," which then might imply as well an aspect of participation in God? This form of cognition might resemble the mystics' experiences of God that are often reported to be intensely somatic, even "erotic." This alchemy of divine understanding, this "eros of cognition" is, then, an aspect that alimentary theology will now explore in the next chapter.[79]

---

[79] The term "eros of cognition" is borrowed from Philip Blond's introduction to id. (ed.), *Post-Secular Philosophy: Between Philosophy and Theology* (London: Routledge, 1998).

2

Sabor/Saber: Taste and the Eros of Cognition

Pedro, hearing [Tita] from the living room, experienced a sensation that was new to him. The sound of the pans bumping against each other, the smell of the almonds browning in the griddle, the sound of Tita's melodious voice, singing as she cooked, had kindled his sexual feelings. Just as lovers know the time for intimacy is approaching from the closeness and scent of their beloved, or from the caresses exchanged in foreplay, so Pedro knew from those sounds and smells, especially the aroma of browning sesame seeds, that there was a real culinary pleasure to come.[1]

Tita, the heroine of Laura Esquivel's novel *Like Water for Chocolate*, has a unique gift: knowledge and wisdom in matters of food. Tita's knowledge is embodied and deeply sensual, and becomes a powerful linguistic medium of communication, particularly with Pedro, the love of her life. The lovers in this narrative grow in knowledge of each other's love by seeing, smelling, touching, and savoring the culinary pleasures that Tita prepares. Food is the means of their erotic cognition of the beloved, and knowledge is intimately related to cuisine:

Tita knew through her own flesh how fire transforms the elements, how a lump of cornflour is changed into a tortilla, how a

---

Some aspects of this chapter were developed earlier in my essay "Nahrung für das Denken. Gott: Banquete de los sentidos – Festmahl für die Sinne," *Wort und Antwort* (Apr./June 2002), 64–9.

[1] Laura Esquivel, *Like Water for Chocolate: A Novel in Monthly Installments, with Recipes, Romances, and Home Remedies*, trans. Carol Christensen and Thomas Christensen (New York: Doubleday, 1992), 62.

soul that hasn't been warmed by the fire of love is lifeless, like a useless ball of cornflour.[2]

Tita's gifts evoke the relationship between knowing and savoring, or knowing as a form of savoring. I will thus look at various ways in which Esquivel's novel evokes this relationship between knowing and savoring (in Spanish, *saber* and *sabor*) which is intimately connected with the body in general and the senses in particular, and is a relationship that is paradigmatic of (although not exclusive to) eating and drinking. This will also point to the Eucharist as a paradigm of a culinary epistemology and ontology.

The etymology of both *saber* and *sabor* is rooted in the Latin *sapio* or *sapere*, meaning to taste, to have a flavor, as well as to understand. *Sapientia*, later translated into English as wisdom, means to have knowledge or wisdom of the world, but also to taste things in the world. Likewise, the word *sapiens* means being wise, and it is also derived from *sapere*, to taste and/or to know.[3] While eating and drinking implicate other senses such as smell, touch, vision, and even sound, it is the sense of taste that predominates. Eating and drinking thus provide a culinary medium for a cognition that is connected with the body and constructions of the world. Thus, by reflecting on Esquivel's novel, I will attempt to demonstrate that to know something is precisely to have a taste of the known, and likewise, to taste is to grow in knowledge and wisdom. To "know" something (*saber*) is also to taste it (*sabor*), and cognition of an object is intensely erotic: an intimate and sensory participation in the known object.

Sor Juana Inés de la Cruz did not find philosophy and cooking incompatible.[4] Cuisine could complement philosophy – as she wrote, "had Aristotle cooked, he would have written a good deal more." Sor Juana's reflection may also sound as a lament for the philosopher's lack of interest in food, the senses, and the body. However, looking at the course philosophy has taken over the past 20 years, perhaps a lament for this apparent lack is no longer necessary.[5] After the rise of phenomenology

---

[2] Ibid., 63.
[3] See Cassell's *Latin–English, English–Latin Dictionary*, 26th edn. (London, 1952), 501.
[4] For a brief reflection on Sor Juana Inés de la Cruz, see chapter 1 above.
[5] The bibliography on the subject of the body is extensive. For an important anthology that also includes a large bibliography on the body see Ramona Michel, Nadia Naddaff, and Feher Tazi (eds.), *Fragments for a History of the Human Body*, 3 vols. (New York: Zone Books, 1989). For a more recent anthology of current thinkers, see Juliet Flower MacCannell and Laura Zakarin (eds.), *Thinking Bodies* (Stanford: Stanford University Press, 1994).

and its influence on thinkers from a variety of disciplines – sociology, anthropology, cultural theory, and theology – one can see a greater attention to bodily perception and somatic means of cognition and meaning construction. And yet, while current thinkers seem more inclined to include the body, and food, in their investigations, there are also philosophers and theologians who do not consider this to be "serious" philosophy or theology.[6] In this chapter I echo Sor Juana's vision and attempt to demonstrate that there is much to explore and learn from the relationship between food and body, and its impact on cognition, hermeneutics, the experience of being in the world, and God's interaction with creation.

In exploring – against a view of cognition as purely disembodied and disinterested – the relationship between *saber* and *sabor*, the main goal of this chapter will be to show how cognition is a powerfully sensual medium of communication. In addition to this, it is also a paradigm of knowledge as participation. This will lead to a discussion of the Christian divine banquet: the Eucharist. From a eucharistic perspective, one could make a more emphatic claim, that to know does not merely mean to cast an aloof gaze from "outside" that which one knows, but rather to participate through intimate savoring of the known. Thus, a notion of participation will lead, in the final section of this chapter, to a reflection on the Eucharist. I will argue that, from a eucharistic account, taste reigns supreme among the senses, and takes primacy over the intellect, becoming a foretaste of the beatific vision – a beatific taste – revealing cognition as profoundly erotic/agapeic.[7]

From the standpoint of what I call alimentary theology (see chapter 1), and in light of this eucharistic account of cognition, knowledge is envisioned as participatory in divine desire: God kenotically (a dis-possessive

---

[6] I am not alone on this view; see e.g. Carolyn Korsmeyer, *Making Sense of Taste: Food and Philosophy* (Ithaca, NY: Cornell University Press, 1999); Elizabeth Telfer, *Food for Thought: Philosophy and Food* (London: Routledge, 1996); Deane W. Curtin and Lisa M. Heldke (eds.), *Cooking, Eating, Thinking: Transformative Philosophies of Food* (Indianapolis: Indiana University Press, 1992); Carole Counihan, *The Anthropology of Food and Body: Gender, Meaning, and Power* (New York: Routledge, 1999); *Food and Culture: A Reader* (New York: Routledge, 1997); L. Shannon Jung, *Food for Life: The Spirituality and Ethics of Eating* (Minneapolis: Fortress Press, 2004).

[7] In the next chapter I will argue further in favor of the simultaneity of the erotic and agapeic, in a fashion that shows how each is constituted mutually, without annihilating or overcoming the other. This view of the relationship between the erotic and the agapeic is mainly inspired by William Desmond, *Being and the Between* (New York: State University of New York Press, 1995). But whereas in Desmond's account the agapeic is a final stage beyond the erotic, in my account the agapeic does not dismiss the erotic, but reintegrates it. This is the main reason why I am using here the combined term erotic/agapeic.

self-giving) gives God-self as bread (body) and wine (blood) in order to be known; but also to love and to be loved, and to integrate the beloved into this dynamic exchange of reception, consumption, and sharing of God's self-giving. Just as Tita and Pedro delight in knowing their mutual love through the savoring of a lavish meal, so at the eucharistic banquet growing in knowledge means growing in love of a God who shares divinity with humanity. Through eating and drinking at the eucharistic banquet, knowledge is no longer envisioned as abysmal distance, but as intimate union. In Oliver Davies's words, at the eucharistic banquet the partakers "are not longer merely observers from without ... but are an intrinsic part of [God's] self-communication."[8] To know is to become aware (through savoring) of Being as participatory in the divine's self-communication and sharing. Such is the ontological (rooted in theology) turn of epistemology.

1   Food as a Sensual Medium of Communication

Like Water for Chocolate tells of how Tita's cooking is her life's vocation. Born in the kitchen, Tita develops "a deep love for the kitchen where she spent most of her life from the day she was born."[9] The kitchen is Tita's own realm, and even though she does not go to school or learn to read and write, her knowledge of cooking is advanced: "when it came to cooking she knew everything there was to know."[10] So great is her knowledge and love for the culinary arts that Tita develops a sixth sense regarding "everything concerning food."[11] Tita's view of life always relates to cuisine, including "the joy of living" which she sees as being "wrapped up in the delights of food."[12] In every meal that she so meticulously prepares, the ingredients of her feelings, emotions, hopes, fears, dreams, joys, and suffering are added. The meals she prepares are infused with her own feelings, and have a powerful effect on the emotions of the diners.

However, in spite of her art, Tita is unable to find happiness. Pedro is the love of her life, the man she would like to take as a husband. Tita's obstacle is her own mother, Elena, a widow who forbids her youngest daughter to marry because of her demand that Tita not break family Mexican tradition. It is the duty of the youngest daughter (Tita is the

---

[8]   Oliver Davies, *The Creativity of God: World, Eucharist, Reason* (Cambridge: Cambridge University Press, 2004), 152.
[9]   Esquivel, *Like Water for Chocolate*, 10.
[10]   Ibid.
[11]   Ibid., 11.
[12]   Ibid.

youngest of three daughters) to remain single in order to provide care for her mother in her old age until her death. The historical context of the story is the Mexican revolution, at the beginning of the twentieth century. The novel portrays this period as a time of rapid social, political, moral, and economic change. Because of a fear that tradition will be undermined, great spatial constraints increasingly dictate life in family households, and particularly the lives of women. In fact, so driven is Elena by this fear of breaking the family tradition that she arranges for Pedro to marry Tita's older sister, Rosaura. Surprisingly, Pedro, who returns Tita's affection, accepts this deal, but only because he wants to be near Tita, his true love.

Unable to communicate with her beloved through conventional means, Tita's food becomes what Carole M. Counihan calls a "sensual medium"[13] of communication. In her reflections on Esquivel's novel, Counihan argues that the great contribution of this story is its view of food as "powerful because it is so intimately connected with our physical, sensual selves – with our strongest feelings of hunger, desire, greed, delectation, and satiety."[14] Frustration and heartache must also be added to this list. For when Tita is obliged by her mother to prepare the cake for Pedro and her sister Rosaura's wedding, she unknowingly infuses it with her frustration and pain. The night before the wedding Tita spends many hours preparing the cake. But she is broken-hearted and cries continually, her copious tears falling into the cake mixture. When the guests start to eat the cake at the wedding feast, "everyone [is] flooded with a great wave of longing," and cannot stop weeping because of such "acute attack[s] of pain and frustration ... wailing over lost love."[15] This ruins the wedding feast, for by now people are both weeping and vomiting because of this powerful "intoxicating" heartache, produced by Tita's own tears.

Tita's cuisine has power to communicate not only frustration, but also love and indeed eroticism. On one occasion, after Tita receives a gift of roses from Pedro, Tita's mother orders her to throw them away. In an act of disobedience, Tita instead decides to use the petals to cook an extravagant, fragrant dish: "quail in rose petal sauce." We learn that this is a "prehispanic recipe" that Tita "seemed to hear" from a voice coming from Nacha, her beloved but now – at this point in the story – dead culinary mentor.[16] Her skillful hands become an extension of Nacha's

---

[13] Counihan, *The Anthropology of Food and Body*, 23.
[14] Ibid.
[15] Esquivel, *Like Water for Chocolate*, 39.
[16] From the time of Tita's birth, Nacha the family's cook, took great care to teach her everything she knew about cuisine. Ibid., 46.

own expertise. Tita kills the quails that were reared in her own home, and prepares them just as if Nacha were dictating to her body with great precision how to "dry-pluck the birds, remove the viscera, [and] get them ready for frying."[17] Tita flawlessly performs all the steps: she tightens the birds' feet together in "a nice shape" that allows them to be browned in butter, salt, and pepper; she applies one of the "many cooking secrets that can only be learned through practice" which recommends keeping a better flavor in the quail by dry-plucking instead of putting them into boiling water;[18] finally, she removes the petals from the roses.[19] It is, however, in performing this last step that Tita, in a turmoil of excitement and anxiety, pricks her fingers on the rose thorns and mingles her own blood with the dish, failing to notice the warning in the recipe that this "might alter the flavor of the dish and even produce dangerous chemical reactions."[20] In effect, this addition of Tita's blood "proved quite an explosive combination," that turns the dish into a potent aphrodisiac experience.[21] The narrator tells the reader:

> It was as if a strange alchemical process had dissolved her entire being in the rose petal sauce, in the tender flesh of the quails, in the wine, in every one of the meal's aromas. That was the way she entered Pedro's body, hot, voluptuous, perfumed, totally sensuous ... Pedro didn't offer any resistance. He let Tita penetrate to the farthest corners of his being, and all the while they couldn't take their eyes off each other.[22]

---

[17] Esquivel, *Like Water for Chocolate*, 47.

[18] Ibid., 48.

[19] The final steps of the recipe are as follows. "After the petals are removed from the roses, they are ground with the anise in a mortar. Separately, brown the chestnuts in a pan, remove the skins and cook them in water. Then purée them. Mince the garlic and brown slightly in butter; when it is transparent, add it to the chestnut purée, along with the honey, the ground *pitaya* and the rose petals, and salt to taste. To thicken the sauce slightly, you may add two teaspoons of cornflour. Last, strain through a fine sieve and add no more than two drops of attar of roses, since otherwise it might have too strong a flavour and smell. As soon as the seasoning has been added, remove the sauce from the heat. The quail should be immersed in this sauce for ten minutes to infuse them with the flavour, and then removed." Ibid., 50.

[20] Ibid., 45.

[21] Ibid., 48.

[22] Ibid., 53. The story also relates how Gertrudis (Tita's other sister) is even more aroused by the dish. Gertrudis is overtaken by an unbearable burning sensation that prompts her to take a shower to calm her erotic heat. Since the shower does not diminish the burning, Gertrudis then runs naked into the fields and is picked up by a revolutionary soldier riding a horse, who is guided by the smell of petals that her body exudes.

Tita's food not only nourishes the body of the one who eats it, it also communicates powerful feelings, becoming a sensual medium of communication that reduces any gap that separates her from her beloved Pedro.

Roland Barthes rightly points out that "[food] is not only a collection of products that can be used for statistical or nutritional studies. It is also, and at the same time, a system of communication, a body of images, a protocol of usages, situations, and behaviors."[23] Following Barthes's line of thinking, food, as a language of communication created between Tita and Pedro, goes beyond mere instrumental utility and becomes a medium, a magical bridge that lessens the imposed gap within their relationship. Through food and cuisine, Esquivel offers a rich body of images that express desire, eroticism, sensuality, and the transgression of boundaries.

Tita and Pedro's unrequited desire to physically consummate their love finds an opportunity for actualization. In savoring and consuming the quails in rose petal sauce, Tita not only reduces the physical gap between herself and Pedro, but she evocatively "enters" into his body, even to the point of penetrating "to the farthest corners of his being." We observe a clash of the structures formerly established for communication with one another, for that which was an expected protocol of communication between sister-in-law and brother-in-law is now sabotaged by a new (as much sensual as it is subversive) possibility of "contact" and exchange. Paradoxically, the avoidance of intimacy is now transcended by the taking of the other's total self "inside" one's own body, heart, and soul. It is as if food provides a locus for a deeper intimacy in the midst of an externally imposed repression of bodily contact.

Food thus becomes a language of intimacy between them; and it is a language not only of the senses but of the soul and the heart as well. This text evokes eating as an act whereby the self loses its center and moves toward the other, only to return to the self, now transfigured, by this ecstatic encounter. Here eating becomes a means for the "indwelling" of self within the other. Nevertheless, in this ecstatic act, the "I" preserves some sort of self-testimony, for the "I" delights in this sensuous exchange. The paradox here is that self-delight requires one to move beyond the self, to experience a sense of self-loss. It is an exodus from the self that leads toward knowledge of the other, as well as to a new, transfigured self-knowledge.

---

[23]   Roland Barthes, "Toward a Psychosociology of Contemporary Food Consumption," in *Food and Culture: A Reader*, 21.

The novel thus evokes the connection between *saber* and *sabor* that I mentioned earlier. The experience of savoring food provides a greater knowledge of the love between Pedro and Tita. To savor is to know, and to know is to savor. Pedro not only conceptualizes Tita's love at a rational level, but he also *feels* and *tastes* it as it penetrates his body. Here knowledge or cognition is viewed as holistic, for it involves the entire self: body, mind, soul, and heart.[24] It is as much a bodily as an intellectual and affective experience of knowledge, not as distance but as intimacy. And the medium is food. Both Pedro and Tita experience the other's love in the concrete materiality of food, in its appearance, its texture, smell, and taste. Every ingredient and element of the quails in rose petal sauce is a sign pointing beyond itself – for these signs point to the reality of the other's love. And this beyond-itself of signification brings awareness of divinity, transcendence: "when Pedro tasted his first mouthful, he couldn't help closing his eyes in voluptuous delight and exclaiming, 'It's a dish for the gods!'"[25] In eating this lavish dish, cognition becomes a hermeneutically erotic play of interpreting signs of love and desire by eating them – signs become edible. Coming to know is an erotic/agapeic process of coming to *love* through edible signs.

2 Bodily Cognition and the Construction of Meaning

There is a knowledge that is acquired in the act of preparing and eating food. Esquivel's novel explores in an evocative narrative style this bodily knowledge and its intimate link with food, love, and desire. Later on in this chapter I will address these connected issues. But first I will briefly reflect on the importance of bodily knowledge as it relates to food and food practices. Attention to the senses in general, and the sense of taste in particular, will be one aspect of this discussion. This will offer clarification on how Pedro's act of eating Tita's food is in fact a powerful erotic encounter between them.

Lisa M. Heldke is a philosopher who argues for a greater appreciation of the bodily knowledge that is acquired in preparing food. As we saw in chapter 1,

> The knowing involved in making a cake is "contained" not simply "in my head" but in my hands, my wrist, my eyes and nose as well.

---

[24] I will use both "knowledge" and "cognition" as exchangeable terms, though they are distinct. Cognition is a process of acquiring knowledge and understanding (rational as well as sensual experiences are integrated in this process). Knowledge is the content of such an understanding, and it is also the act of coming to understanding.
[25] Esquivel, *Like Water for Chocolate*, 48.

The phrase "bodily knowledge" is not a metaphor. It is an acknowledgment of the fact that I *know* things literally with my body, that I, "as" my hands, know when the bread dough is sufficiently kneaded, and I "as" my nose know when the pie is done.[26]

Heldke criticizes the Cartesian separation of body and mind whereby bodily experience is considered as merely external somatic data in need of the conducting cognitive function of an internal mind that produces "objects of knowledge."[27] Heldke explains that the cognition that takes place in preparing and eating food is embodied knowledge, for the body and the senses become not something external to cognition, but integral to it, the actual medium of knowledge before, and often beyond, the controlling of reason. This does not assume that bodily cognition is irrational; rather, Heldke moves beyond a dualistic separation of body and mind (a position which usually disregards the body in favor of the "highest" intellectual function employed by reason), and instead argues in favor of an account of knowledge that does not dismiss the body.

In addition to integrating the body as a means of cognition, Heldke also argues that foodmaking contains an emotional and erotic knowledge that can serve as an alternative to that of the traditional notion of knowledge as "dispassionate objectivity." She suggests that this

> dispassionate objectivity, the standard for scientific inquiry, is not the ideal in cooking; good cooking is good in part because of the emotional attachment you have to the people for whom you're cooking, to the tools you're using and to the foods you're making.[28]

Cuisine is not only a cognitive practice that offers information about the subjective experience of cooking and eating, but, as Heldke argues, it also connects to objects and people in the world and draws attention to the construction of both social and communal meaning. Heldke also points out that the philosophical tradition has not given much attention to the senses, particularly the senses related to eating (smell, touch, and taste), largely because of an attitude that considers the body to be a "lower" form of knowledge.

---

[26] Lisa M. Heldke, "Foodmaking as a Thoughtful Practice," in Curtin and Heldke (eds.), *Cooking, Eating, Thinking*, 218.
[27] "Theories like Descartes's conceive of my body as an external appendage to my mind, and see its role in inquiry as merely to provide a set of (fairly reliable) sensory data on which my reasoning faculty then operates to produce objects of knowledge." Ibid.
[28] Ibid., 222.

Carolyn Korsmeyer explores the positioning of bodily perception in a hierarchy of knowledge. She develops an argument that explores the cognitive and symbolic significance of the senses, particularly the gustatory sense, which is most involved in eating and drinking.[29] Korsmeyer coincides with Heldke's reading of the Western philosophical tradition (initiated by Plato and Aristotle) wherein touch, smell, and taste are considered the lowest forms of knowledge, while vision and hearing are located at the top of this hierarchy.[30] This is not to say that from early Classic Greek philosophy there was no attention to or appreciation of the body whatsoever. Korsmeyer is aware that Greek philosophers such as Plato and Aristotle had a positive appreciation of the senses because they thought to bring some light to the human "natural desire" to know. Nevertheless, she points out that there was also a great suspicion of the senses because they were considered distorters of the knowledge of "the truth of things."[31] And the senses of smell, touch, and taste were considered the ones that had a greater propensity to bring about distortions than the "higher" senses of vision and hearing.

Korsmeyer points out that one reason for this epistemological hierarchy is a traditional understanding of vision and hearing as senses that preserve a "distance" from the object perceived.[32] This account maintains that such a distance allows a more objectifying and scientific construction of the perceived objects, since they bring attention *outwardly* to the objects perceived, rather than *inwardly* to the body or sense experience. The philosophical tradition considers smell, touch, and taste as senses that are more "intimate," even more "bodily" (than vision and hearing) in their relation to the object sensed, and thus are more likely to provide subjective rather than objective accounts. According to Korsmeyer, this traditional view considers taste "a *subjective* sense that directs attention to one's bodily state rather than to the world around, that provides information only about the perceiver, and the preferences for which are not cogently debatable."[33] Above all, Korsmeyer argues that the strongest reason for a suspicion of taste as the

---

[29] Korsmeyer, *Making Sense of Taste.*
[30] I shall later address how Thomas Aquinas offers a reversal of this hierarchy, and gives a privileged role to taste in the construction of meaning, particularly after a conjecture upon the experience of tasting and eating as enacted in the eucharistic feast.
[31] Korsmeyer, *Making Sense of Taste,* 18, 19.
[32] This strong account of distancing, however, is not present in Plato's account of the relationship between knowledge and the senses. I appreciate Catherine Pickstock pointing this out to me.
[33] Korsmeyer, *Making Sense of Taste,* 68 (emphasis in original).

"lowest sense" is that it is considered more intimately connected with humanity's tendency to vice, and thus is in greater need of scrutiny and control, since it "can deliver pleasures that tempt one to indulge in the appetites of eating, drinking, and sex."[34] The equation of taste with bodily sexual pleasure reaches a peak with Kant's attempt to bring aesthetics into a universal category, and thus disqualify sexuality from his schema. In this Kantian equation, "only vision and hearing qualify as aesthetic senses," and touch and taste are reinforced as the lowest categories.[35] Even today, this legacy of what has been called "Western visualism" is the result of a primary role that the "gaze" plays in Western culture (particularly with regard to visual images in modern consumer societies), which usually neglects or ignores the "other" senses.[36]

Besides her deconstructive reading of a philosophical tradition that is highly suspicious of the gustatory sense, Korsmeyer also presents an alternative account that considers taste an important cognitive element for the world and bodily knowledge, and also for a greater understanding of the complexities of meaning construction.

To support her argument, Korsmeyer first relies upon scientific research that considers both smell and taste to be "chemical senses." The relevance of such investigations is the understanding of the complex mechanisms and operations involved in the relationship of the organs of sense (taste, for instance) with substances, creating a series of chemical reactions that stimulate neurotransmitters to send "messages to the brain and produce sensations."[37] If this condition is pre-linguistic, it seems that it is a fixed reality that can be applied universally to every human being. At times it appears as if Korsmeyer wants to argue for such a physiological fixity for the purpose of anchoring taste experience to what she explains as the "physiological factors that furnish and restrict the ability to taste." And, she adds, "these factors are as it were hardwired in the individual and not subject of alteration. They consist of certain basic universal taste dispositions as well as unchangeable individual differences."[38] Korsmeyer is therefore trying to move beyond a

---

[34] Ibid., 3.
[35] Kant quoted ibid., 57.
[36] See e.g. S. Ewen, *All Consuming Images: The Politics of Style in Contemporary Culture* (New York: Basic Books, 1988); Rachel Bouldy, *Just Looking: Consumer Culture in Dreiser, Gissing, and Zola* (New York: Methuen, 1985); Constance Classen, *Worlds of Sense: Exploring the Senses in History and Across Cultures* (New York: Routledge, 1993).
[37] Korsmeyer, *Making Sense of Taste*, 71.
[38] Ibid., 95.

philosophical tradition that sees taste as an "inward" or merely "subjective" experience, and instead argues in favor of more objective and universal account.

A potential problem with this position is that it might intensify subjectivity rather than the reverse, for it points to the mechanics or "hardwired" physicality of all individuals, and thus tells us more about the body's own constitution than about the object perceived. Nevertheless, Korsmeyer insists that there is also an "outward" experience when we taste objects. A cook tasting a stew or a professional wine taster both taste the properties of the product, rather than simply examining the state of their tongues or gustatory senses.[39] Thus, the physical constitution of the sense of taste exposes us to a twofold reality: both the body and the properties of the objects perceived. The senses of smell and taste, she argues, tell us something about the chemical constitution of objects, even though such constitutive elements are further "digested" or filtered by bodily organs, and thus are never fully transmitted in their unmediated form. What is important to realize is the vital function of bodily sense organs in a greater understanding of the objects sensed.

The knowledge that is acquired in smelling, touching, savoring, and digesting food is not only knowledge of the chemical world and the mechanics of the bodily organs of sense; it is also knowledge regarding the construction of meaning. Thus, Korsmeyer is not arguing in favor of a "mechanistic" understanding of taste, for she is also aware of the many complexities, such as eating habits and cultural factors, that play a crucial role in the varieties of forms of cognition relating to food and the senses. She explains that "tastes for particular foods are to a large degree inculcated by culture and learned by experience, as well as chosen according to individual predilection"[40] The notion of what is or is not edible, for instance, is not a merely biological and/or physiological reaction that can be universally applied, but is rooted in particular cultural interpretations and in social, including religious, regulations. The same goes for the development of notions such as "good and bad taste," and "low and high cuisine."[41] It is therefore important to incorporate the research of ethnic, cultural, social, and anthropological scholars – among other disciplines – in order to better understand these complexities of the

---

[39] Both examples are given by Korsmeyer (ibid., 97).
[40] Ibid., 89.
[41] See e.g. Jack Goody, *Cooking, Cuisine and Class* (Cambridge: Cambridge University Press, 1982).

construction of meaning and the relationship between the body, the senses, and cognition.[42]

In order further to support her view of food and the construction of meaning, Korsmeyer integrates Nelson Goodman's account of what he calls "symbolic typologies."[43] While Goodman developed a hermeneutics of art and aesthetics in general, Korsmeyer's main goal is to apply these categories to food in order to argue for the cognitive and symbolic functions associated with eating. That is to say, Korsmeyer's project is to explain how food can point at something beyond itself while at the same time displaying a complex network of the construction of meaning. I cannot here do justice to the full breadth of her examples; instead, I shall offer a brief summary that highlights some of her ways of typologizing food.

1   Food and *representation*: this is when food points beyond itself and symbolizes or represents something else. The sugar skulls in the Mexican feast of El Día de Los Muertos (the Day of the Dead) represent more than just an object of consumption, for the forehead of each skull has the name of a dead person (usually a family member or loved one) inscribed on it as a memorial to them.

2   Food also *exemplifies* the qualities or properties contained in the object, as well as some structures of the cultural construction of meaning. For some groups or cultures, for instance, oatmeal is an example of a breakfast food. The structuralist approach (mainly following the anthropological works of Lévi-Strauss) strongly advocates this account of exemplification.[44] In a less universalizing fashion than that of Lévi-Strauss, cultural anthropologist Mary Douglas views food as a "system of communication." Douglas's research is valuable for bringing a greater awareness to eating practices as examples or

---

[42]   It is worth mentioning that politics also play an important role in the construction of meaning. I shall develop this aspect of the politics of food further in chapter 4. For a reflection on the political regulations of the senses, see esp. "The Odor of the Other: Olfactory Codes and Cultural Categories," in Classen, *Worlds of Sense*.

[43]   Korsmeyer is here mainly basing her arguments on Nelson Goodman's *Languages of Art* (Indianapolis: Bobbs-Merrill, 1968), and id., *Ways of Worldmaking* (Indianapolis: Hackett, 1978).

[44]   Here Korsmeyer has in mind mainly Lévi-Strauss's work on the "raw" and the "cooked" which reads binary oppositions as being "isomorphic with other binaries (such as nature–culture and male–female) which taken together illuminate the myths and social practices of vastly divergent societies." However, Korsmeyer quickly notes that this view has been criticized by anthropologists, including Mary Douglas, "for imposing too rigid a structure of analysis on the phenomena under question." Still, this is just one illustration on how food exemplifies something which is not too unrelated to the cultural construction of meaning. Korsmeyer, *Making Sense of Taste*, 129.

illustrations of social codification and relations such as class and social boundaries. As such, food practices are carriers of meaning.[45]

3   Foods can also be *expressive*. By this Korsmeyer means the metaphorical aspect of food. In the story of Snow White, for instance, an apple can be read as "sinister" because of the poison contained in it and the role it plays in the story. In Korsmeyer's own words, "there are numerous cases in which expressive properties attach to foods the particular context of a story, but there are also more ordinary cases in which foods come to express certain properties because of the traditional or routine circumstances of their preparation."[46] Regarding this later "ordinary case" of the expressiveness of food, Korsmeyer provides the example of chicken soup (as it is popularly made in the USA), a dish whose implicit properties are in some cultures associated with adjectives such as "soothing" and "comforting," and which is used as a home remedy for minor illnesses such as colds.

4   Food and the role it plays in ceremonials and rituals provides another important illustration of food practices as constructing meaning. Here again, food points beyond itself and serves a broader purpose than mere nourishment. For instance, the Eucharist is, for Catholics, an element of a sacramental ritual-liturgical practice governed by the belief that God becomes food (bread re-presenting Christ's body and wine re-presenting Christ's blood) for the purpose of sharing divinity with humanity. Another example is the tea ceremony, described by the Zen master Takuan as the embodiment of an entire philosophy and tradition within Japanese culture.[47] There is

---

[45]   Korsmeyer quotes Mary Douglas: "Each meal carries something of the meaning of the other meals; each meal is a structured social event which structures others in its own image. The upper limit of its meaning is set by the range incorporated in the most important member of its series. The recognition which allows each member to be classed and graded with the others depends upon the structure common to them all. The cognitive energy which demands that a meal look like a meal and not like a drink is performing in the culinary medium the same exercise that it performs in language. First, it distinguishes order, bounds it, and separates it from disorder. Second, it uses economy in the means of expression by allowing only a limited number of structures. Third, it imposes a rank scale upon the repetition of structures. Fourth, the repeated formal analogies multiply the meanings that are carried down any one of them by the power of the most weighty." Mary Douglas, "Deciphering a Meal," *Daedalus* (Winter 1972), 69–70, cited in Korsmeyer, *Making Sense of Taste*, 130–1.

[46]   Korsmeyer, *Making Sense of Taste*, 132.

[47]   For her examples of the Eucharist, Korsmeyer is mainly relying on Louis Marin, *Food for Thought*, trans. Mette Hjort (Baltimore: John Hopkins University Press, 1989). For her example of the tea ceremony she uses D. T. Suzuki, *Zen and Japanese Culture* (Princeton: Princeton University Press, 1970).

something "epiphanic" about food practices in ceremonials and rituals, for they attempt to express that which is inexpressible: mystery, and the reaching out to some experience of transcendence, somehow activated in the ceremonial event around food.

There are many more typologies that could be included in this list. What is important to underline with such typologies is that food and food practices can be linguistic systems of communication that bring light to the bodily experience of knowledge, construction of meaning, systems of valuation, and so forth.

Recipes are another important example of this construction of meaning as they are passed on by individuals, families, and cultural traditions through time and space. At times, these traditions are passed on in written form through notes, or even as books.[48] *Like Water for Chocolate* is an example of a novel constructed around monthly recipes and home remedies which are passed on to the next generation. But at other times these culinary traditions are transmitted not by writing but verbally, and with accompanying stories. This was the case with the Mexican baroque *mole* discussed in chapter 1, which was a tradition first passed on orally within religious communities and then became part of people's culinary traditions, usually accompanied by folk stories of its invention. Time and space are important elements in this inherited knowledge, as they are in the case of *molli*. During the baroque era in Mexico, nuns and monks incorporated the culinary wisdom of pre-Colombian times, and so the original *molli* was later adapted to and re-created and syncretized in a different time and space.

In addition, there are recipes that may involve very few, or even nonverbal, instructions. Many recipes are learned just by "doing." One has to bodily "perform" the actions over and over in order to achieve a refined skill as well as to obtain the desired final product.[49] Again, this form of performative knowledge relates to the body. Here the body is not just a series of bodily mechanical motions, but also (among other

---

[48] This is indeed a whole fascinating genre that sheds light on how food is constructed, written styles, views about food, world-views about eating and social rules, and so forth. See e.g. Goody, *Cooking, Cuisine, and Class.*
[49] Regarding alternative forms of knowledge that are more "performative" and include few (or no) verbal or alphabetical elements, see Walter D. Mignolo, *The Darker Side of the Renaissance: Literacy, Territoriality, and Colonization,* 2nd edn. (Ann Arbor: University of Michigan Press, 2003). Mignolo's research is helpful for a critique of the "Eurocentric" (a form of colonization) notion of knowledge that not only values verbality/literacy over non-verbal practices, but also used its own epistemological and linguistic categories as strategies of control, government, and colonization, which often violently wiped out "other" practices.

things) a developed sense of smell, an awareness of texture that one learns by touching and manipulating food products, and a sense of taste that one learns by savoring foods and dishes. Food practices such as cooking demonstrate the role of performance (which is intrinsically bodily) in building knowledge, and, as Graham Ward correctly argues, thus imply that knowledge is "inseparable from experience and socialization." Ward explains that knowledge is always "interactive," for it performs a web of social "transcorporeal" relations:

> Knowledge becomes a performance demonstrating that one knows how to. But it is also only relational. That is, *that* performance takes place within the context of other performances. Knowing, then, is implicated in economies or movements of response, exchange and declaration. It is continually caught up in communicating and in the communication of others. Even when asleep the ensouled body communicates – by how it lies, turns, moans, snores or is simply still. It communicates with respect to others, in answer to others, as a declaration to others. I am not some monadic centre of my knowing and my knowledge; I am immersed in a transcorporeal exchange of knowledge in which sensing is always simultaneously sensibility. ... I am caught up in an interactive knowing that issues from micro acts of interpretation that concern what the body is in contact with and that become necessary, inevitable, because I am placed within intricate webs of communication.[50]

Through food practices, the body interactively performs and develops information, and access to a web of knowledge, aesthetic experience, and wisdom that complements mind and reason, while it also "quickens awareness of physical being itself," of which the experience of tasting – Korsmeyer underlines – "takes us to the most intimate regions of these phenomena."[51] Taste and intimacy are, then, the next aspect of food that I shall explore, and one that is pivotal in Esquivel's construction of Tita and Pedro's gastroerotic relationship.

3 Cognition as Relationality, Intimacy, and Participation

From that day on [early on when Tita was born], Tita's domain was the kitchen, where she grew vigorous and healthy on a diet of

---

[50] Graham Ward, *Christ and Culture* (Oxford: Blackwell, 2005), 95.
[51] Korsmeyer, *Making Sense of Taste*, 10.

teas and thin corn gruels. This explains the sixth sense Tita developed about everything concerning food. Her eating habits, for example, were attuned to the kitchen routine: in the morning, when she could smell that the beans were ready; at midday, when she sensed the water was ready for plucking the chickens; and in the afternoon, when the dinner bread was baking, Tita knew it was time for her to be fed.[52]

Cognition has to do with *relations*: between subject and object, the perceiver and the perceived, the individual and the world she or he lives in. In these networks of relationality, the body plays an important role. The problem is that, as George Lakoff and Mark Johnson lament, disembodied notions of cognition usually suffer "an unbridgeable ontological chasm between 'objects,' which are 'out there,' and subjectivity, which is 'in here.' "[53] Extreme accounts of objectivism (a view that further splits the object–subject schema) and subjectivism (and intersubjectivity, which only refer to social constructions of the world, and leave the world untouched) are outcomes of such dichotomous views. To overcome such a dichotomy, Lakoff and Johnson propose "embodied realism," which, they explain, "relies on the fact that we are coupled to the world through our embodied interactions. Our directly embodied concepts (e.g., basic-level concepts, aspectual concepts, and spatial-relations concepts) can reliably fit those embodied interactions and the understandings of the world that arise from them."[54] This position also echoes Korsmeyer's attention to the body and the senses in general, and particularly the sense of taste, as a strategy to overcome the crisis of a disembodied (and de-sensualized) epistemology. It is also a position that avoids the error of creating an abysmal gap between the "outside world" and the inward realm. Embodiment insists on the in-betweenness, which is always mediated by the body, as well as connecting social and linguistic constructions. Even accounts of what might at first suggest a notion of "pure disembodiment" (such as the soul, spirit, transcendence, etc.) are also, in a human context, intimately related to the body.

Taste, precisely because of its corporeal closeness and relationship (indeed, intimacy) with the world, can become a paradigm of embodied cognition as an instance of the in-betweenness or the relational aspect of

---

[52] Esquivel, *Like Water for Chocolate*, 10–11.
[53] George Lakoff and Mark Johnson, *Philosophy in the Flesh: The Embodied Mind and its Challenge to Western Thought* (New York: Basic Books, 1999), 93.
[54] Ibid., 93.

knowledge. Tasting through eating and drinking is a sensuously rich experience that literally requires taking the object into our mouth and body. Constance Classen explains that taste is a form of touch, only more intense. In fact, as Classen points out, the origin of the English word taste is "the Middle English *tasten*, to feel, derived from the Latin *taxare*, to feel, touch sharply, judge."[55] Classen explains that it was around the fourteenth century that taste became associated with savoring. Accordingly, the sense of taste gives an account of knowledge as something "savorable," so that to know something means, to some extent, to have a taste of it, to feel and touch and enter into a relationship with it.

The etymology of the word "taste" has an affective dimension that has perhaps been lost until recently. Laura Esquivel's novel is so evocative precisely because she reintegrates taste with affectivity, sensuality, and eroticism. At the same time, the etymology also indicates that one has right discernment, a judgment about what tasting something is about. Therefore, taste is not absolutely disconnected from intellectual and aesthetic – or from ethical – discernment. Again, this recalls what I said earlier regarding the relationship between the Spanish words *saber* and *sabor*, for to know is to have tasted, and discerned the truth of that which is known, in a fashion that does not disregard the body, but rather intensifies embodied sensuality. Knowledge is not a merely "interiorist" or a purely "exteriorist" event, but is, rather, a shareable act whereby interiority is constituted by exteriority, as much as the reverse.

While taste implies some form of correspondence, it is not an absolute mirroring whereby the body and intellect are mere passive epistemological registers. Somehow things are touched and constructed by the act of tasting. On the one hand, as Merleau-Ponty has demonstrated, to touch is also to be touched by that which one touches.[56] In touching one can be damaged or even killed (as for instance, by a sharp knife that penetrates the skin and the organs). This means that taste, as an intense form of touching, also implies being touched, affected, transformed, and even destroyed by the act of tasting. But, on the other hand, a transformation can also occur into that which one touches. Language, cultural and social constructions of the world, physical, chemical, and bio-neurological impulses – all enter into contact and interact with the sense of taste in such a way that

---

[55] Classen, *Worlds of Sense*, 75.
[56] See esp. Maurice Merleau-Ponty, *The Visible and the Invisible*, trans. Alphonso Lingis (Evanston, ILL: Northwestern University Press, 1968).

these interactions also cast some light on the world. It is as if through tasting the world is made: re-created or recrafted.

This action could be compared to an aesthetic event, a creative action, a sense of *poiesis*, if you wish, that crafts and brings new light to the truth of being in the world. Graham Ward explains the etymology of the word, as well as providing an Aristotelian account of *poiesis* that is intimately related to *praxis*, but also to a Christian envisioning of a human power to transform or re-create. It is worth citing Ward at length:

> The Greek word means "making" as in "creating" and relates directly to the verb *poieo*, to produce, perform, execute, compose or, more generally, be active. Put in structuralist terms, "poetics" is synchronic, ahistorical explanatory map, while *poiesis* is a diachronic, historical operation concerned with creative action. As such, *poiesis* would constitute one aspect of a theory of action – cultural action – and in this way it is associated with praxis, from the Greek verb *prasso* meaning to act, manage, do or accomplish. For Aristotle there appears to have been a distinction between a specific form of making or production (*poiesis*) and the more general notion of doing and being involved in an activity (*praxis* or *pragma*). *Praxis* would relate to ethics and politics, for example. I am wishing to view *poiesis* in a complex sense that would not over-distinguish aesthetic production from political and ethical activity … [From a Christian perspective] *poiesis* differs from social behaviour more generally, with respect to its power to create a new, to transform; it announces a production not a mindless reproduction.[57]

Perhaps this dimension of *poiesis* in the experience of taste is one of the reasons why cuisine has been considered by some cultures to be an art.[58] Through tasting not only are data and substances incorporated into our bodies and intellect, but also an entire dimension of emotions, feelings,

---

[57] Graham Ward, *Cultural Transformation and Religious Practice* (Cambridge: Cambridge University Press, 2005), 7–8. Unlike Ward, however, I do not dismiss a notion of "crafting" in this understanding of *poiesis*. On this issue, see chapter 1, esp. n. 51.

[58] Although Korsmeyer's main point in *Making Sense of Taste* is not to argue in favor of considering taste/food/cuisine as an art form, she strongly argues in favor of giving more attention to the aesthetic dimension of taste as an important form of human cognition. For a more direct argument in favor of considering food as an art form (albeit a "minor" rather than a "major" one), see Telfer, *Food for Thought*. Finally, for a historical development of cuisine as a culinary art, see Massimo Montari (ed.), *El Mundo en la Cocina: Historia, Identidad, Intercambios*, trans. Yolanda Daffunchio (Barcelona: Paidós, 2003).

and memories is brought into play. There is an evocative aspect of tasting. As *Like Water for Chocolate* illustrates, this evocative dimension is more intensified when the eating and drinking take place within particular personal and communal contexts. There is a sense of being shaped by these experiences, but also a sense that memories, stories, boundaries, and rules are created and shaped by societies around the experience of tasting food and drink. In tasting through eating and drinking, the world enters us, but we also enter the world. We are made by that which we eat and drink, but we also "make" the world. We are what we eat, but also eat what we are. To know is, then, to savor, and thus enter into an intimate relationship with another that shapes us, while it is being shaped by us. Knowledge is interaction, a form of participation with a rich diversity of contexts. Tita's encounter with food is inseparable from her location in early twentieth-century Mexico, its colonial past and revolutionary times, and Laura Esquivel's own constructions are likewise inseparable from her own context.

Fergus Kerr echoes Thomas Aquinas in his argument that to know is to participate in the known. Kerr explains that, against a passive account of knowledge (that is, that the mind and body are only passively open to the reality of the world), in the Thomistic approach, knowledge is active collaboration and participation. Kerr explains it as follows:

> The Thomist wants to say that knowledge is the product of a collaboration between the object known and the subject who knows: the knower enables the thing known to become intelligible, thus to enter the domain of meaning, while the thing's becoming intelligible activates the mind's capacities. Knowing is a new way of being on the part of the object known. For Thomas, meaning is the mind's perfection, the coming to fulfillment of the human being's intellectual powers; simultaneously, it is the world's intelligibility being realized.[59]

In Kerr's Thomistic approach to knowledge as participation, there is a sense of both object and subject being mutually constituted.[60] If, as I have been arguing in this chapter, taste is a form of knowledge, it is one that is profoundly intimate, to the extent that it requires both trust and

---

[59] Fergus Kerr, *After Aquinas: Versions of Thomism* (Oxford: Blackwell, 2002), 30.
[60] For a similar positive and theological argument for constructing truth as a manifestation of participation in God's creativity, see Robert Miner, *Truth in the Making: Creative Knowledge in Theology and Philosophy* (London: Routledge, 2004). See also Davies, *The Creativity of God.*

risk. As I have mentioned, eating and drinking give strength and life, but can also produce illness, or even death. We are *affected* by the things we consume, for they become part of the body, mind, and soul. Moreover, for Aquinas, besides being affected by that which is known, the intellect also displays a desire, impulse, or "appetite" to know: "intellect only moves anything by virtue of appetition."[61] Through taste, our appetite to access the world becomes utterly direct and intimate, so much so that it is somehow digested by us, and becomes part of us as much as we also become part of the known. To taste is also to make things intelligible, to add new dimensions of "being on the part of the object known" as Kerr rightly puts it.

4 Eucharistic Desire and the Eros of Cognition

Knowledge as participation via the tasting in eating and drinking is well illustrated in *Like Water for Chocolate*. Through Tita's meal, Pedro becomes a part of her as much as she becomes a part of him. The desire of the one for the other is somehow consummated in the sensual and erotic act of eating and drinking. Paradoxically, in this Mexican narrative, food and drink signify more than the act of eating and drinking: these activities are a performance of spiritual union whereby the lover participates in the beloved, in and through the materiality of food and drink. Matter and spirit constitute one another and illuminate the intellect, but only insofar as the intellect allows itself to be instructed and guided by the senses, particularly by that of taste. A reversal takes place here, for the so-called "lower" senses are now primary in this erotic pilgrimage of further dimensions of knowing. The erotic has to do with the movement of desire to satisfy the appetite for the other: the quails in rose petal sauce that directly nourish the body, just as another (the lover) nurtures body, soul, mind, and heart.[62]

---

[61] Thomas Aquinas, *Commentary on Aristotle's De Anima*, trans. Kenelm Foster, OP, and Silvester Humphries, OP (Notre Dame, IN: Dumb Ox Books, 1994), 245, cited in Ward, *Christ and Culture*, 103. It is also important to remark that Aquinas' epistemology integrates a theology of "grace" as that which *elicits* nature to particularly desire the beatific vision, so that knowledge is also enacted by a "grammar" of grace and not by mere logical or rational abstractions. On this relationship between grace, knowledge, and language, see Jeffrey Stout and Robert MacSwain (eds.), *Grammar and Grace: Reformulations of Aquinas and Wittgenstein* (London: SCM Press, 2004).

[62] It might be argued that not all appetites are "erotic." However, in this particular text of Tita's recipe given to Pedro it seems that the appetite for food meets the appetite for the lover. The two hungers meet in this one erotic desire. The argument for desire as an erotic appetite will be explored in this section.

In a fashion akin to Octavio Paz's intimations, I would like to suggest that Esquivel's novel shows that, in fact, eroticism and gastronomy are intimately related in the eros of cognition. I will then advance this reflection further and incorporate a notion of the Eucharist, bringing together the main points discussed in this chapter. In doing so, I will reflect on notions of knowledge, embodiment, and the construction of meaning through the experience of savoring that takes place in eating and drinking in general, and the Eucharist in particular.

In 1972 the journal *Daedalus* published Octavio Paz's article "Eroticism and Gastrosophy."[63] In this essay, Paz echoes the central idea of Charles Fourier's *Le Nouveau Monde Amoureux*, that eroticism and gastrosophy (the love of food and gastronomy) are the most fundamental pleasures of human life: the former is the most intense, and the latter is the most extended. For Paz, these two forms of pleasure are ultimately related to the reality of desire itself, a desire that "simultaneously reveals to us what we are and beckons us to transcend ourselves in order to become the *others*."[64] Paz describes desire as "the active agent, the secret producer of changes, whether it be the passage from one flavor to another, or the contrast among flavors and textures. Desire, both in Gastronomy and Erotica, initiates a movement among substances, the bodies, and the sensations. It is the force that regulates connections, mixtures, and transmutations."[65] Paz argues that eroticism is not (as for Georges Bataille) transgression, but representation. Eroticism is invention and envisioning in its desire for the other. Paz's connection of eroticism and gastrosophy in the act of desiring is incarnated in the reality of the body and the senses, whereby humans endlessly reinvent themselves. And here Paz, linking eroticism and gastrosophy in the act of desiring, can be read as actually *incarnating* the reality of desire in the sensuality of the flesh, where human bodies endlessly reinvent themselves spiritually in a touch and taste that also go beyond touching and tasting. In this union of the erotic and food, love is reimagined and re-enacted; for love, like gastrosophy and eroticism, is a communion that lifts the senses toward spiritual perfection.

What is most remarkable about Paz's essay is his connection between eroticism and gastronomy, the body and the senses, and love and communion. His analysis lends itself to a description of the love between Tita

---

[63] Octavio Paz, "Eroticism and Gastrosophy," *Daedalus* (Fall 1972), 67–85. This section on Octavio Paz and the eucharistic desire is an edited and expanded version of my earlier work, "Divine Alimentation: Gastroeroticism and Eucharistic Desire," *Concilium*, 2 (2005), 14–25.

[64] Paz, "Eroticism and Gastrosophy," 74.

[65] Ibid., 75.

and Pedro that meets both desires via a culinary feast which opens up, in and through the bodies and the material, an ecstatic pathway to transcendence. I believe that these connections may seem even more pointed when looking at the Eucharist. Indeed, from the perspective of a Catholic narrative, the Eucharist harmonizes these complex elements in their most *polygeusic* sense. In other words, the meaning of the Greek word *poly* (many or multiple) is not only exclusively related to the well-developed traditional perspective of sound, *phoné* (as in *polyphony* or *polyphonic*).[66] Instead of this auditory term, I prefer here to use a word that better describes the eucharistic reality as intimately related to the sense of taste (*geusis*).[67] Here, using a eucharistic imagination, what is envisioned is a dynamic multiplicity of tasting as it is intimately related to an erotic/agapeic gastronomy, to a lavish banquet, an eternally divine–human *gustus*.

Ultimately, what takes place in the Eucharist is a dynamic of desire: both God's desire to share divinity with humanity and humanity's desire for God. In theological terms, desire is as much a human reality as it is a divine one. Echoing Augustine, Graham Ward suggests that there is a fundamental *appetitus*, a radical hunger at the heart of humanity. Humanity perpetually hungers for another – this other being a piece of bread or another person. *Appetitus* is hunger that is desire, and in Augustinian terms it is an ultimate desire for God. Desire also exits within a relational God: as the mutual craving of the Father for the Son and the Son for the Father, as well as the eternal craving maintained by and united through the Holy Spirit.[68] In this Trinitarian community desire is ultimately enacted not from a reality of fundamental lack, but rather from one of plenitude. Because God loves God, God desires God, and God's desire does not go unfulfilled. God feeds God with God's

---

[66] For a reflection on the crucial role of music (harmony, polyphony, rhythm, sound, silence, and so forth) in theological discourse in the Augustinian tradition, see Catherine Pickstock, "Music: Soul, City, and the Cosmos After Augustine," in John Milbank, Catherine Pickstock, and Graham Ward (eds.), *Radical Orthodoxy: A New Theology* (London: Routledge, 1999), 243–77. Also, in a similar note on Augustine's *De Musica*, John Milbank reflects on the complex interaction between the "whole" and the "unit," which casts light on our earlier discussion of the Mexican *molli* and the eucharistic taste: "Not only, therefore, is there a structural parallel between the 'whole' and the unit; in addition, the 'whole' is in some sense present within the unit, because the unit *exists* in a position fully defined by the unfolding of an infinite sequence": *Theology and Social Theory: Beyond Secular Reason* (Oxford: Blackwell, 1990), 405 (emphasis in original).

[67] The Greek word *geusis* was later Latinized as *gustus*, which in Spanish was then transformed into the word *gusto* (savoring, flavor, or tasting).

[68] Graham Ward, "The Church as the Erotic Community," in L. Boeve and L. Leijssen (eds.), *Sacramental Presence in a Postmodern Context* (Leuven: Leuven University Press, 2001), 192–3.

excessive love. Within this Trinitarian festive community, something is cooking. Like Tita, God cooks a lavish meal infused with God-self: a sort of *molli*, a mixture, a "hypostatization" of Same and Other without annihilating, but rather celebrating, diversity.

To maintain that the Trinitarian divine nourishment is a type of *molli* is not as daring as it first sounds. Recall what I said earlier in chapter 1, that in the Náhuatl world *molli* actually means feeding,[69] implying interdependence, relationality, and connectivity. God's being is community: desire and fulfillment among intimately related persons. From a Trinitarian perspective, desire is the erotic/agapeic reality of the divine giving-and-receiving of love's plenitude that is further shared (as an act of kenosis or self-dispossession) with all creation. Creation is a cosmic banquet wherein God is (like Tita) the perfect chef.[70] As Tita infuses her very self into her meals, God imprints in the cosmic banquet, that is creation, God's own divinity.

Divine self-sharing performs a more radical gesture of kenosis at the Eucharist, whereby God becomes food, the most excessive form of self-presencing as nourishment itself. As Tita becomes present to Pedro by feeding him with her own desire incarnated in her meals, God's desire becomes present as food. In the Eucharist, desire-as-alimentation becomes the active agent for a relationship with God and with one another. Like the love between Tita and Pedro, the hybrid divine–human desire within the Eucharist is not abstract, but rather intensely embodied, an incarnate desire already preceded or anticipated by the Trinitarian love-exchange, the act of creation, as well as God's incarnation in Christ, the Word made flesh. In the Eucharist, food is the body of Christ, and drink is his blood, and this through the materiality, the elements of creation, of bread and wine.

The Eucharist is a banquet of the senses. More intimately, it is a feasting of the sense of touch because tasting, eating, and drinking are forms of proximity, a form of touching. Hence Aquinas's keen desire to see touch not only as the foundation to sensitivity as a whole, but also as a skill that, in becoming more refined, increases the intellectual capacities:

---

[69] I realize that there are elements of syncretism in my adding pre-Colombian concepts and grammar to the Christian Eucharist. But in the Eucharist there are also elements of syncretism: Roman and Greek banquets, and Jewish religious meals. See e.g. Dennis E. Smith, *From Symposium to Eucharist: The Banquet in the Early Christian World* (Minneapolis: Fortress Press, 2003).

[70] In the next chapter I will further expand these themes of Trinity, agape/eros, and creation. For a reflection on the Trinity as communion and its socio-political implications, see Leonardo Boff, *Holy Trinity, Perfect Community*, trans. Phillip Berryman (Maryknoll: Orbis Books, 1998).

Yet it might seem that mental capacity corresponded rather to excellence of sight than of touch, for sight is the more spiritual sense, and reveals better the differences between things. Still, there are two reasons for maintaining that excellence of mind is proportionate to fineness of touch. In the first place touch is the basis of sensitivity as a whole; for obviously the organ of touch pervades the whole body, so that the organ of each of the other senses is also an organ of touch, and the sense of touch by itself constitutes a being as sensitive. Therefore, the finer one's sense of touch, the better, strictly speaking, is one's sensitive nature as a whole, and consequently the higher one's intellectual capacity. For a fine sensitivity is a disposition to a fine intelligence.[71]

If touching is also being touched, as I earlier pointed out, then in the Eucharist the partaker is also in some way being touched by God.[72] Thus, above all, in the Eucharist it is the sense of taste (in lips, mouth, and tongue) that moves toward the most intimate ecstatic union with God. What could be more intimate than "ingesting" God?[73]

In eating this divine food, sensuality – particularly the sense of taste – is paradoxically intensified to the point of becoming a powerful mystical experience, yet in a way that does no violence to the material and the somatic.[74] In the Eucharist the sense of taste, *gustus*, becomes the medium and guide to the soul and the intellect (rather than the other way around) leading them to participation with God. This is not only an epistemological event, but also includes an ontological component – is a deification of both the partakers and the eucharistic elements. As I will argue in the next chapter, in this theological account of ontological deification is envisioned as an eternal banquet. In this *sacrum convivium* (sacred banquet) the sense of taste – which is prior to any sensory data, and even prior to the intellect – turns into a foretaste of the beatific vision, as

---

[71] Aquinas, *Commentary on Aristotle's De Anima*, 152–3, quoted in Ward, *Christ and Culture*, 101.

[72] Here I am using allegorical and analogical language. This is not a *literal* description, since we cannot directly touch/taste God, who is incorporeal. Nevertheless, the event of Incarnation in general, and the Eucharist in particular, make the analogy trustworthy.

[73] See Jane S. Webster, *Ingesting Jesus: Eating and Drinking in the Gospel of John* (Atlanta: Society of Biblical Literature, 2003).

[74] See e.g. Caroline Walker Bynum's study on the mystical experience of medieval women and their intensively somatic spiritual experience which was intimately connected with the Eucharist and practices of feasting and fasting: *Holy Feast and Holy Fast: The Religious Significance of Food to Medieval Women* (Berkeley: University of California Press, 1987).

Aquinas realized.[75] To know God is to savor God. This is not to say that the intellect is defeated by the sense of taste, but, rather, means that the intellect becomes more transparent or better attuned to such a divine exquisite taste. Since – as I have argued earlier – the tendency of the intellect toward knowing God is constructed by a *desire* to know, and since, likewise, this desire to know God is framed by the intellect's curiosity, in this case both intellect and desire meet and shape one another in the sensual and erotic performance of savoring God's own and prior (to human will) desire to be known.

Predominantly, in the beatific vision epistemology turns into ontology, since cognition performs an intense erotic *ekstasis* (a desire that moves from the "I" toward the other) and more intimately participates in the known "object," only to discover a deeper truth of Being as beyond objecthood.[76] Octavio Paz argues that desire is representation, yet here, in the beatific experience, desire moves from representation to participation in its most intense sensual fashion. This transit toward participation does not nullify representation, but rather brings it into a space of greater transparency because of the shared intimacy and affinity with God who touches us in the human act of touching and savoring. The transparency that representation acquires also includes creativity, for the act of imagination is triggered and set in play in the participatory happening that is the beatific vision. No wonder patristic and medieval thinkers read the biblical text of the Song of Songs as an allegory of this "exquisite" union of divine and human desires, and depicted it as a feast for the senses in general, but most particularly for the sense of taste.[77]

---

[75] This particular reading of Aquinas regarding taste as foretaste of the beatific vision and deification is inspired by John Milbank and Catherine Pickstock, *Truth in Aquinas* (London: Routledge, 2001); see esp. ch. 3, "Truth and Touch."

[76] This ontological dimension will be further explored in next chapter. For heuristic reasons only, I separate epistemology and ontology. In reality, they are mutually constitutive, just as reason and faith inform and shape one another.

[77] On this relationship between desire and the Song of Songs, see e.g. Carey Ellen Walsh, *Exquisite Desire: Religion, the Erotic, and the Song of Songs* (Minneapolis: Fortress Press, 2000). Moreover, this emphasis on the sensuous union with God is consistent with the primacy of the senses in the Bible in general and the Johannine literature in particular. On this, see John Pilch, "Smells and Tastes," in id., *The Cultural Dictionary of the Bible* (Collegeville: Liturgical Press, 1999), 153ff. See also Pasi Falk, "Towards a Historical Anthropology of Taste," in *The Consuming Body*. (London: Sage Publications, 1994), ch. 4. Furthermore, on this same issue James Smith explains that, in the opening of 1 John, the author "emphasizes that God spoke in Christ a sensible and sensuous Word: 'What was from the beginning, what we have *heard*, what we have *seen with our eyes*, what we beheld and *our hands touched*, concerning the Word of Life ... what we have seen and heard we proclaim to you also' [emphasis added by Smith, quoting 1 John 1:1, 3 NASB]. This is the correlate of the Johannine emphasis on the incarnation and the

The beatific vision reorients the hierarchy of the senses as well as the traditional primacy of the universal over the particular. For the sense of taste becomes the guide to the intellect and reveals the particular (bread, wine, matter, body, and so on) as being already divinized. Yet to call it a (beatific) "vision" no longer fully expresses the significance of such an alimentary beatitude. For in the Eucharist the beatific vision is not primarily a visual experience, but is, rather, a reality to do with tasting, drinking, and eating. It has to do with the sensuality of being nourished: a festive partaking-as-tasting of God's divine banquet that makes the partaker a *participant* in God's nurturing love (which is God's very self). It is an ecstatic "beatific savoring," to be more precise. And here again, the relationship between knowing and savoring is reaffirmed, but now in an ontological fashion.

Knowing – via a gastroerotic event – is becoming aware of Being as participatory of divinity. This knowing as a knowledge of self and other participating in the superabundance of divinity – this mindfulness of Being – is what William Desmond calls the locus of "ontological intimacy" that joins together the subject/object poles, and discloses the *metaxu* or the "dynamic happening of being in the between."[79] Here, knowledge is a dynamic and open process of coming to be in the coming to know as coming to love. Cognition is not left behind in this love journey, for the experience of beatification is an experience in which knowing and loving happen both at once and constitute one another. This is most particularly the case in the Eucharist, wherein knowing is savoring God as nourishment, which, more than incorporating God into the human body (although this is only one level of being nourished that is never canceled), is a feeding that incorporates humanity into Godself, and renders the knower (the beloved) part of the known (the lover). The Eucharist evokes the ecstatic realm of beatification as itself being a gastronomic (gastroerotic) event.

enfleshing of God (John 1:14)." James K. A. Smith, *Introducing Radical Orthodoxy: Mapping a Post-Secular Theology* (Grand Rapids: Baker Academic, 2004), 224. One could also add that this same Word is what our *mouths have tasted*; for such an affirmation will be consistent with the primacy of the senses in John, but, even more so, with the discourses of the bread of life as well as the many narratives of eating and drinking, food and drink in the Gospel of John. See e.g. Webster, *Ingesting Jesus*.
[78] However, this is not to dismiss Aquinas's high estimation of both hearing and vision as playing a crucial role in the encounter with God. Unfortunately, for the most part theology only pays attention to this prioritization of vision and hearing while dismissing the *paradox* in Aquinas's restructuring of the hierarchies of the sense under the guidance of taste as it is experienced in eucharistic practice.
[79] In the next chapter I will explore further this ontological dimension of the between. See Desmond, *Being and the Between*, 4, xii.

At the end of Esquivel's novel, Tita and Pedro finally come together to make love. But the intensity of their love is such that Pedro dies in the ecstatic act, as if Tita's inner fire has consumed his own life. Tita then eats all the matches in a box she has with her in order to be also consumed by her inner fire and the fire of her beloved:

> She began to eat the matches out of the box one by one. As she chewed each match she pressed her eyes shut and tried to reproduce the most moving memories of her and Pedro. The first time she saw him, the first time their hands touched, the first bouquet of roses, the first kiss, the first caress, the first time they made love. In this she was successful; when the match she chewed made contact with the luminous image she evoked, the match began to burn. Little by little her vision began to brighten until the tunnel again appeared before her eyes. There at its entrance was the luminous figure of Pedro waiting for her. Tita did not hesitate. She let herself go to the encounter, and they wrapped each other in a long embrace; again experiencing an amorous climax, they left together for the lost Eden. Never again would they be apart.[80]

Such is the fire produced by the lovers that it ignites everything in the ranch, leaving only ashes and Tita's cookbook with her love story, which is passed on to the next generation. Life and fertility come out of the ashes: "they say that under those ashes every kind of life flourished, making this land the most fertile in the region."[81] Tita and Pedro's desire is united in eternity, and God and God's creatures are also eternally united in the eucharistic banquet.

5   Gastroeroticism and Eucharistic Semiotics of Excess

I would like to name this event "gastroeroticism," a connectivity of elements united by desire-love via gastronomy. However, the term gastroeroticism will here be constructed from an angle of a theology of alimentation that is primarily founded upon the extravagant reality of the in-betweenness (divine–human) that takes place in the eucharistic practice, and which imitates a prior gastroerotic performance within the intra-Trinitarian alimentation. Moreover, by virtue of God's desire, the Eucharist allows the partaker to enter into a deeper unity between the human and the divine, the immanent and the transcendent. Matter is divinized, but only through its own materiality. Humanity is deified but

---

[80]   Esquivel, *Like Water for Chocolate*, 220–1.
[81]   Ibid., 221.

only in the midst of its own situatedness. The bread and the wine become Christ's body and blood, but without setting aside their edible characteristics of bread and wine. In this sense, transubstantiation is not a mere extrinsic act but intrinsic, a radical expression of divine intimacy and love enacted by the Holy Spirit from within creation and at the core of human flesh. The gastroeroticism that takes place in the Eucharist is this divine desire-love already nourished from within the situatedness of the particularity of creation and local communities – all participating in one and the same bread, one mystical body of Christ.

Tita's quail in rose petal sauce signifies something beyond itself. It is not "just food"; it is also the signification of desire and love between the lovers. What is invisible and impossible in Tita and Pedro's love for one another becomes visible and even savorable through food. The impossibility of consummating their love is transformed into a realm of possibility by the act of eating and drinking. In eating the quail in rose petal sauce, the self moves beyond the "I" toward the other, and in this movement the other becomes more present and "penetrating" (as Esquivel puts it). It is a truly gastroerotic experience. In the Eucharist as well, there is an erotic play of signs moving beyond their own signification toward otherness. In a reciprocal motion, the visible moves into the invisible. The bread and wine point beyond themselves to the body and blood of Christ. And at the same time, the signification of the body and blood of Christ is similarly displaced into the elements of nature. Christ's body and blood are in the elements of creation (bread and wine), but also are signified in the priest and the community of believers partaking in this erotic/agapeic banquet. In this playful movement between one sign and another, there is never a final semiotic stasis, never a claim for absolute ownership. The Eucharist reveals that "isness" implies relationality, a dynamic in-betweenness. In addition, the local community signals the global ecclesial community, which signifies beyond itself, yet again, to Christ, and Christ to the Father.

As I have already pointed out regarding Mexican *molli*, in the Eucharist the body displays a series of endless movements of signification. From this eucharistic perspective, the body is in flux, being constantly re-created, reinvented. The Eucharist presents the body as a body of desire: it moves toward otherness, into other corporeal vicinities. For in the Eucharist the physical and sensual individual body is now traced or shaped by other and more complex realities of corporeity: communal, ecclesial, and divine bodies. In all these signs, there is never a semiotic resting-place because signs exceed their own signification by virtue of their participation in God's superabundant alimentation. Although always excessive, this is not a restless melancholic flux, because there is a point of encounter that enables cognition, which in the Eucharist implies a touching, and a manner of alimentation. In this banqueting, cognition is enacted in the eating of signs. To know is already to participate in this erotic feasting of edible signs. Knowledge and understanding are gained in eating Christ's bread/body and drinking his wine/blood, which are signs of Christ's nourishing, self-giving love. Thus, as I said earlier about Tita and Pedro's experience of love through food, the act of coming to know is coming to love through edible signs. As in the eating of the rose petal sauce, the gastroeroticism that takes place in the Eucharist displays a succulent semiotics of excess that renders knowledge as an act of love.

To a certain extent (as Paz describes it) by this gastroerotic act of the Eucharist, the self becomes the other. And yet in the eucharistic feast there is a movement beyond Paz's favoring of alterity and overcoming of the self. In the Eucharist the self is transfigured by the other, but never becomes totally alien to its own self since it rediscovers a deeper reality of who it is. Through such a rediscovery it realizes that the other is intrinsic to its own configuration and self-constitution. In the Eucharist, self and other are no longer juxtaposed, but mutually constituted. The Eucharist *is* communion: with God and with one another. This act of participation in the Eucharist transforms the partakers into eucharistic people: Christ's body, an erotic/agapeic community that is called to feed both physical and spiritual hungers. Therefore, as I argued in chapter 1, the Eucharist is not a merely aesthetic realization and performance. At its core, it is a radical ethical expression of the *for-you* of a God who is not indifferent to the other, a God whose caring gesture of self-giving nourishes. God becomes the cook, the host, and food itself in this eucharistic banquet. This divine *for-you* does not end at the table. Just as God feeds humanity, the partakers are called to feed their neighbor, and are challenged to transform a world of hunger, exclusion, and violence. Herein taste moves from solipsistic experience to a communal event, for the Eucharist calls for *eating together*, which is to say that the intimacy of tasting together is being transformed into the *for-you-ness* of this communal or collective savoring whereby everyone is fed.

6 Conclusion

In this chapter I have looked at the relationship between *saber*, "to know," and *sabor*, "to taste." I first explored this relationship as it is expressed in Laura Esquivel's novel. In this evocative love story, knowledge is enacted through the savoring and eating of food, so that coming to know is coming to love in and through the sensual practice (a performative cognition) of eating and drinking. The cognition achieved in savoring and tasting food and drink is complex. I followed these complexities by exploring various aspects of this intricate relationship between the subject and the object of cognition, and argued in favor of a non-dualistic notion of embodied knowledge, which becomes paradigmatic in the sensually intimate experience of taste. But I also argued that taste and cognition are mediated not only by the body and the senses, but by cultural-linguistic structures as well. I argued that cognition casts light on the world as much as on the individual doing the tasting. What is more, in tasting through eating and drinking not only is the individual shaped, but the world is also shaped by the experience. World and the self are thus mutually reconfigured in the performative knowledge that is tasting.

The in-betweenness of self and other, subject and object, led me to conjecture on the relational dimension of knowledge. In order to move toward an argument of knowledge as participation, I integrated a view of the Eucharist as that where self and other, divine and human, the material and the spiritual enter into a space of intimate encounter and mutual constitution. Herein is found an instance of the eros of cognition, for the knower only knows in receiving the other's love that is kenotically given in and by edible signs as bread/food and wine/drink. I called this event "gastroerotic" because it evokes the unity of divine and human desires coming together in the context of a banquet that not only nourishes but also incorporates the partaker into God's body – namely, the body of Christ who already participates in the intra-Trinitarian erotic/agapeic corporality. In this view, knowledge is not only rational or intellectual, but it is first sensual, integrating affectivity, while simultaneously reshaping the intellect. The traditional view of the primacy of the intellect over the bodily senses (particularly the sense of taste) is reversed, for now savoring/tasting becomes a guide for the intellect, and a foretaste of the beatific vision – a beatific savoring. And here again, knowledge is no longer contemplated as aloofness, but, on the contrary, as intensely intimate with the known. For this reason, the cognition enacted in the Eucharist is not only aesthetic but profoundly ethical. The beautiful is also the good, given in a context of a shared table, *our daily bread*, to be shared with those who physically and spiritually hunger.

It is impossible in this small book to look at all forms of cognition. I have concentrated on the cognition that takes place in tasting food and drink, which I hope will offer a foretaste of knowledge as participation. One knows by entering into contact with the known, that is, by somehow savoring the known which is given as edible signs, further recrafted in the digestive act of interpreting these nourishing signs. But when these signs intimate the presence of the divine one faces superabundance and the infinite plenitude of meaning that always surpasses what it is possible to know. God is actuality in surplus, and humanity can only understand that as an infinitely dynamic mystery.

Such a mystery is a form of knowing, but not as mere correspondence, for there is no system of signification that could possibly be equivalent to the infinite surplus of meaning that is God. And yet, in the face of mystery, humanity is not left malnourished, in absolute silence, incapable of utterance and of knowing God. God gifts creation with edible signs that nurture speech and cognition. Creation, Being, revelation, and so forth are signs that point to God's intimacy and desire to communicate. God is also Logos, the "erotic Word" made flesh for the purpose of intensifying communication – that is a form of encountering, entering into a relationship, being transformed by this intimate knowledge of God.[82] Beyond correspondence, cognition is here envisioned as relationality: a knowledge that is also a sharing of God's *sapientia* (wisdom or Sophia), as we shall see in the next chapter. God's sharing of edible signs performs a further kenotic offering in the Eucharist, where God becomes nourishment itself. In the Eucharist the erotic Word is given as food and drink to sate our appetite and incorporate humanity into the Body of Christ – making the partakers participants in a Trinitarian community as well as becoming members of a social communion that is the ecclesia.

From this eucharistic perspective, one could argue that there is a reverse intentionality of cognition, for the point of departure is not the "I" that intends objects, but rather a prior gesture of God's gifting of signs exceeding all signification, yet rendering signification not empty but nourishing, because of their superabundant source. The "I" is constructed from the *other* that nourishes, and promises yet more to fulfill. As in the Mexican *molli* that we explored in the previous chapter, there is always more to taste, new flavors yet to discover, not from a horizon of melancholic imagining of the impossible, but rather from already savoring the giftedness of the other, despite the partiality of tasting edible signs. One is captivated by the other who pours itself upon oneself, and one falls in love with it, as Pedro falls in love with Tita by savoring and eating her lavish meals. In this erotic/agapeic pilgrimage of savoring as knowing and knowing as savoring there is the perpetual rediscovery that, at the end, knowing the self is becoming aware of *Being* as participatory in the known – the other given as food.

In the next chapter I shall explore this (participatory) ontological (which is profoundly theological) dimension of the gift, and the invitation to reception – that is also a call to sharing – of such superabundant giftedness.

---

[82] For a biblical approach to the relationship between eros and God's Word, see David M. Carr, *The Erotic Word: Sexuality, Spirituality, and the Bible* (Oxford: Oxford University Press, 2003).

3

Being Nourished: Food Matters

In his *Theory of Religion*, Georges Bataille remarks that "the world of things is perceived as a fallen world."[1] However, he argues that, in the prelapsarian world, all creatures stand in a relationship of difference but without transcendence, and thus within a realm of pure immanence. In Bataille's prelapsarian vision both the eater and the eaten, though distinct, are part of the same immanent reality. But in the world after the Fall there is subjugation, and thus to eat something is to posit the "thinghoodness" of that which is eaten. According to Bataille this process of objectification is intensified by men's use of tools, for these are instruments of the subjugation of nature. The human history of war and violence is a result of this long genealogy of subjugation. For Bataille economy and religion go hand in hand, for both are humanity's search for a lost intimacy, whereby violence and sacrifice serve as practices for such a recovery. Thus Bataille suggests that economics and religion promote violence and destruction rather than peace and communion.

In this chapter I will argue with Bataille that the fallen world initiates a severance not only between creatures and creation, but also between creatures and the Creator. I offer a brief "digestive" exercise on the Hebrew Scriptures' narrative of the Fall in the book of Genesis 2–3, and emphasize how food and eating are central in this story of severance from God. Furthermore, and echoing Bataille, eating suggests consumption of another, a certain destruction and transgression. From this perspective, eating is a mark of the transient: a mark of finality, and of mortality. Mikhail Bakhtin points out that, in every act of eating,

[1] Georges Bataille, *Theory of Religion*, trans. Robert Hurley (New York: Zone Books, 1992), 2.

the body transgresses … its own limits: it swallows, devours, rends the world apart, is enriched and grows at the world's expense. The encounter of man with the world, which takes place inside the open, biting, rending, chewing mouth, is one of the most ancient, and most important objects of human thought and imagery.[2]

But not only food is destined to be consumed by the transgressive act of eating. Death is also the eater's fate. While eating sustains life, nonetheless the eater himself shall – just like the eaten products – die. From this perspective of the ephemeral and transgression, food signifies death. Thus, a conventional reading of the narrative of the Fall could echo this same line of thought: death and transgression are inevitable, and it is significant that they both arrive through an eating mouth.

However, beyond Bataille, I will argue for a more positive reading of creation and food and eating, which simultaneously looks at the origins and destiny of creation. In this alternative "alimentary" reading, God is presented as a superabundant banquet gifting creation both at its beginning and its end. God's gift to creation does not presuppose sin. In this Catholic "alimentary theology," eating is not only a sign of communion with one another and with God, but also a means of deification that constructs a space for peaceful community. Two Eastern Orthodox theologians, Alexander Schmemann and Sergei Bulgakov, will be invited to this table of reflection, helping to find a more positive theological reading of food and eating. Furthermore, creation itself will be envisioned as a sign of deification, wherein the Eucharist becomes the main item on this theological menu, since this partaking of God-as-food is a Christian-Catholic paradigm of being nourished.

The feminine figure of Sophia – the Wisdom of God – will be also invoked in this theological understanding of God's superabundant banquet. In the sapiential scriptural texts, Sophia is portrayed as a woman who counsels God before the creation of the world, and is both hostess and cook at a lavish banquet. She nurtures creation, but, more astonishingly, she is also food itself. After looking at some biblical texts on Sophia, I will then revisit Bulgakov's own sophiological account. Bulgakov understands Sophia as God's divine essence shared within the Trinity, gifting creation with a kenotic act of nurture. The eucharistic sharing of God in and through the material elements of bread and wine is a *continuation* of Sophia's gesture of self-giving, intensifying deification. From this perspective, Being is "sophianic," for it participates in God's

---

[2] Cited in Carolyn Korsmeyer, *Making Sense of Taste: Food and Philosophy* (Ithaca, NY: Cornell University Press, 1984), 188, from Mikhail Bakhtin, *Rabelais and his World*, trans. Helen Iswolsky (Cambridge, MA: MIT Press, 1968), 281.

own sharing (a God whose essence is a perpetual "to be"). Bataille is correct in finding a link between economy and religion, for, according to Bulgakov, all economy is already sophianic by virtue of its participation within a prior Trinitarian economy. All creation is God's own sophianic economy, a cosmic banquet that is nurtured by God's eternal generous source of Life and Love. Creation is not an expression of thinghoodness multiplied, a sum of "things" or autonomous items put together in the world. Rather, within Bulgakov's sophianic economy, the world is already the "household of God."

Instead of constructing a prelapsarian world of pure immanence – as Bataille does – my theological argument will look at food, eating, and creation as already sharing in God's own supernatural feast. In this divine feast, transcendence is not finally overcome. While there is a "communal" status of all created Being that shares the same divine banquet, such a status is not a space of pure immanence, since this would evacuate any notion of transcendental sharing, thus leaving ontic reality starved. But neither is the immanent surpassed by a new stage of pure transcendence. In this divine feast, the immanent and the transcendent constitute one another, and this mutual constitution invites us to reflect on why, precisely, "food matters." The intimation of divine sharing, this sophianic economy that is a cosmic banquet, challenges us to question the world's own economic exchanges.

1 Eating the Forbidden Fruit

Early in the second account of Creation in the book of Genesis, the narrative describes Eden as a bountiful garden containing trees that are "enticing to look at and good to eat, with the tree of life and the tree of knowledge of good and evil in the middle of the garden" (Gen 2:9).[3]

---

[3] The book of Genesis includes two accounts of Creation. The first (Gen 1–2:4a) is attributed to what biblical scholars call the "priestly" or "P" source (around the sixth century BCE). This version is written as a poem or a hymn, and narrates how the Creation took place over seven days, with humanity occupying a privileged position, blessed by and created in God's image, and culminating on the seventh day, the Sabbath, when God rests. The second account (Gen. 2:4b–25), which is generally attributed to the "J" or Yahwist source, describes God in more anthropomorphic terms than P. The narrative of the Fall is attributed to the J source. In the New Testament, St. Paul (Rom. 5:12ff.) remarks that sin and death entered into the world by Adam's act of disobedience. Paul's version is later revisited by St. Augustine (fifth century CE) who developed the so-called doctrine of "original sin": the transmission of sin from Adam that is passed on to all generations. See Bruce M. Metzger and Michael D. Coogan (eds.), *The Oxford Companion the to the Bible* (Oxford: Oxford University Press, 1993), in particular the entries on Creation, the Fall, "J," and "P."

God tells the first human that he is to cultivate and take care of the Garden of Eden. At this point of the narrative there is the impression that, in addition to being pleasurable and good, eating in the garden is an open and free affair. Later on however, God issues an explicit admonition: "You may eat indeed of all the trees in the garden. Nevertheless of the tree of the knowledge of good and evil you are not to eat, for on the day you eat of it you shall most surely die" (Gen 2:16–17). This is the first time that the notion of death is introduced into the narrative, and it is connected with food, a fruit from a tree.[4] A warning against eating from the tree of life is not mentioned in this particular admonition. But after Eve and Adam eat from the tree of knowledge of good and evil, the narrative relates that God is concerned about the possibility of them reaching the tree of life, and thus decides to expel humanity from Eden, and, further, posts cherubs with flaming, flashing swords "to guard the way of the tree of life" (Gen 3:24). Therefore, although there is not an explicit warning in God's first admonition, it later becomes clear that eating from the tree of life is also forbidden.

After these prohibitions, there is a description of God's fashioning all sorts of companions for the first human, for, in God's view, "it is not good that the man should be alone." Even though the first human enjoys some company and also has the power to *name* all creatures, still "no helpmate suitable for man was found for him" (Gen 2:21). In order to bring about the right helpmate, God induces deep sleep in the man and makes a woman out of a rib taken from his side. Flesh of flesh, bone of bones, both man and woman live naked and with no apparent conflict in this divine garden. So far the narrative describes great harmony, including eating, as a part of the whole orderly and pleasurable life of Eden.

Things start to turn sour when the serpent, "the most subtle of all the wild beasts," suddenly appears to speak with the woman, and asks her if God *really* said "not to eat from *any* of the trees of the garden" (Gen 3:1; the emphasis is mine). Here the narrative hints at the subtlety of the serpent, for it is clear that God did not issue this admonition, and thus leads the interlocutor to highlight that which has been forbidden. The woman paraphrases God's admonition as follows: "You must not eat it, nor touch

---

[4] The biblical narrator does not say what kind of tree or fruit this is. Although there might be a hint that it is a fig tree (for instance, when the man and woman realize they are naked they cover themselves with large leaves), traditionally, it has been associated with the apple tree. Stewart Lee Allen argues that this tradition started around AD 470 during the Celtic–Roman conflict in which the Romans rejected the Celtic symbolism of apples as containers of divine wisdom. See Stewart Lee Allen, *In the Devil's Garden: A Sinful History of Forbidden Food* (Edinburgh: Canongate, 2002).

it, under pain of death" (Gen 3:3). Initially it is not clear which tree in the middle of the garden she is referring to, but later, during the serpent's reply, it becomes clear that it is the tree of the knowledge of good and evil. It is interesting that the woman's account of God's admonition adds an injunction against "touching," which is not mentioned in the first narrative. On this point, for instance, Katherine Doob Sakenfeld, in her brief essay entitled "Eve," suggests that the woman's adding a prohibition against touch to God's admonition is not so much a lie as an exaggeration made with the purpose of emphasizing a desire not to break the divine command.[5] Doob also suggests the fact that the woman is directly addressed by the serpent – instead of the serpent addressing the man – makes Eve the "first theological thinker, rather than the more gullible of the couple."[6] In the same way as Doob interprets Eve's actions in a more positive light than conventional theology, Vanessa Ochs also suggests greater wisdom on Eve's part. Ochs remarks that, "for Eve, seeking wisdom was about noticing, registering, and making sense."[7] Eve's conversation with the serpent shows her openness to dialogue, a desire to learn, and a willingness to wonder about the world and God which I firmly believe are essential qualities for theologizing. Thus this connection between theological thinking and food suggests that one of the primary forms of theological thought is in fact food, and the practice of eating.

In this dialogue between the serpent and the woman, the narrative pays special attention to the senses, while also connecting them with a notion of judgment. The serpent quickly denies that death will come after eating the forbidden fruit, and so implies that God in fact lied to the man and woman. It further suggests that behind God's admonition there might be an unwillingness to elevate the humans to divine status: "God knows in fact that on the day you eat it your eyes will be opened and you will be like gods, knowing good and evil" (Gen 3:5). As the woman adds forbidding touch to God's admonition, the serpent adds three effects of eating this fruit: opening the eyes; becoming like gods; and gaining knowledge of good and evil.[8] The serpent's words arouse Eve's curiosity.

---

[5] I am grateful to Professor Vanessa Ochs, who pointed out to me that in Jewish thought this practice is called "placing a fence around the Torah," which means taking further precautions to ensure that something forbidden cannot be done.

[6] Katherine Doob Sakenfeld, "Eve," in Metzger and Coogan (eds.), *The Oxford Companion to the Bible*, 206–7.

[7] Vanessa L. Ochs, *Sarah Laughed: Modern Lessons from the Wisdom and Stories of Biblical Women* (New York: McGraw-Hill, 2005), 7.

[8] These two additions, however, had different motives: Eve's addition of forbidding touch is motivated by a desire to be more scrupulous, while the serpent's motive is to be more enticing. I am grateful to Vanessa Ochs for this clarification.

She first looks at the tree. Prior to touch and taste, sensual stimulation is activated by vision. Vision is connected to desire, and leads Eve to judge the object's edibility: "The woman saw that the tree was good to eat and pleasing to the eye." Recall that in God's admonition there is no mention of vision, but it is only the serpent that brings attention to the eyes, saying that they "will be opened." Perhaps the serpent's statement implies vision as judgment or self-awareness, for having one's eyes opened promises a realization of becoming "like gods," in addition to acquiring knowledge of good and evil. We later learn that the serpent did not lie regarding vision: after eating the forbidden fruit, the eyes of the woman and man are indeed opened and they become aware that they are naked, a discomforting realization. Moreover, since this is a dialogue, it implies a degree of both hearing and speaking. Hearing is thus also involved in this set of actions. In hearing, there is also a judgment, that is, a capacity to discern the credibility and plausibility of speech content with the capacity to make a choice. The sense of touch is also mentioned: first, when the woman refers to a prohibition on touching the tree, and later, as part of an action, when she *takes* the fruit prior to eating it. Therefore, this narrative involves all the senses (with the exception of smell). But it is the sense of taste that intensifies the proximity to the forbidden fruit, and subsequently brings all the senses into the final consummation of transgressing God's admonition.[9]

The reader is not immediately told of the effect of eating the fruit. The narrator first relates that, after eating "some of its fruit," the woman gives "some also to her husband who was with her" (Gen 3:6). He does not refuse it, but instead and with neither question nor reply, eats it. Patristic and medieval Church Fathers portray the woman as a temptress; she is the initiator of disobedience and thus the one who tempts the man into sin.[10] However, the fact that he is *with* the woman while the dialogue between her and the serpent is taking place also implicates him (this is, of course, if the reader assumes that the man, by being with the woman, is actually listening and observing her actions; nothing in the narrative indicates the contrary). First, the man silently grants approval of what goes on during this verbal exchange. Or if he disapproves, he makes no utterance nor takes any action to stop the series of events. He is thus indirectly complicit. Secondly, he seems concerned with his

[9] There is no mention of the actual taste of the fruit. Whatever this might have been, it is interesting that – as I argued in the last chapter following Korsmeyer's analysis – this is one of the textual instances giving evidence of an early tradition of setting the sense of taste as the lowest in the hierarchy of the senses.

[10] See e.g. Caroline Walker Bynum, *Holy Feast and Holy Fast: The Religious Significance of Food to Medieval Women* (Berkeley: University of California Press, 1987).

own safety, for he chooses to eat only after the woman has chosen to eat. Only after seeing no immediate negative effect does the man also partake of the forbidden fruit.

The narrative describes how after they both eat the fruit their eyes are opened. On this point at least, the serpent did not lie. But soon they realize that they are naked – an effect that the serpent failed to mention – and so cover their bodies with fig leaves. It is not clear at first why they do so, but later, when they hear God walking in the garden, the narrator relates how they hide because they are "afraid," as if feeling shame at being seen in this newly realized state. When God asks the man if he has eaten of the forbidden fruit, the man immediately blames the woman, and remarks upon God's having made her (thus indirectly blaming God as well): "It was the woman *you put* with me; she gave me the fruit, and I ate it" (Gen 3:12; emphasis added). Then the woman, when interrogated by God, blames the serpent, saying that it tempted her and so she ate the fruit. Notice that, unlike the man's remark, the woman's answer does not make any direct reference to God's making. Yet neither man nor woman takes direct responsibility for their actions, but rather blame someone else. Furthermore, this attitude of blaming also depicts the origins of a self-construction as divided or severed from the other. The "I" stands alone in the midst of the "other" (the woman, creation, and the Creator) who is antagonistic, and even in potential conflict with oneself. After the Fall, the world becomes not a space of community, but a divided place.

The consequences of this eating are irreversible, and will affect their relationship with food and eating in the post-Eden era. The serpent is accursed and told to "eat dust every day" of its life. The woman is to experience great pain in childbearing; her "yearning" will not be explicitly for food, but for her husband who will "lord it over" her. The man is told consequences that explicitly affect his relationship with food and eating (and which may also include the woman's own): food will come from the soil, he must labor to obtain it with great suffering, wild plants will be his food, and with the sweat of his brow he will eat bread. In the narrative the term "bread" is used for food or nourishment in general, suggesting that nourishment will come with effort and struggle, a common feature of agricultural civilizations.[11] This condition is for life. Only death terminates it, or, as God puts it, "until you return to the soil, as you were taken from it. For dust you are and to dust you shall return" (Gen 3:19). Although man and woman are not accursed as the serpent

---

[11] See e.g. Charles B. Heiser, Jr., *Seed to Civilization: The Story of Food*, 2nd edn. (San Francisco: W. H. Freeman, 1981).

is, their act of eating from the tree of knowledge becomes also a cause for their being expelled from Eden in order to prevent them from eating the fruit of the tree of life.

The serpent is partly right: eating from the forbidden fruit does bring a new vision. Moreover, it seems here that the sense of vision is directly connected to the knowledge of good and evil, which – the narrative tells us – is a God-like quality. This idea of divine knowledge as analogous to a likeness with God becomes explicit in God's own words: "See, the man has become like one of us, with his knowledge of good and evil" (Gen. 3:22). The serpent seems to be right here: humans become "like god." However, John Milbank is correct in invoking Augustine's analysis of the Fall for arguing that it only issues in a "false vision" that ultimately separates creation from the Creator. For in the prelapsarian world the will is always oriented to the good, "under the compulsion of the vision of the good, and no choice between good and evil at all."[12] The postlapsarian "fictional" vision invents reality as independent of God's goodness, and erects a self-governance of the will, now with a potential for willing a distorted desire: "The reality of Adam's election is revealed first and foremost as loss of the vision of God and as physical death and incapacity of the body. As a result of this twin impairment, will as desire lacks both vision and capacity, and degenerates into concupiscence: the original sin of Adam which through ignorance and weakness we tend to repeat."[13] This sense of likeness that the serpent speaks about might be a "fictional" analogy that in reality is a loss of Being participating in God. Moreover, the serpent also declared that death was not going to follow from breaking God's eating boundaries. Certainly, the man and woman do not immediately die after ingesting the forbidden fruit. Nonetheless, death does arrive as a result of that forbidden eating. Hence, the long (particularly Christian) tradition of directly associating death with food and eating.[14]

---

[12] John Milbank, *Being Reconciled: Ontology and Pardon* (London: Routledge, 2003), 8.
[13] Ibid., 9.
[14] This association is not explicit in the Hebrew Scriptures. It is a later formulation (particularly by St. Paul and the Church Fathers). In addition to associating food with death, there is a long Christian tradition of associating it with sexuality and lust. However, it is important to notice that in this tradition the act of eating is not sinful per se; it becomes sinful when desire is "disoriented" (as in gluttony – one of the seven deadly sins – for instance). On this issue see how, in *The Confessions*, Augustine tells of an occasion in his childhood when he stole fruit from a tree, not to satisfy his hunger but for the mere act of stealing, as if it was an end in itself: "I simply wanted to enjoy the theft for its own sake, and the sin" (Book II, 4, 9; see also Book I, 19, 30). For a reflection on gluttony, see Francine Prose, *Gluttony* (Oxford: Oxford University Press, 2003). Also, for some interpretations in the Christian Scriptures, see Rom. 16:17; Phil. 3:18–19.

Nevertheless, from a Christian theological perspective, the death that comes from ingesting the forbidden fruit consummates neither history nor ontology. The narrative of Genesis 2–3 says that mortality was neither the origin nor the final destiny of the story of eating food.[15] Prior to the Fall, there is only life – or, at least, death seems not to occur at this stage. The Garden of Eden that God so carefully crafts is a sign of abundant life, wherein death has neither dominion nor even ontological warrant. God fashions humanity out of dust from soil and breathes life into the nostrils of the first human being. Here the breathing mouth of the Creator is not a consuming, chewing mouth, as Bakhtin remarked in the text quoted at the start of this chapter, but it is rather a divine opening that is life-giving, and a sharing of God's divinity.

I would like to suggest that there are two movements that are established in this ingesting of the forbidden fruit. The first movement points toward a self-realization from the viewpoint of the past, the origins of creation as already participating in divinity, an Edenic economy. The second movement is a future-oriented self-realization, that is, one that moves towards a *telos* or future fulfillment or promise of total restoration from the Fall whereby Christ's incarnation takes a crucial role. It is therefore in this twofold movement that I would like to posit an envisioning of food and eating as life-centered, rather than rooted in death.

In other words, food is envisioned as life that overcomes death, and simultaneously, as a symbol of deification. In the previous chapter I argued that coming to know is coming to love through tasting or savoring that which is given to be known. But if knowledge is participation in the known, I argue that this form of knowledge presents Being as participatory in divinity, whereby food is not irrelevant or peripheral, but is instead central. We become God through God constantly becoming us through a practice of eating. In the next two sections I will explore Alexander Schmemann's and Sergei Bulgakov's understanding of food and eating from a perspective of life rather than death, as well as their being symbolic of deification. In these two accounts, creation is envisioned as a "cosmic feast" that manifests God's self-sharing.

2 Schmemann: Food and the Cosmic Sacrament

Alexander Schmemann, in his book *For the Life of the World*, reads the Creation narrative of the book of Genesis (1–3) in a fashion that reclaims Feuerbach's assertion that "man is what he eats."[16] Schmemann explains

---

[15] This view is also complemented by the priestly (P) account in Genesis 1.
[16] Alexander Schmemann, *For the Life of the World: Sacraments and Orthodoxy* (New York: St. Vladimir's Seminary Press, 1973), 11.

that such an assertion was Feuerbach's attempt "to put an end to all 'idealistic' speculations about nature."[17] For Feuerbach, the "isness" of the eater (the human eater) points to matter itself, a world of pure material ontic realism, whereby eating is an end in itself. Schmemann argues that Feuerbach's assertion unknowingly expresses "the most religious idea of man."[18] Contrary to Feuerbach's de-spiritualized account, Schmemann claims that from the beginning of creation humanity is presented as "a hungry being," within a world that is offered by God as a divine banquet. As created by God, the whole cosmos bears the inscription of its maker, but in a way that expresses a cosmic feast: "all that exists lives by 'eating.' The whole creation depends on food."[19] For Schmemann, such dependence is an expression of participation in God's divine gift of life. The "isness" of humanity points to the practice of eating, which then points to the centrality of life, and this further signifies the human vocation to participate in God's eternal life (God's kingdom):

> Man must eat in order to live; he must take the world into his body and transform it into himself, into flesh and blood. He is indeed that which he eats, and the whole world is presented as one all-embracing banquet table from man. And this image of the banquet remains, throughout the whole Bible, the central image of life. It is the image of life at its creation and also the image of life at its end and fulfillment: "… that you eat and drink at my table in my Kingdom."[20]

According to Schmemann, all that exists is filled with God's love and goodness, making all that is "exceedingly good" (Gen 1:31). God's delight in creation is God's blessing, which makes the cosmos "a sign and means of His presence and wisdom, love and revelation: 'O taste and see that the Lord is good.' "[21] The blessings of God (God's goodness) imply that the materiality of the world is a doxological expression of God's gift: creation is *eucharistic* (a sign of thanksgiving). No dichotomy between the spiritual and material spheres is present in this biblical narrative of Creation, for matter is God's gift to humanity, "and it all exists to make God known to man, to make man's life communion with God.

---

[17] Schmemann, *For the Life of the World*, 11.
[18] Ibid.
[19] Ibid., 14.
[20] Ibid., 11.
[21] Ibid., 14.

It is divine love made food, made life for man."[22] People are what they eat, but their hunger is neither a mere material craving nor a pure spiritual yearning; it is, instead, a desire for God that is satisfied in the materiality of a world blessed by God.

Schmemann's reading of Genesis 1 interprets the material world as an all-embracing Eucharist that places humanity as the priest within this cosmic sacramental banquet. In this ontological (which is deeply theological) sense, food *matters*: "the world was created as the 'matter,' the material of one all-embracing Eucharist, and man was created as the priest of this cosmic sacrament."[23] For Schmemann, unlike Feuerbach, eating is not simply a utilitarian function, but rather is ultimately a sacramental act that sustains, gives meaning to, and transforms the life of humanity into a greater communion with God. Schmemann points out that, while both the universe and humanity depend on divine nourishment, humanity occupies a privileged position in creation: humans are the only ones who bless and name creation *for* and *in* God's gift of creation's goodness. Blessing is "the very *way* of life." But what makes man's blessing so unique is that it is a doxological act that expresses "gratitude and adoration," and in so doing returns, non-identically, the gift as blessing God for and in it. Naming is also a human act that signifies the awareness of the world as not being an end in itself, but as participatory in God's divine gift. Gratitude and adoration are ways of seeing, tasting, knowing God, and thus naming matter in its intrinsic relation to God. In this material relation humanity is

> "*Homo sapiens*," "*homo faber*" ... yes, but, first of all, "*homo adorans*." The first, the basic definition of man is that he is *the priest*. He stands in the center of the world and unifies it in his act of blessing God, of both receiving the world from God and offering it to God – and by filling the world with this Eucharist, he transforms his life, the one that he receives from the world, into life in God, into communion with Him.[24]

It is within this notion of food and eating as a sacramental communion with God that Schmemann reads the story of the Fall not as a disobedience to God's command but as a failure to see God as the ultimate source

---

[22]   Ibid.
[23]   Ibid., 15.
[24]   Ibid.

of divine food. The Fall inaugurates the "secular" space by which a distorted vision of the world as an end in itself sets creation apart from God's sacramental presence. In a similar way to Bataille's reflection, in Schmemann's account the secular space would construct matter as mere "thing," severed from communion with the divine. Herein lies the origin of constructing a dichotomy between the sacred and the profane. The world is wrongly reduced to the sphere of the profane, while God occupies the *exclusive* space of the "sacred." Schmemann argues that, after the Fall, humanity lost its eucharistic dynamism, and instead entered into an alienated world of "pure materiality" possessing its own signification outside of God; therein lies the mark of its own agony, indeed its own death. In Schmemann's own words,

> The world of nature, cut off from the source of life, is a dying world. For one who thinks food in itself is the source of life, eating is communion with the dying world, it is a communion with death. Food itself is dead, it is life that has died and it must be kept in refrigerators like a corpse.[25]

Sin is not disobedience, but the ceasing of hunger for God. The material world in and for itself is an invention of a distorted vision of the world: under this sinful economy of the merely material as the quantifiable exchange of products and nominal calculations life is no longer understood within the superabundant order of sacramental communion with God. In a sinful world, religion (from the Latin *religare*, meaning binding or bridging over) mediates the wall that separates God from humanity, the sacred from the profane, nature from the supernatural. In this severed notion of reality, religion is an economy of exchange that properly administers with quantifiable acts of sacrifices and cults the suitable trade that would gain God's favors. In this way, Schmemann's account is comparable to Bataille's presentation of religion and economy as the source of sacrifice and violence.

However, unlike Bataille, Schmemann argues that, in spite of this fallen vision, humanity and the world are not originally distorted but instead originally graced. He upholds that through God's incarnation humanity assumes divinity through Christ, who re-founds the world in its original communion with God. From a Christian perspective, however, such a community is not a return to a lost paradise, but is the re-foundation of a new community, the church whose head is Christ. The

---

[25] Schmemann, *For the Life of the World*, 17.

church's main source of nourishment is the body and blood of Christ – the eucharistic banquet – from which it comes into being and through which it practices day by day its true communion with God. For Schmemann Christianity is the locus of the post-religion that reorients the world's economy within the gift of the eucharistic practice.

3   Bulgakov: Food and the Communism of Being

While Schmemann contrasts Feuerbach's secular economy of alienation from God with his notion of the eucharistic economy within a space of the cosmic sacrament and the church's eucharistic practice, Sergei Bulgakov, in his *Philosophy of Economy: The World as a Household*, contrasts Marxism and positivism with a biblical notion of divine Sophia – the wisdom of God. Sophia plays an important role in Bulgakov's economic analysis. In the next section of this chapter I will further explore this notion. For now, I would like to point out that Bulgakov takes some relevant features of the scriptural feminine figure of Sophia (particularly from the book of Proverbs 8–9:1–6), which characterizes her as being in intimate relationship with God from the beginning of creation, as well as sharing eternity with God. Sophia establishes an intimate bond with God (she is God's own delight), but also with creation, and most particularly with humanity (Prov. 8:30–1). In this sense, then, Sophia is an expression of the divine–human union: God's shared wisdom from the beginning of creation, and for all eternity. The element of nourishment is vital to Bulgakov's notion of Sophia and his philosophy of economy. In this sense of nourishment, Bulgakov echoes Proverbs 9:1–6, where Sophia shares a banquet, and alludes to her metaphorical identification with meat, bread, and wine. Food points to the root of being as ultimately relational – the very character of Sophia. Sophia is, for Bulgakov, the true expression of the metaphysical, social, and economic life. A similar analogy could be drawn with regard to food. At the metaphysical level, being is the food/substance offered as a gift from God, and thus intimately related to or participatory in the divine. At the social level, food expresses the interdependence between individuals and societies. And at the economic level food is an expression of exchange per se.

Food is vital for survival yet it also anticipates a movement toward finality and mortality, hence the existential struggle to overcome it. Bulgakov remarks that both the animal and the human worlds resemble one another in "the struggle for life," which "is therefore a struggle for food."[26]

[26] Sergei Bulgakov, *Philosophy of Economy: The World as a Household*, trans Catherine Evtuhov (New Haven: Yale University Press, 2000), 71.

All human economy, according to Bulgakov, is founded upon this condition characterized as the "biological struggle for existence."[27] The term "economy" is taken by Bulgakov in a broad sense to mean "household management," a term mainly taken from its Greek's roots, *oikonomia* (*oikos* = house; *nemein* = to manage). For Bulgakov, economy is the process of managing or mastering life in the midst of struggle for survival, and here food assumes a vital role.

Bulgakov envisions the whole world as a household entrusted to humanity with the purpose of the fulfillment "of God's word – *In the sweat of thy face shalt thou eat bread* – and this includes all bread, that is, spiritual as well as material food: it is through economic labor, in the sweat of our face, that we must not only produce material goods but create all of culture."[28] The world is a household, for it is a product and object of labor. Labor is an activity that is intrinsic to such an economy. Beyond Karl Marx's material definition of labor as "the expenditure of nervous-muscular energy," Bulgakov attempts to integrate a counter-notion that could also express living being and life in general: "The capacity of labor is one of the characteristics of a living being; expresses the flame and sharpness of life. Only he lives fully who is capable of labor and who actually engages in labor."[29] The necessity of labor for bringing about physical and spiritual nourishment is another god-like characteristic of humanity, which, as I earlier remarked, also echoes the serpent's words regarding the eating of the tree of knowledge of good and evil, as well as God's own words. In the same gesture as God's crafting the universe in the Genesis story of Creation, human labor is also a re-creation of the world, including nature. Here Bulgakov makes a distinction between economy and nature, explaining that while the former is about "re-creation and expansion of life through labor," the latter is "the totality of what is given (to man), the 'natural' forces of life and its growth."[30] In this sense, economic activity – which involves labor – is "a part of the life of the universe, a moment in its growth."[31] Bulgakov claims that economy is a necessary moment in the universe because both nature and the universe are interpreted and read by humanity in a gesture

---

[27]   Bulgakov, *Philosophy of Economy*.
[28]   Ibid., 75.
[29]   This is a counter-notion because, for Bulgakov life and labor escape axiomatic definitions (ibid.).
[30]   Ibid., 76.
[31]   Ibid.

of constant re-creation, a remaking of God's gift. But re-creation is not only a one-way act: humanity is constantly being reshaped by nature, and by God as well. And in this mutual constitution between nature and subject economy continues to shape the path of history.

However, this economy of the mutual constitution of humanity and creation, people and God, has been interrupted. Bulgakov notes how scientific positivism has reduced nature and matter to mere observable objects that can only be described and quantified under the calculations made by positive laws of correspondence. Nature and matter are then reduced to things entirely separate from humanity, and yet absolutely controlled by human subjectivity (recall a similar analysis in Bataille's account of thinghood and tools as a form of subjugation of nature imposed by humans). This abysmal gap between subject and object, nature and humanity, has also created a disenchanted world, devoid of divinity. That is to say, a "fallen world." In a similar fashion to the Schmemann's reading of the narrative of the Fall in Genesis, Bulgakov argues that the Fall opens up an era of radical separation between the natural and the spiritual, the object and the subject, God and humanity. Original sin is the loss of this organic interrelation that existed at the Edenic stage. Bulgakov argues that Marx followed this "fallen state" of humanity and the material world and built his entire doctrine of economic materialism upon it, where history marches in constant struggle toward the establishment of the utopic teleology of the proper distribution of goods.

In a similar way to Schmemann's reading of Genesis, Bulgakov's answer to Marxism and positivism takes as a point of departure not the world of original sin, but the world in Eden that signifies an organic whole in harmonious existence. Bulgakov conjectures that, at the heart of such an "organic whole," there is ultimately a *living* unity between matter and spirit, object and subject. As it was in Eden, Bulgakov believes that at the heart of reality there is the unifying dimension of life, rather than death. He was nevertheless aware – like Schmemann – of the world's fallen situation that breaks with its original state of harmony and brings about death. In spite of this fallen state, Bulgakov believes that Christianity can provide the means of establishing a "sophianic economy" that would not necessarily regress into paradise, but would instead create a discipline to constantly help humanity to discern its restored nature in and through Christ, who is God made human flesh. Bulgakov claims that God's incarnation divinizes the human flesh, and thus reintegrates and reorients humanity into its initial unity with God. He also believes that Christ's resurrection overcomes death, and thus anticipates a future promise of divine union.[32] In order to sustain his argument of divine identity, Bulgakov reads Schelling's version of identity against Kant's egocentric account.

At the heart of his *Philosophy of Economy*, Bulgakov endeavors to answer the question: "*how is economy possible*, what are the conditions and presuppositions, the a priori of objective action?"[33] Bulgakov believes that Schelling rather than Kant was the founder of a notion of philosophy of economy, because it was the former who properly answered the question of the possibility of economy. According to Bulgakov, Schelling demonstrates that the Kantian division between subject and object which subsequently determines the subject's hegemony ultimately incarcerates nature and the world within the confines of the rational: nature becomes the "sublime object" that the subject contemplates as existing beyond the boundaries of thought, while being immanent to consciousness. This Kantian egocentricity does not correctly describe the a priori nature of objective action, because Kant's rational scheme fails to describe the dynamic of exchange and interaction that is implicit in reality. Bulgakov argues that, for Schelling, the condition and presupposition of every exchange and economy are rooted in a dynamic intra-relationality between subject and object, spirit and nature. Schelling's philosophy of identity describes the dynamic of an exchange whereby humanity is in nature as much as nature is in humanity:

> "Nature must be the visible spirit, and the spirit must be invisible nature. Thus the problem of how nature is possible outside ourselves is resolved here, in the absolute identity of the spirit within us and nature outside of us." In the light of the philosophy of identity, the universe looks like a ladder with rungs or "potentials," like an evolutionary development whose general content is the expression of the spirit.[34]

---

[32] The divinization of the flesh that Bulgakov reflects on points to God's incarnation and resurrection in Christ, surpassing Platonism and Neoplatonism, for it claims a higher unity between flesh and spirit: "Christianity is also a philosophy of identity ... Neither Platonism nor Neoplatonism, viewing the body as an envelope for the soul or as a dungeon for it, nor the new idealism, which turns flesh into a subjective image, can know the unity of spirit and flesh that Christianity teaches. This is the basis for the doctrine that the human incarnation of God brought about a divinization of the flesh. And the incarnation took place not just for show or externally but in reality and with finality. Christ retains the flesh that he took upon himself forever; he was resurrected with this flesh and will retain it at the Second Coming – such is the teaching of the church." *Philosophy of Economy*, 88.

[33] Ibid., 78.

[34] Ibid., 85. The quotation is taken from Schelling's *Ideen zur Philosophie der Natur*, in *Werke*, 1: 152.

Both materialism (which sees matter as an independent mechanism capable of coercing the subject) and idealism (which "denies nature by reducing it to a mere [subjective] image"[35]) fail to give a sufficient account of this "living unity" between subject and object. For Bulgakov, the Schellingian notion of a highest unity between object and subject describes Christianity's resolution of dichotomies by its teaching of the living unity between flesh and spirit, which ultimately points to the fact that life cannot be conquered by death.

Philosophy of economy is based on this objective action: a principle of unity that connects and makes possible all exchanges. For Bulgakov, all life is an economy, "a metabolic process" which he compares with the course of action of "circulation or an alternation of inhaling and exhaling."[36] Economy is a perpetual cycle consisting of two acts or essential functions: production and consumption. For the purpose of this chapter I will mainly concentrate on the aspect of consumption, for it is this phase that will illuminate an understanding of the theological relevance of nourishment; the alimentary theology that this book is concerned with.

Bulgakov contemplates all living organisms as existing in a perpetual interaction with one another. The universe is an organic whole that expresses the reality that nothing exists apart and totally independent from the whole, "for the universe is a system of mutually connected and mutually penetrating forces."[37] The essence of being is mutuality rather than disconnection:

> The unity of the universe, the physical communism of being, means that, physically, everything finds itself in everything else, every atom is connected with the entire universe; or, if we compare the universe to an organism, we can say that everything enters into the makeup of the world body.[38]

In the end, even death and life are not totally disconnected but imply the other through a "mysterious identity" that expresses the most fundamental pillar of being, its life-capacity. The universe is in a perpetual movement or exchange that is sustained by "the development of infinite potentials of life." In this sense, the cosmos is a living organism nourished by a life-giving principle that connects all living and nonliving

35 Ibid., 87.
36 Ibid., 95.
37 Ibid.
38 Ibid., 96.

organisms. And, for Bulgakov, nourishment is precisely that which expresses this primordial identity and principle.

To better understand what he means by this notion of nourishment, it is important to quote Bulgakov in full:

> By *nourishment* in the broadest sense we mean the most general metabolic exchange between the living organism and its environment, including not just food but respiration and the effects of the atmosphere, light, electricity, chemistry, and other forces acting on our organism, insofar as they support life. Nourishment understood even more broadly can include not just metabolism in the indicated sense but our entire "sensuality" (in the Kantian sense), that is, the capacity to be affected by the external world, to receive impressions or irritations of the sense from it. We eat the world, we partake of the flesh of the world not only with our mouths or digestive organs, not only with our lungs and skin in the process of respiration, but also in the course of seeing, smelling, hearing, feeling, and general muscular sensation. The world enters us through all the windows and doors of our sense and, having entered, is apprehended and assimilated by us. In its totality this consumption of the world, this ontological communication with it, this communism of being, lies at the foundation of all of our life process. Life is in this sense the capacity to consume the world, whereas death is an exodus out of this world, the loss of capacity to communicate with it; finally, resurrection is a return into the world with a restoration of this capacity, though to an infinitely expanded degree.[39]

The world becomes food that we consume and integrate into our own bodies, into our own self. By eating, we communicate and make communion with the world, and in so doing, eliminate all boundaries between interiority and exteriority. The process of eating manifests the essence of every economic exchange.

Bulgakov looks at food on the physical and biological level. But, more radically, food also has a metaphysical component:

> How can matter that is alien to my organism become my flesh, enter into my body? Or, to put the same question backwards: How does my flesh, a living body, turn into dead matter, entirely after death but partially over the course of my entire life, in the form of

---

[39] Bulgakov, *Philosophy of Economy*, 101–2.

excrement, falling hair, nails, evaporations, and so on? Here we have the most vivid expression of the cosmic communism ... The boundary between living and nonliving is actually removed in food. Food is natural communion – partaking of the flesh of the world. When I take food, I am eating world matter in general, and in so doing, I truly and in reality find the world within me and myself in the world, I become a part of it.[40]

For Bulgakov, as for Schmemann, food *matters*. Food is an act of partaking, of being in communion with the world-matter that becomes bread for humanity. Food is connectedness with the bread of the world made flesh, and which already contains a history of constant transformations from atoms into particles and into matter, and which further becomes transformed by the very act of eating: "And not only this bread, but every particle of the food we eat (and every atom of the air we breathe) is in principle the flesh of the world."[41] The world is the flesh that nourishes; it is that which sustains life, and connects to the history of the entire universe. "Food in this sense uncovers our essential metaphysical unity with the world."[42] Eating is more than assimilation, for it is "a moment of the universal nourishing, incarnating, body-creating process, as opposed to the equally universal process of destruction of the body."[43] Because humans are incarnate beings, food becomes this point of intersection with the universe; it is a means of communion with the world.

In a similar way to Schmemann, Bulgakov addresses the radical message of God's incarnation and its presence in the eucharistic banquet. In Christ God becomes flesh – "the divinized flesh of the world" – which furthermore becomes bread for humanity.[44] The eucharistic meal is a means of receiving the divinity's own gift of life eternal as it is already preceded by the ordinary act of eating:

Eucharistic meal means to partake of immortal life, in which death is conquered once and for all, and the deathlike impenetrability of matter is overcome ... God's incarnation created a new, spiritual flesh – the flesh of the world is raised to a higher, immortal potential, and we anticipate its imminent transfiguration in the sacrament.

---

[40]   Ibid., 103.
[41]   Ibid.
[42]   Ibid.
[43]   Ibid., 301–2 n. 3. Bulgakov is here citing Johannes Claassen, *Baader*, 2: 63.
[44]   Ibid., 104.

In this sense we can say that the holy food of the Eucharist, the "medicine of immortality" ... is food, but potentialized food; it nourishes immortal life, separated from our life by the threshold of death and resurrection ... In this sense we can say that the greatest Christian sacrament is anticipated by such a simple act of daily life as eating.[45]

For Bulgakov, the holy food of the Eucharist is a healing communion. It is anticipated by a natural consumption of the flesh of a world already graced by God, and which incorporates humanity into a life of communion – a "metaphysical communism" – with the universe: just as the Eucharist activates a deeper human incorporation into communion with God. And at the heart of this communion there is, for Bulgakov, Sophia, the Wisdom of God that invites and nurtures human desire for a greater unity with God.

4 The Sophianic Banquet

Sophia is not only crucial for understanding Bulgakov's general philosophy of economy, but also for articulating the relationship between a Christian understanding of creation and alimentation – and particularly from a perspective of eucharistic nourishment. In this section I will first provide a brief outline of the figure of Sophia taken from few selected sapiential texts.[46] Given that Sophia is a complex scriptural notion, I do not offer a thorough analysis, but rather concentrate on the scriptural relationship between Sophia and God's creation, and in a fashion that mostly relates to food.[47] I will then revisit Bulgakov's articulation of Sophia with the hope of bringing light to why nourishment is so central to a Christian eucharistic discourse, as well as for building a theological ground for a non-dualistic account of Being and materiality.

---

[45] Bulgakov, *Philosophy of Economy*, 104–5.

[46] For further research on biblical wisdom literature see Metzger and Coogan (eds.), *The Oxford Companion to the Bible*, 801–3.

[47] The main source of inspiration for this biblical reading of Sophia comes from Maurice Gilbert and Jean-Noël Aletti, *La Sagesse et Jésus-Christ* (Paris: Editions du Cerf, 1980). See also John Barton and John Muddiman (eds.), *The Oxford Bible Commentary* (Oxford: Oxford University Press, 2001), and Metzger and Coogan (eds.), *The Oxford Companion to the Bible*. For a postcolonial reading of Sophia, see Mayra Rivera, "God at the Crossroads: A Postcolonial Reading of Sophia," in Catherine Keller, Michael Nausner, and Mayra Rivera (eds.), *Postcolonial Theologies: Divinity and Empire* (St. Louis, MO: Chalice Press, 2004), 186–203.

In the Hebrew Scriptures, Sophia is the personification of wisdom, or *hokhmah*. At times wisdom means "skillfulness," "ability," or "craftsmanship" in general; at other times, it is an achieved skill for intellectual penetration and eloquence of speech in particular. Related to intellect and speech, wisdom could also mean knowledge, insight, and instruction (an ability to live a disciplined life). In addition, wisdom is a divine gift that provides a foundation for "fear of the Lord."[48] But, more than a noun, wisdom in the Bible (particularly within the context of wisdom literature) is personified as a *woman*. Among her many public roles, Sophia is depicted as a sister, prophet, wife, counselor, and teacher of wisdom.[49] In the book of Proverbs, for instance, she first appears as a messenger raising her voice in the streets, crossroads, and public squares, and at the city gates.[50] Mayra Rivera rightly points out that there is something about Sophia's figure that is perplexing and ambiguous. She is a woman taking a public stand – usually the exclusive domain of males – in a patriarchal society. Also, this *strange* woman might not be a native of Israel, but a foreigner, for nobody knows exactly where she comes from. Rivera also observes how some scholars have noted that Sophia appears to be "the daughter of somebody else's goddess, be it the 'Canaanite love goddess Maat, the Semitic mother goddess ... the Hellenized form of a Egyptian goddess Isis.'"[51] To add to this list of Sophia's unsettling characteristics, she also appears to be riskily crossing the border between being a creature and being God. In the book of Ecclesiasticus, Sophia comes from the mouth of God.[52] In the book of Wisdom, she is portrayed as being *with* God, a fountain of divine spirit, and the "emanation of the glory of the Almighty ... she is a reflection of the eternal light, untarnished mirror of God's active power, image of

---

[48]   See esp. the didactic discourses in Proverbs 1:1–9:18. Most of these descriptions of Wisdom are taken from K. T. Aitken, "Proverbs," in Barton and Muddiman (eds.), *The Oxford Bible Commentary*, 405–22.

[49]   See, Prov. 1:20–33, 7:4, 8:6–10, 14, 31:10.

[50]   Prov. 1:21, 8:1–3.

[51]   Rivera, "God at the Crossroads," 188. Rivera is here quoting Elizabeth Johnson, *She Who Is: The Mystery of God in Feminist Theological Discourse* (New York: Crossroads, 1992), 92. Regarding these possible goddesses' influence on the construction of Sophia, Mary Joan Winn Leith also points out that the biblical figures of the "foolish woman," the "seductive/adulterous woman," and the woman who brings about death are Sophia's counterparts, which may have been used as a deliberate tool to undercut the neighbor goddesses imagery (see Prov. 2:16, 18–19, 5:3–20, 6:24–35, 7:5–27, 9:13–18). Mary Joan Winn Leith, "Wisdom," in Metzger and Coogan (eds.), *The Oxford Companion to the Bible*, 800–1.

[52]   Ecclus. 24:3.

his goodness."[53] Sophia stands at the crossroads, at the borders between male and female, native and foreigner, creature and God, god and goddess.

The role that Sophia is said to play at the beginning of creation is crucial. Sophia's speech in Proverbs 8:22–31 is perhaps the passage that most resonates among the wisdom literature texts with her central role in creation. As the "oldest of creation," she "is there" in the crafting of the created world. Standing at the side of God's creativity, she is an artist, the master craftswoman of creation.[54] And, in performing this "playful" role, she delights God: "day after day, ever at play in God's presence, at play everywhere in God's world."[55] Like the life that comes out of God's mouth at the creation of humanity, the book of Ecclesiasticus depicts Sophia coming forth "from the Mouth of the Most High," and covering all creation both in space and time (for she is eternal).[56] Just as she delights God with her playfulness and insight at the beginning of creation, she is also and most particularly the pleasure of humankind from the moment of their creation: "delighting to be with the sons of men."[57] For men and women who "hold her fast," Sophia is the *tree of life*," and so recalls the tree of life in Eden.[58] Moreover, the life that she provides is superabundant, for it is a vital source of "happiness" and priceless treasures.[59] In this sense then, Sophia may help recover some of the blissfulness and fructifying life of the lost Eden.

Sophia not only accompanies (and perhaps, also counsels) God in crafting the world and becoming a source of life, but her artistry and superabundance are also at work in building a house with "seven pillars," and preparing a banquet:

> Wisdom has built herself a house, she has erected her seven pillars, she has slaughtered her beasts, prepared her wine, she has laid her table. She has despatched her maidservants and proclaimed from the city's heights: "Who is ignorant? Let him step this way." To the fool she says, "Come and eat my bread and drink the wine I have prepared! Leave your folly and you will live, walk in the ways of prudence."[60]

[53] See Wisd. 7:22–8:1, 9:1–3, 9, 17.
[54] Prov. 8:30.
[55] Prov. 8:30–1.
[56] Ecclus. 24:3–10. This passage also mirrors Wisd. 7:25–6, where Sophia is the breath of God and God's active power.
[57] Prov. 8:31.
[58] Prov. 3:18 (my emphasis).
[59] Prov. 3:13–18.
[60] Prov. 9:1–6.

Aitken suggests that Sophia's building a "seven-pillared house" may symbolize "the world as fashioned by Wisdom; the cosmic temple of Wisdom"; and her splendid house suggests a gesture of hospitality that "accommodate[s] all who accept her invitation."[61] In this passage, Sophia's menu includes wine, meat, and bread. As I have mentioned, the notion of "bread" is usually a general term that most likely means alimentation (of both food and drink) in general.[62] As far as Sophia's menu goes, John Pilch also points out the importance in the Bible of food and drink – products such as wine, meat, and wheat for making bread (along with the milk, honey, and olive oil that are also frequently mentioned). The high value given to these products has to do with their availability and varieties of use. The soil of Palestine, for instance, was favorable for the cultivation of grapes. Wine was considered to be the "blood of the grapes," an alcoholic beverage that helped in quenching thirst, particularly in an area that suffered from scarcity of water, and that also did not have the disadvantage of turning sour without refrigeration, as milk does. As for meat, Sophia's banquet menu probably indicates sheep or goat (or both), since they were ancient domesticated animals that were very common in the Middle East. Slaughtering an animal was also considered a gesture of hospitality, and a symbol of banqueting. Finally, wheat was used with great frequency, for it was "the most important cereal grain in Israel."[63] Wheat was also a grain used for multiple purposes: "eaten as a parched grain, and in the form of bread. Its stems served as fodder, bedding for the animals, mulch, compost, and fertilizer. Stems were also woven into hats, baskets, chair, seats, and beehives."[64]

Architect and cook, Sophia is also a commanding housekeeper who dispatches her servants to issue invitations, particularly to those who are most hungry or needy (the fool and the ignorant) to dine at her well-prepared table. But Sophia is not the only one keeping herself busy in preparing a banquet for her guests. The book of Proverbs contrasts Lady Wisdom's banquet to that of Dame Folly:

Dame Folly acts on impulse, is childish and knows nothing. She sits at the door of her house, on a throne commanding the city, inviting the passers-by as they pass on their lawful occasions, "Who is

[61] Aitken, "Proverbs," 411.
[62] See e.g. John J. Pilch, "Drinking and Eating," in id., *The Cultural Dictionary of the Bible* (Collegeville: Liturgical Press, 1999), 52–8.
[63] Ibid., 56.
[64] Ibid.

ignorant? Let him step this way." To the fool she says, "Stolen waters are sweet, and bread tastes better when eaten in secret." The fellow does not realize that here the Shades are gathered, that her guests are heading for the valleys of Sheol.[65]

As I have already suggested, the negative feminine figure of Folly contrasting with the "positive" figure of Sophia could have been created in order to criticize the goddess-worship of peoples in neighboring territories that presented a threat to preserving the patriarchy of Israel's monotheistic deity. This position, however, must still deal with the fact that Sophia is, despite the predominantly male figure of Israel's God, a feminine figure that intimates a very close relationship with God – and even at times seems to be God's own manifestation. But it could also be, as Rivera argues, that this Dame Folly figure is the result of a male-dominated society that constructs both positive and negative feminine typologies in order to maintain strict gender control, and thus promote moral social expectations of what is "ideal" in a woman (Sophia's character) as opposed to what must be censured (Folly's character). Aside from these interpretations, the comparison between these two women and their banquets is, nonetheless, illuminating. Dame Folly is not wise: she is impulsive, childish, and lacking in knowledge. In contrast to Sophia's formal protocols of inviting guests, Folly lacks decorum, for she merely commands people to attend. Mirroring Sophia's inviting the ignorant and foolish, Folly also addresses them. Yet Folly's menu is water and bread, and there is no mention of meat or wine.

However, the differences in menu between these two banquets might not be so relevant. After all, Folly's provisions are also a source of nourishment. Aitken suggests that in fact the attractiveness of Folly's banquets may mirror the "the magnetic power of the forbidden fruit" in Eden.[66] Thus, here again we may have a conventional reading of the eating of the forbidden fruit as related to a female temptress (Eve/Dame Folly): a symbol that also reinforces the negative construction of the female gender from a male perspective. But, more importantly than the menu, the two attitudes of providing food sharply contrast with each other. Sophia is the cook, she prepares the food, and her food brings about life, creates community, and provides correct perception. In contrast, Folly does not prepare the menu, for water is stolen and it is said to be "sweet," perhaps a reference to the attractive forbidden fruit in Eden, which was also somehow "stolen." In addition, Folly says that

---

[65] Prov. 9:13–18.
[66] Aitken, "Proverbs," 412.

bread tastes better when eaten in secret, which also contrasts with the communal gathering of Sophia. Finally, while Sophia's meal "promotes and celebrates life, to dine with Folly is to feast with the 'dead' of Sheol."[67]

Sophia not only provides nourishment, she is also food itself. At times, wisdom is compared to the sweetness of honey: "Eat honey, my son, since it is good; honey that drips from the comb is sweet to the taste: and such is knowledge of wisdom for your soul."[68] In the book of Ecclesiasticus, for instance, wisdom is not only compared to honey, but also exhales perfume and flowered scents; and like the vine, wisdom bears fruit "of glory and wealth":

> I have exhaled a perfume like cinnamon and acacia, I have breathed out a scent like choice myrrh, like galbanum, onycha and stacte, like the smoke of incense in the tabernacle. I have spread my branches like a terebinth, and my branches are glorious and graceful. I am like a vine putting out graceful shoots, my blossoms bear the fruit of glory and wealth. Approach me, you who desire me, and take your fill of my fruits, for memories of me are sweeter than honey, inheriting me is sweeter than the honeycomb.[69]

Here again, the image of fruit could recall the forbidden fruit in Eden; yet wisdom's fruit brings about pleasure and satisfaction rather than punishment. Wisdom is superabundant food and drink and explicitly calls to be ingested, to open up a desire for *more*:

> They who eat me will hunger for more, they who drink me will thirst for more. Whoever listens to me will never have to blush, whoever acts as I dictate will never sin.[70]

Sophia is God's Wisdom. She is at the beginning of creation with God, and from the beginning she offers herself as a gift that nourishes and brings people closer to God in her act of nurturing. While the forbidden fruit in the narrative of the Fall suggests a severance between God and creatures, divinity and matter, Sophia's fruit intimates a recovered sense of inner connection with God. And this notion of a deeper unity – a reconnection with the Edenic dimension – is perhaps what most fascinated

---

[67] Ibid.
[68] Prov. 24:13.
[69] Ecclus. 24:15–20.
[70] Ecclus. 24:21–2.

Bulgakov in his construction of Sophia's gift that renders the harmonious unity of the economy of being.

5 Being Sophianic: Being Nourished

Bulgakov is fascinated by the figure of Sophia; she plays a central role in his thought in general, and in his *Philosophy of Economy* in particular.[71] Bulgakov believes that every human being contains the inner organic connection of humanity with God, and that this proceeds from the harmonious beauty of divine Sophia. "Humanity is and always remains the unifying center of the world in the eternal harmony and beauty of the cosmos created by God."[72] But not only humanity "but the whole world is really the artistic re-creation of the eternal ideas that together make up the ideal organism, the divine Sophia, the Wisdom that existed with God before the Creation and whose joy is 'with the sons of man.'"[73] The same gesture, the same gift of God, re-creates itself, that is, repeats itself non-identically into multiple exchanges of the same gift, the same force acting in the world as a unifying harmonious principle.

As we have explored, there is a *positive* reading of food in Bulgakov's sophiological account. For Bulgakov, the original unity of all humanity, a dynamic human essence or "Adamness," shares in this same sophianic and inexhaustible force. Just as all humanity inherits the same original sin of Adam, by virtue of this primordial unity it is also made possible for humanity to equally recover some of the original unity in the prelapsarian world. In this act of recovery, Bulgakov looks at the figure of Christ's incarnation as a continuation and manifestation of Sophia's own work, which pronounces with greater transparency God's own Word, God's Logos becoming flesh, and who further becomes food and drink in the Eucharist, thus extending Sophia's invitation to her banquet.[74] And this unifying principle between God and the Logos is further manifested in a practice of collective unity that is the church, which is

---

[71] For a general analysis of the role that Sophia plays in Bulgakov's thought, see Rowan Williams, *Sergii Bulgakov: Towards a Russian Political Theology* (Edinburgh: T&T Clark, 1999), and John Milbank, *The Suspended Middle: Henri de Lubac and the Debate Concerning the Supernatural* (Grand Rapids: Eerdmans, 2005). See also Milbank's unpublished paper, "Sophiology and Theurgy: The New Theological Horizon." I am grateful to Professor Milbank for providing me with a copy of this.

[72] Bulgakov, *Philosophy of Economy*, 144–5.

[73] Ibid., 137.

[74] It is not uncommon to associate Sophia with Christ, God's Logos, particularly as presented in the prologue to John's Gospel. See e.g. Gilbert and Aletti, *La Sagesse et Jésus-Christ*. I prefer not to confuse the figure of Sophia with that of Christ but to render them

deified via food and drink at the eucharistic sharing: "Christ through the church as a new unifying center; humanity becomes the body of Christ so that Christ as a person can re-create human nature, thus becoming a new Adam of whose flesh and blood humanity partakes."[75] In Bulgakov's reading of Sophia's banquet, her gesture of hospitality and generosity points to a metaphysical sharing of God's own being, which at the end points to humanity's deification – a new Adamness. This notion of "partaking" as a way of re-creating (and, even more, deifying) human nature is therefore central in Bulgakov's metaphysical construction, and can provide a more positive reading of creation in general, and food in particular. Human beings are part of Sophia, who partakes of the Logos, who is a further participant in God's intra-Trinitarian relationship. What allows this mediation or in-betweenness (humanity and divinity, persons in the Trinity, and so forth) is, for Bulgakov, Sophia. The unity of being is participation as such, a metaphysical banquet united by divine sharing prepared by Sophia. Bulgakov points out that such a unity is not mechanical, but a "dynamic process over time and manifested in history, in knowledge, and in economy."[76]

The unity that Bulgakov describes does not devolve into an impersonal monism, which, as the Irish philosopher William Desmond has pointed out, would only resolve into a mere univocal predication of autonomous being, devoid of difference from and dependence on God.[77] But neither is this relation just sheer difference, mere equivocity without communion. Instead, and akin to Desmond's account of complex unity

---

distinct. However, I do observe a certain continuity with Christ, who inherits some of Sophia's gestures: Jesus is a wise master, attends banquets and speaks of eschatological banquets, and offers himself as food and drink. The feminine dimension of Jesus as it was later explored in some of the devotional and discursive practices of women in the Middle Ages, for instance, could also be understood as the continuity of a theological tradition that speaks on behalf of a feminine face of God. On this see Caroline Walker Bynum, *Jesus as Mother: Studies in the Spirituality of the High Middle Ages* (Berkeley: University of California Press, 1984), and Julian of Norwich, *Revelations of Divine Love* (Baltimore: Penguin, 1984), chs. 57–63.

[75]   Bulgakov, *Philosophy of Economy*, 140.

[76]   Ibid.

[77]   As John Milbank points out in "Sophiology and Theurgy," Desmond is aware of Bulgakov's own writings, which favor the Platonic term *metaxu* to articulate Sophia's mediation. It is also not a coincidence that this Platonic term is presented in the *Symposium*, where Plato deals with issues of eros/agape within the context of a post-banquet discussion. See William Desmond, *Being and the Between* (New York: State University of New York Press, 1995). See also Plato, *The Symposium*; my discussion is based on the Spanish version, *El Banquete*, trans. Luis Gil (Madrid: Tecnos, 1998).

of being, Bulgakov envisions Sophia as the "in-between" of communion: Sophia as the one who brings about communion. Nevertheless, and as John Milbank comments on Desmond's analysis, this sense of communion surpasses a dialectical version, which is a self-mediation that usually ends up favoring either univocity or equivocity. Rather, and in Milbank's own words,

> Sophia names a *metaxu* which does not lie between two poles but only stands simultaneously at both poles at once. As such it does not subsist before the two poles, but it co-arises with them such that they can only exist according to a mediated communication which remains purely occult, a matter of utterly inscrutable affinity.[78]

Sophia's *metaxu* (middle, in Greek) is the mediated communication of Being. The *metaxological* is an understanding of Being as relationality without a final human-mediated dialectical resolution, for it is an opening up to the "excess of being's plenitude that is never exhaustively mediated by us."[79] It includes individuality, self-discernment, and determination, yet it is not ultimately rooted in the subject – for the subject and singularity are not self-creations – but rather in a gift-exchange. Thus, individuality and singularity are not self-mediated, for they are opened by the ineffable otherness that is not indifferent to the same, but communicates and creates a space of mutual affinity. From a sophiological perspective, individuality and difference allow all economic exchange by virtue of this other-reception of Sophia's superabundance and hospitality: "the oneness of humanity is not empty but consists of coordinated and united multiplicity, for individuality as a particular ray in the pleroma of Sophia in no way contradicts the notion of the whole, which allows its part to develop."[80] Sophia is the divine Wisdom that guides and brings about awareness of the primordial union or affinity with one another, and humanity's original communion and affinity with God. This sort of affinity and communion does not imply a final dialectical moment, but is in fact the *intermediate* space that is perpetually open-ended, and so leads to a journey of perplexity or mystery that kindles a desire to taste more and more the unknowability that is God's Wisdom.

[78] Milbank, "Sophiology and Theurgy," 4.
[79] Desmond, *Being and the Between*, 177.
[80] Bulgakov, *Philosophy of Economy*, 140.

Sophia provokes desire – an *appetitus* – for this otherness, only to reveal that the other is not extrinsic, but is rather intrinsic to self-constitution, since the self is a gift, a "great art of God."[81] From the beginning of creation, all that is becomes a sign of God's goodness, for God explicitly pronounces that which is created to be "good." And Sophia is there also, delighting in God's creation and delighting God as well. The movement toward the other's goodness, which is a hunger for the other, is a mark of being that never stands on its own, but it is always *in relation to*. "To be" is to enter into the very dynamics of love as it is manifested in the reciprocity that takes place within the Trinitarian community:

> To dissolve in the supraindividual, to find oneself in others, to love and be loved, to reflect each other, to see the possibility of newborn person – this is to realize the ideal given to humanity and expressed in Christ's words: "That they all may be one; as thou, Father, art in me, and I in thee." (John 17:21)[82]

"To be" is, then, to enter into an erotic/agapeic community that echoes a prior Trinitarian relationship.

Desmond argues that the consummation of being is the agapeic stage (the astonishment of the goodness of Being) that surpasses eros (a restless craving for that which it lacks). I want to argue that Being is ultimately and simultaneously both erotic and agapeic (erotic/agapeic). If Being is an expression and foretaste of excess, there is always much more to taste in the agapeic stage, and therefore the erotic is not totally eliminated, but transfigured and even intensified as it ascends into higher dimensions of agape's intercommunication with eros: it is eros and agape at once. Pope Benedict XVI, in his encyclical letter *Deus Caritas Est*, rightly points out that "eros and agape can never be completely separated," for both are nourished by one and the same divine source of Love.[83] The erotic is not a mark of mere lack, but a movement of desire toward the infinite agapeic plenitude that is a participation in the divine banquet of love.

Sin is what blinds humanity to the truth of this original state of erotic/agapeic communal harmony. Sin also prevents self-awareness of a redeemed and restored nature that opens up a future eschatological destination. As a result of this distortion, human beings strive to love and be in solidarity with one another, and this perpetual struggle, this

[81] Desmond, *Being and the Between*, 187.
[82] Bulgakov, *Philosophy of Economy*, 141.
[83] Benedict XVI, *Deus Caritas Est*, part I, 7: <www.vatican.va/holy_father/benedict_xvi/encyclicals/documents/hf_ben-xvi_enc_20051225_deus-caritas-est_en.html>.

perpetual discernment and determination, which is at times expressed as "social ideals," is the putting into practice of the "hypothetical formulation of the higher unity and harmony that actually exists in the metaphysical world."[84] To be sure, all economic activity is an expression of this inner vocation to participate in God's own perpetual creative activity.

Bulgakov affirms that the world is "plastic."[85] By this he means that humanity has been endowed with the power to transform it, to "constantly create a cultural reality – new goods, new feelings, new beauty – alongside the 'natural' world that is given to him."[86] But the source of this power and creativity is not purely human, but sophianic: Sophia partaking of "the cosmic activity of the Logos"[87] – that which *is* in virtue of its own intra-Trinitarian communion within God. To co-create with the ability of sophianic wisdom means to discover the world as not being fixed or static but quite the contrary, for the world is fluid, and in a constant process of manifesting in new and multiple expressions its inner beauty and goodness.

Bulgakov believes that humanity is capable of seeing its own reflection in Sophia's perpetual blooming: it is "through her" that humanity "takes in and reflects in nature the wise rays of the divine Logos."[88] Bulgakov builds up his metaphysics of Being upon this unifying principle, a "living interaction, like a plant's nourishment through its roots."[89] Here we observe a continuation of the wisdom literature in the Bible, which depicts Sophia as nourishment, with Bulgakov's own imagery of Sophia's nurturing dimension. In this sense, Bulgakov's depiction of being is intimately connected with an intimation of Being as already participatory in divine nourishment.

Since every economic process is a product of creativity, Bulgakov insists that such creativity is in fact an act of re-creation. Only God creates out of nothing, and thus grants all that *is* as itself a gift. Subsequently, creativity (including economy) is a re-creation of a pre-existing gesture of God's own gift.

Human creativity is really a re-creation of that which pre-exists in the metaphysical world; it is not creation *from nothing* but replication of something already given, and it is creative only insofar as it is free re-creation through work. There is nothing *metaphysically new* in human

---

[84] Bulgakov, *Philosophy of Economy*, 141.
[85] Ibid., 142.
[86] Ibid.
[87] Ibid., 145.
[88] Ibid.
[89] Ibid.

creativity; we can only reproduce a likeness of the images that are divinely given to us.[90]

To construct a sense of creativity outside of the Creator – and, more explicitly, outside of divine Sophia – is, for Bulgakov, to construct a "parasitic world" upon "nonbeing."[91] And, in my own view, this would be equivalent to repeating the gesture of Folly, who ultimately brings about death and malnourishment, rather than Sophia, who invites us to her superabundant banquet.

But for Bulgakov, human economy is "sophianic" in its metaphysical basis precisely because it partakes of both Sophia and empirical reality. At the end, however, all that is (all life), "proceeds from the Source of Life outside of this world, the living God, who does not know envy and who creates life through divine love."[92] To extend this image, one could say that, inasmuch as humanity drinks freely of God's Wisdom (that is Life and Love) as an infant is nourished at its mother's breast, humanity is fed and sustained and able to grow and mature, to re-create, and reinvent itself and participate in the same divine community – a divine banquet.

Moreover, Sophia expresses a maternal feasting, which also recalls Mary's breastfeeding of Jesus Christ, God incarnate.[93] Here, again, we can find a more positive reading of the eating of the forbidden fruit, which was the first theological moment initiated by a woman's wisdom. Thus, regarding Eve's wisdom, Vanessa Ochs, "midrash-like," remarks:

> Eve teaches us that life gets us wise, bit by bit, and we need to notice, appreciate, and celebrate each step of the way as we carve it out for ourselves, no matter how hit-or-miss. Eve celebrates the path of getting there, however complex or convoluted. In *Women's Ways of Knowing*, a collaboration of four women authors, we learn that women "view reality and draw conclusions about truth, knowledge, and authority in distinctive ways" – including accessing understanding through shared experience, through feeling empathy, through dialogue, and through the questioning of authority and accepted truths.[94]

---

[90]   Ibid., 145–6 (emphasis in original).
[91]   Ibid., 146.
[92]   Ibid., 147.
[93]   I am grateful to Professor John Milbank who introduced me to this fascinating subject of "gender reversal." I am aware that this subject can be developed even further, so my reflection is only too brief, and open to further investigation and dialogue.
[94]   Ochs, *Sarah Laughed*, 12.

Eve's wisdom is, then, recaptured by Sophia's becoming food as a means of deification. And deification via alimentation is further evoked by Mary's becoming pregnant with God, and her breastfeeding of God. The maternal feeds God, the One who redeems us by also becoming a maternal feeding, as food and drink in the Eucharist. Redemption ensures a form of maternal feeding, for it offers nourishment from Christ's own body and blood. Yet Mary's feeding is bloodless, and so intimates a non-sacrificial feeding, a recovery of deification beyond sacrifice. Hence the pre-modern figure of Christ as "mother" (as in Anselm and Julian of Norwich, for instance).[95] Christ must first be fed by his mother, and, in saving us, he continues his mother's nurturing action. In addition, the church also becomes a new female figure, the bride of Christ, which is nurtured by Jesus-as-mother, while simultaneously becoming a maternal feeding of the entire ecclesial community. By transmitting nourishing, edible signs, this maternal eucharistic feeding mirrors Sophia's nurturing gesture (which echoes Eve's initial eating). From a perspective of Christian-Catholic alimentary theology, all these forms of maternal feeding sustain the ecclesial pilgrim's advancement to the eschatological banquet.

Conclusion

From the perspective of a traditional Christian theological interpretation, the eating of the forbidden fruit of Eden marks a severance from one another, and from God. It creates a "fictional" vision of self-governance over and against God's will and desire. In the postlapsarian world sin is understood as a loss of Being participating in God. Such a severance and loss of sight also initiate a condition of eating as a struggle for life (and thus an understanding of life as inherently "lacking"), as well as positing the thinghoodness of the eaten that must be destroyed for individual survival. In this sense, and following Bataille's theory of religion, the world after the Fall constructs eating as an act of subjugation of an-other, and leaves behind the Edenic realm of harmonious community of the created world with God. From this perspective, one could construct food and eating in a negative fashion, always pointing to a lack (a recurrent state of being hungry), death (the finite nature of both the eater and the eaten), and destruction or violence (the necessity to destroy an-other in order to survive).

However, and as I have attempted to argue in this chapter, from the perspective of a Catholic alimentary theological understanding of the Eucharist, there is a positive alternative interpretation of eating. While

[95] On the development of this figure, see Walker Bynum, *Jesus as Mother*.

death comes from eating, it is nevertheless *not* the final stage of the story of consumption. An alternative Catholic reading of eating affirms that, through eating in the Eucharist, unity with God is restored, and a promise of resurrected life is opened up. From this eucharistic perspective eating is not a condition of lack, but a foretaste of divine plenitude: a physical and spiritual tasting that kindles a desire for more, for that beautiful *excess* wherein there is yet more to savor.[96] In the eucharistic feast, death is therefore not the end of the eater, but a promise of reintegration into the resurrected life of Christ – the Father's offering of resurrection to the Son's death, which is then shared in and through the Holy Spirit with the partakers of the eucharistic Paschal banquet.

God's Trinitarian gesture of hospitality and kenotic sharing in the Eucharist nourish the erotic/agapeic community that is the church. God becomes food and drink, so that God can be a part of the partaker's body, and, even more, so that humanity can become part of God's own body. In this way, the proclamation in Catholic liturgies of the *O felix culpa!* points to the eating of the forbidden fruit not as a curse, but rather as a blessed proleptic moment of a future eating of God's own body and blood that is a gift and promise of deification. For retrospectively – and paraphrasing John Milbank – from the perspective of the eucharistic feeding, the sin of the first Adam is unmasked in Jesus, the second Adam's, crucifixion, so that, by finally knowing sin as a refusal of God's love-as-nourishment, the partaker of the Eucharist can be radically healed, transfigured into the resurrected body of Christ. Moreover, as we shall see in next chapter, the sacrificial offering of the church at the eucharistic table is an "idiom" that the church learns and imitates from a prior communication of the Logos's self-offering idiom (who, by identifying with the victim, teaches forgiveness and peace).[97]

This eucharistic vision of a communal divine–human body nourished by God's self-offering gesture is not without precedent. Eve's wisdom initiates this theological gesture as being, intrinsically, "food for thought." Furthermore, Sophia also anticipates and prepares a divine feast. Sophia allows an understanding of eating from both protological and eschatological poles. She nourishes from the beginning of creation, and she will offer nourishment at the end of creation, for she is, in eternity, the delight of God's self-sharing. Sophia's invitation, "Come and

[96] This is the main thesis of Ann W. Astell, *Eating Beauty: The Eucharist and the Spiritual Arts of the Middle Ages* (Ithaca, NY: Cornell University Press, 2006).

[97] See Milbank, *Theology and Social Theory Beyond Secular Reason* (Oxford: Blackwell, 1990), 397–8. For a positive analysis regarding the doctrine of "original sin," see James Alison, *The Joy of Being Wrong: Original Sin through Easter Eyes* (New York: Crossroad, 1998).

eat my bread and drink the wine I have prepared!", anticipates the bread
and wine that in the Last Supper Jesus identifies as his own body and
blood. To understand Being from both a eucharistic and a sophianic perspective is to intimate Being as inherently the reception of a gift that nourishes, while simultaneously being an expression of gratitude (and return)
of that same gift. Echoing Milbank's articulations of Being, and from a
eucharistic and sophianic perspective, one could construct Being as

> dynamic self-expressive life, but as such it is also the otherness of
> active reception of this dynamism. It is, indeed, super-eminently
> sperm and womb, forever conjoined and forever apart. But this
> eminent life is also eminent intellect, or precisely "wisdom,"
> because, in our experience, the reception of oneself as a gift, or the
> receiving of a gift such that one *is not* outside reception, is ... most
> of all characteristic of conscious life, capable of gratitude.[98]

This "conscious life" that Milbank speaks of is a sign of the mutual
constitution of the same and the other. It is a mark of communal life
sustained by the reception of the other's gift and the return in gratitude
for such a donation.[99] In the midst of this gratitude (*eucharistein*) for a
gift that nourishes, Being is posited as inherently eucharistic.

Being is not lacking but it is nourished by God's superabundance,
which is also a gift *to be*. Being is not self-grounded, but is the generous
sharing of God's perpetual "to be." Being, like God, is relational. That
is why analogy helps to clarify the linguistic and ontological relationship
with God – a relationship rooted primarily in gift, reception, and return.
Analogy articulates the inherent "likeness" of Being with God, which is
the ever-dynamic relationship of affinity that shapes and reshapes Being
into God's excessive image. In this analogical sense, Being is an "unfinished" project or process; it is a continuous process of "coming to be,"
since it is perpetually open to the infinite mystery and superabundance
that is God's self-sharing. The "isness" of Being is always in excess of its
own existentiality, for it is perpetually open to God's infinity. One can
only intimate a complex harmonious relationship in this analogue that
allows both difference and affinity, distance and communion, to mysteri-
ously co-arise albeit without reaching a final stasis or inert stage.

Moreover, the notion of eucharistic alimentation helps to evoke this
aspect of relationality in Being: God descends into the material elements

[98] Milbank, "Sophiology and Theurgy," 7.
[99] In the next chapter I will explore further this notion of the gift, particularly in relation
to the figure of *manna*.

of creation, and so elevates creation to divine status and permits the making of an analogy (though a limited one). Creation is God's ecstatic self-exceeding: it is an expression of God's superabundance and sharing. The descent of God, like that of the manna, is a gesture of nurturing, yet it does not accomplish a total satiation or saturation, since, as it is infinite, there is much more to taste and to be fed by; but neither is it a mere promise of future alimentation that leaves us starving, since there is here and now already some form of feeding. This reality of "Being-nourished" intimates the relational aspect and interdependence of Being. Also, this sort of Christian ontology does not intend to abolish traditional ontology, but rather is a counter-ontology to those articulations of Being as the ultimate univocal foundation of all being (and an erroneous vision devoid of God's participation).

Sophia is God's own sharing that gifts creation with a food and drink that is God-self, God's love: "God's love for what he creates implies that the creation is generated within a harmonious order intrinsic to God's own being."[100] God offered as food and drink is further radicalized in the eucharistic sharing where the elements of bread and wine become a source of that same divine-sophianic sharing. This is the most physical and material aspect of deification. Therefore, rather than merely constructing an ontology or metaphysics from the abstract, "flattened" mapping on a single plane and from non-corporeal hypotheses, a sophianic and eucharistic ontology intrinsically intensifies the materiality, corporeality, and contingency of Being, and displays a complex, metaxological – to use Desmond's account – realm. For divinity reaches beyond humanity, into the realms of the material (bread and wine), only to reconstitute the mystery of materiality as eucharistic: an expression of thanksgiving, that is, a reception and return of God's gift. Materiality and the natural world are, thus, transfigured by the supernatural. Matter and nature are oriented to a supernatural end, but in a way that does not do violence to the material and contingent. Materiality and contingency are re-intensified, or even recovered or reoriented in a way that offers at once a taste of Eden (from the past perspective) and a foretaste of the Eschaton (from the future perspective). The intimations of an Edenic stage are not, as Bataille argues, a longing for a world of pure immanence. Instead, in this vision of Being-nourished, the immanent is nurtured by the transcendent maternal feeding, yet not in a merely extrinsic fashion, but from within, at the core of immanence and contingency.

From this perspective, then, food matters. This is to say that the materiality of food, far from leaving the physical world (and contingency,

[100]   Milbank, *Theology and Social Theory*, 429.

immanence, Being, and so forth) malnourished or starving, recalls a prior maternal sharing of God's nurturing materiality with divinity. Food matters: this should not be as marginal as it presently is to theological thought. From a theological perspective, and from the Creation narrative, food is a central theme of God's superabundant self-sharing.

The dialogue between the woman and the serpent on the subject of the forbidden fruit also suggests that one of the most primary forms of theological thought is in fact food and eating. The eating of the forbidden fruit identifies sin as not so much disobedience but a refusal, denial, the ceasing of hunger for God. But God does not let humanity starve to death. In this chapter I have examined the figure of Sophia as an instance of God's gesture of hospitality and generous sharing: Sophia prepares and invites all to a banquet, and, what is more, she is food itself. In line with the previous chapter, I recall that wisdom is knowledge as a savoring of the known (*sapientia-sapere*). And, as I have already argued, this savoring of the known brings deeper participation with the known. To know God is to taste God, and, more, to be divinized. This biblical theme of God's nourishment is intensified in God's self-kenotic gesture in the Eucharist wherein God becomes food and drink that not only promise eternal life, but also provide a foretaste of deification. Here, the body of Christ becomes the intersection of participation: God's body in humanity, and humanity's body in God. Theology, then, must not be indifferent to the reality that food matters. But this thinking through food and eating must not be detached from the concrete individual and communal body.

The Eucharist not only envisions an ontology of participation and deification. It is also a model for discipleship, and thus it is profoundly ethical and political. If God is superabundant sharing, then theologians must look at how – or not – this divine sharing is repeated in the world's daily exchanges of food. If the Eucharist is an expression of God's own body offered to humanity for the purpose of constituting communion from within the embodied spheres of materiality and sacramentality ("This is my body given for you"[101]), then what sense are we to make of the multitude of starving bodies in this world? It looks as if that marginal woman, Sophia, still continues to cry out at the crossroads, publicly protesting, and challenging our careless exchanges. But it is in this divine stranger that men and women the better discover who they are. This is the arena where theology meets politics, for it is a question of communal identity and the sharing of God's generous gift that constitutes the practice of communities.

Thus I shall now turn, in the next and final chapter, to this "theopolitical" dimension of food.

[101] See Matt. 26:26–8; Mark 14:22–4; Luke 22:19–20; 1 Cor. 11:23–7.

4

Sharing in the Body of Christ and the Theopolitics of Superabundance

Blessed are those who hunger and thirst after righteousness, for they shall be filled.

Introduction

In the previous chapter I offered a reading of the narrative of the eating of the forbidden fruit in the book of Genesis. In this narrative, sin is symbolically inaugurated by this eating, which brings about the disruption of the harmonious participation of humanity in God. Sin constructs an illusory space severed from God, and, subsequently, a space where human communion is broken: the realm of individuality and enmity. I stated that sin is what blinds humanity to the truth of the original state of erotic/agapeic communal harmony. I also argued that there is a Catholic alternative to surrendering to the effects of sin; it is not a denial, but a reorientation of vision. This alternative envisions Being as sophianic, all that "is" participates in God's superabundant nurturing Love and Wisdom. Sophia, the Wisdom of God, is with God before the beginning of creation, where God is "the preeminent gardener, working to produce vital, edible wisdom-food, engendering and sustaining humans who should respond to God and each other in kind."[1] God's sophianic sharing is further and more radically expressed in the Eucharist, wherein God becomes food and drink itself, and in doing so opens up a space for a collective performance or communal practice that reincorporates humanity into Christ's Body, and this within the context of a shared

[1] Gillian Feeley-Harnik, "Meals," in Bruce M. Metzger and Michael D. Coogan (eds.), *The Oxford Companion the to the Bible* (Oxford: Oxford University Press, 1993), 507.

table. From these sophianic and eucharistic perspectives, food is not severance, nor does it bring about ultimate destruction and final death. Instead, what Sophia and the Eucharist convey is food as a material – as much as it is also a divine – sign of relationality, interdependence, and sharing of life eternal. The eucharistic banquet tells a story of the enactment of the Body of Christ that shapes and nurtures communal life.

If William Cavanaugh is correct in his argument that politics is "a practice of the imagination" (because it constructs space, time, a sense of civil, national, and global territoriality and identity, and so forth), then alimentation in general, and the Eucharist in particular manifest a political reality as well.[2] Alimentation is a practice of human imagination that reflects complex interactions and exchanges that go from local and micro realities to a more global or macro ones. Carole Counihan and Penny Van Esterik also argue that alimentation is "a central pawn in political strategies of states and households. Food marks social differences, boundaries, bonds, and contradictions. Eating is an endlessly evolving enactment of gender, family, and community relationships."[3] The political reality of alimentation reflects, among other factors, the willingness and capacity of individuals and societies to express solidarity by sharing food, while "food scarcity damages the human community and the human spirit."[4]

From a sophianic and eucharistic angle, food is also political: it is a practice that imagines divine sharing as the locus (spatial and temporal) of "holy communion" with one another and with God – the One who is a loving community of persons. The political dimension of divine sharing speaks about alimentation as incorporation into Christ's Body. This alimentary divine–human Body is the "endlessly evolving enactment" of mutual transformation, harmonious difference, reciprocal relations, and ecstatic love. This eating, however, is not an "erasure" of sin. Nor is it an attempt to go back to Eden; it is, rather, a recognition or awareness that God loves and generously shares divinity in spite of and in the midst of sin (the refusal of God's gift). Yet such a divine generous sharing is,

---

[2] William Cavanaugh, *Theopolitical Imagination: Discovering the Liturgy as a Political Act in an Age of Global Consumerism* (Edinburgh: T&T Clark, 2002), 1.
[3] Carole Counihan and Penny Van Esterik (eds.), *Food and Culture: A Reader* (London: Routledge, 1997), 1. On the relationship between food and politics, see Sidney W. Mintz, *Tasting Food, Tasting Freedom: Excursions into Eating, Culture, and the Past* (Boston: Beacon Press, 1996); Marion Nestle, *Food Politics: How the Food Industry Influences Nutrition and Health* (Berkeley: University of California Press, 2002); David Bell and Gill Valentine (eds.), *Consuming Geographies: We Are Where We Eat* (London: Routledge, 1997).
[4] Counihan and Esterik (eds.), *Food and Culture*, 1.

like Babette's own gift in Isak Dinesen's *Babette's Feast*,[5] transformative: from sin to redemption and deification, from scarcity to superabundance, from individualism to communion. The Eucharist speaks of the body politics of – in Graham Ward's terms – "co-abiding": the Father with the Holy Spirit in the Son, Christ in the eucharistic elements and in the partaker, and the material elements as well as the partakers in Christ and in the Holy Spirit.[6] This complex co-abiding relies on the theopolitics of alimentation, which is endlessly enacted through this communal sharing in the Body of Christ.

In this final chapter, then, I will explore the theopolitical dimension of alimentation.[7] I say theopolitical because politics here is not envisioned as an autonomous figure apart from God. My political perspective is fundamentally theological only because my understanding of the Greek term *polis* (a city or "community embodying the fulfillment of human social relations") is intrinsically derived from a vision of divine sharing, a co-abiding in the Body of Christ, which constitutes the ecclesial body; a divine–human *body politic*.[8] Just as humanity does not *have* a body, but *is* a body, the church – as James K. A. Smith rightly points out – "does not have a politics; but it *is* a politics."[9] The church expresses a corporate existence where divine agency interacts with human affairs, and such an interaction nurtures, that is to say gives life and shape to, the ecclesial body. I will show how a theopolitics of Christ's Body in the Eucharist is rooted not exclusively in power, but, in a more primary sense, in divine caritas, which is expressed with a radical gesture of kenosis, reciprocity, and concrete communal practices. This is not to say that power is herein dismissed, or that the Eucharist is a sign of disempowerment. There is a politics of power here. Yet it is a power that integrates plenitude of desire; it is the paradoxical force of sacrifice on the cross; it is the humble power of bread broken into pieces for the purpose of sharing; it is the washing of feet that means a life of service

---

[5] Isak Dinesen, *Babette's Feast*, in *Anecdotes of Destiny and Ehrengard* (New York: Vintage Books, 1993).

[6] See Graham Ward, *Christ and Culture* (Oxford: Blackwell, 2005).

[7] The term "theopolitical" or "theopolitics" is taken from Cavanaugh, *Theopolitical Imagination*.

[8] This definition is taken from the Philip Babcock Gove (ed.), *Webster's Third New International Dictionary of the English Language* (Springfield: Merriam-Webster, 1993), cited in Matthew Whelan, "The Responsible Body: A Eucharistic Community," *Cross Currents* (Fall 2001), 359–78. Also, "body politics" is defined as "people organized and united under an authority."

[9] James K. A. Smith, *Introducing Radical Orthodoxy: Mapping a Post-Secular Theology* (Grand Rapids, MI: Baker Academic, 2004), 253.

to one another; it is the power of giving one's life for the other. In other words, this is the theopolitical power of caritas, where the extraordinary embraces and transfigures the ordinary: God's "sovereignty disclosed at the breaking of the bread," as Samuel Wells remarks.[10]

Taking the same approach that I have used in earlier chapters, my point of departure here will be a concrete narrative of food: Isak Dinesen's novel, *Babette's Feast*, where something extraordinary takes place. The act of eating food not only satiates human hunger but also becomes an ecstatic experience that transforms self and community. Babette gives away her riches, her own self-expression. And yet this giving does not impoverish her, but, rather, highlights the excess (the infinite creative caritas) of giving itself. From the Christian narrative we could also envision God as a sort of Babette, the cook par excellence whose superabundant edible gift is the very source of caritas that creates and sustains the world while inviting humanity to share this same (yet repeated differently, perpetually) divine gift with one another.

After discussing *Babette's Feast* I will explore the Hebrew and Christian figure of God's feast communicated as the "manna from heaven," which, like Dinesen's story, shows something extraordinary and "strange" taking place: God not only cares for his people by satiating hunger, but God's desire to be near humanity is further expressed with an intimate kenotic gesture of becoming food and drink, nourishment itself. Christianity believes that through the ingestion of this divine manna (Christ's body and blood) God abides in the partaker as much as the partaker also abides in God. The Eucharist is a practice of this divine and human co-abiding that constitutes the Body of Christ.

The figure of the manna will be further explored from the perspective of the gift – an edible gift. As Babette offers her culinary gift in the midst of a gift-exchange community, and transfigures the community by her lavish gift, so the eucharistic gift is a reintensification and revitalization of a complex gift-exchange system: the Trinitarian gift exchange that is perpetually shared with – and from within – creation, and is then repeated non-identically in further examples of caritas among human communities, by humanity with creation, and by all of creation in Christ, with the Holy Spirit returning the gift to God as a doxology.

The final section of this chapter will explore the dilemma of superabundance, and how a theopolitical horizon offers an alternative for a practice to orienting desire toward God, for whom superabundance and caritas constitute one and the same divine gift.

---

[10] Samuel Wells, *God's Companions: Reimagining Christian Ethics* (Oxford: Blackwell, 2006), 210.

1 Babette's Transformative Sharing

Babette enters into the life of a small town with puritanical and rigid religious practices where – in the words of Dinesen's narrating voice – "its members renounced the pleasures of this world, for the earth and all that it held to them was but a kind of illusion, and the true reality was the New Jerusalem toward which they were longing."[11] This strange woman, Babette, breaks into the earthly life of these townspeople because she is escaping from the consequences of the French Revolution, which has brought death to her own family and taken away all her belongings. Poor, and deprived of all her possessions and beloved family, she begs to be welcomed. She is received by two elderly sisters (Martine and Philippa) who have become, after the death of their father, the spiritual leaders of this religious community. Since these sisters are very poor, and since the idea of having a cook in their house is too extravagant for them, the women are at first skeptical about taking Babette into their household. Nevertheless, in an act of charity and after reading a letter of recommendation from an old friend (a French opera singer, Monsieur Papin, who in his younger years had fallen in love with one of the sisters), they finally decide to welcome Babette into their lives.

Babette's culinary skills are evident right from the start. Not only is she an extraordinary cook, but she also has a profound sense of service to the community, particularly toward the ill and infirm. She even reduces the costs of housekeeping: "And they soon found that from the day when Babette took over the housekeeping its cost was miraculously reduced, and the soup-pails and baskets acquired a new, mysterious power to stimulate and strengthen their poor and sick."[12] However, the initial harmony and wellbeing of the community created by Babette's presence are soon disturbed.

Babette receives a letter from France confirming that she has won a lottery. In her astonishment, she announces to the sisters her new fortune of ten thousand francs. While the sisters share in the joy over Babette's new wealth and good luck, they also seem troubled by the idea that she might leave them because of this new financial status. Turbulence seems to be in the air, for Babette's news coincides with a new experience of division and discord among the members of the community. Individual and communal harmony start to dissipate: "they had endeavored to

---

[11] Dinesen, *Babette's Feast*, 21.
[12] Ibid., 32.

make peace, but they were aware that they had failed."[13] In the midst of this turbulence Babette asks the sisters to allow her to prepare and cook for the upcoming celebration of the birthday of their dead father, who was the patriarch of the community's religious practices. She insists, indeed begs, that they should let her pay with her own money for the celebration. The sisters cannot resist this plea, for they know that she has never asked them for anything while she has been working in their house.

But soon not only the sisters but also the entire town are deeply troubled by the animals (a gigantic turtle, a cow's head, birds) and other extravagant and strange items (wines, champagne, silverware) that Babette uses to prepare this mysterious dinner. They start to see her in a new light: as an evil medium, a witch who will poison them with her strange food. The whole town fears that soon the deserved punishment for their own personal and communal sins will come upon them. But the townspeople vow to one another that they will endure in profound silence the punishment (even death) that might be visited on them by means of this meal and vow not to say anything about the food that Babette cooks for them.

The day of the celebration finally arrives. Everyone in the town, and even some friends from the past (a highly honored general and his elderly mother), is gathered at the sisters' house.[14] It would be impossible to reproduce the exquisite prose of Dinesen's description of this meal; I would only highlight that not only the food, but also the preparation of the dinner table that Babette so meticulously arranges, is indeed extravagant and beautiful.[15] Such beauty intensively awakens all the senses of the celebrants despite their vow to suppress them: their senses of sight, hearing, taste, and touch are intensified by Babette's art. Not only are their physical senses transfigured into an ecstatic experience, but also, and subsequently, their hearts and souls start to light up:

> The *convives* grew lighter in weight and lighter of heart the more they ate and drank. They no longer needed to remind themselves of

---

[13]   Dinesen, *Babette's Feast*, 34.

[14]   Like Monsieur Papin, the general in his youth fell in love with one of the sisters. But, like Papin, he was discouraged from declaring his love, because the sisters' father did not want his daughters to marry but rather to consecrate their lives to the service of the community.

[15]   *Babette's Feast* was made into a film directed by Gabriel Axel. It won the Academy Award for best foreign-language film in 1987. Axel's version is quite artistic, particularly in its visual refinement, which reaches its climax with Babette's lavish meal.

their vow [to say nothing about the meal and to suppress their senses, particularly that of taste]. It was, they realized, when man has not only altogether forgotten but has firmly renounced all ideas of food and drink that he eats and drinks in the right spirit.[16]

What was broken is suddenly repaired, and what was wounded is miraculously healed.

The dinner culminates in the general's toast and speech, in which he expresses his astonishment at such a miraculous dinner. He recalls the story of a female cook at a famous French restaurant, the Café Anglais, where the cook used to turn her culinary art "into a kind of love affair – into a love affair of the noble and romantic category in which one can no longer distinguish between bodily and spiritual appetite or satiety!"[17] In his speech, the general also reflects upon the reality of grace as a pure expression of (divine) giving:

> We tremble before making our choice in life, and after having made it again tremble in fear of having chosen wrongly. But the moment comes when our eyes are opened, and we see and realize that grace is infinite. Grace, my friends, demands nothing from us but that we shall await it with confidence and acknowledge it in gratitude. Grace, brothers, makes no conditions and singles out none of us in particular; grace takes us all to its bosom and proclaims general amnesty.[18]

Indeed, Dinesen's narrator describes this experience at the table as an occasion of pure grace that fills the heart to the point of immersing self, community, and time into eternity:

> Of what happened later in the evening nothing definite can here be stated. None of the guests later on had any clear remembrance of it. They only knew that the room had been filled with a heavenly light, as if a number of small halos had blended into one glorious radiance. Taciturn old people received the gift of tongues; ears that for years have been almost deaf were open to it. Time itself had merge into eternity.[19]

---

[16] Ibid., 50.
[17] Ibid., 51.
[18] Ibid., 52.
[19] Ibid., 53.

Babette's feast becomes a "foretaste" of the heavenly banquet, a beatific vision – or better, a beatific savoring – experienced through the body and the senses, and particularly through the act of eating:

> They realized that the infinite grace of which the General Loewenheim had spoken had been allotted to them, and they did not even wonder at the fact, for it had been but the fulfillment of an ever-present hope. The vain illusions of this earth had dissolved before their eyes like smoke, and they had seen the universe as it really is. They had been given one hour of the millennium.[20]

Another moment when the novel speaks of this beatific experience of the effects of eating Babette's feast is when, after the meal, the community steps outside the house to play like children, once it has stopped snowing:

> The town and the mountains lay in white, unearthly splendor and the sky was bright with thousands of stars. In the street the snow was lying so deep that it had become difficult to walk. The guests from the yellow house wavered on their feet, staggered, sat down abruptly or fell forward on their knees and hands and were covered with snow, as if they had indeed had their sins washed white as wool, and in this regained innocent attire were gamboling like little lambs. It was, to each of them, blissful to have become as a small child; it was also a joke to watch old Brothers and Sisters, who had been taking themselves so seriously, in this kind of celestial second childhood. They stumbled and got up, walked on or stood still, bodily as well as spiritually hand in hand, at moments performing the great chain of a beatified *lanciers*.[21]

Food in this story is not only an aesthetic experience. Yes, Babette is an artistic genius who expresses her art for the sake of bringing forth the truth of beauty. Yes, art and beauty express their own truth in one way or another, regardless of resistance and opposition. But Babette's expression is not only aesthetic; it is also ethical, a true act of caritas. At the end of the story we learn that Babette is the famous cook from the Café Anglais that the general described in his speech. We also learn that in Paris she risked her life fighting for justice and against the cruelties of evil men who – in Babette's words – "left the people of Paris [to] starve;

---

20 Dinesen, *Babette's Feast*, 54.
21 Ibid., 54–5.

they oppressed and wronged the poor."[22] Furthermore, and more relevant to the story, we also learn that she spent the whole ten thousand francs that she won in the lottery on preparing her lavish dinner. "So you will be poor now all your life, Babette?" – Martine, one of the sisters, expresses her concern. But Babette quickly points out that a great artist is never poor. She has given all her riches for the benefit of others and her caritas has transformed the community. Her art and her caritas do not impoverish her, but, on the contrary, her gesture only reveals the reality of superabundance, which is the gift that knows no end. Like Babette, the one who gives self to others will never experience poverty but rather a rich recompense and self-assurance that the gift is never impoverishment but superabundance, and that the gift of caritas is the transformative plenitude that in one way or another always returns. One of the sisters affirms to Babette that, despite her current lack of material possessions, her rich art and her sharing will see no end: " 'I feel, Babette, that this is not the end. In Paradise you will be the great artist that God meant you to be! Ah!' she added, the tears streaming down her cheeks. 'Ah, how you will enchant the angels!' "[23]

In the introduction to this chapter I remarked – following Cavanaugh – that politics is an art, a practice of the imagination. Babette's feast also imagines a sort of *polis*, a community that encounters fulfillment in its most bodily practice: eating and drinking, which, paradoxically, is much more than eating and drinking. Time and eternity, beauty and goodness, aesthetics and ethics are interrelated and mutually constitutive in Babette's feast. The political imagination in this story is founded upon a narrative of the gift that shapes the individual and the community: Babette firsts receives the gift of hospitality, and she who is gifted with an artistic culinary skill offers her gift to others. Babette's culinary art is her own self-giving, her own self-expression, and in this novel that creativity reaches its climax in a lavish banquet that transforms people's hearts and lives. Her culinary gift is both erotic and agapeic, or "gastroerotic" – to use a term I introduced in chapter 2, where I emphasized how the erotic and agapeic are re-created, together, in and through food. While being an epiphany of beauty, Babette's gift is simultaneously an expression of goodness and trust, for she does not mind sharing her riches with others. And this kenotic act does not leave her empty. There is a self-rejoicing in her nurturing gift. In this story, the sharing of Babette is ecstatic, illuminating, transformative, and healing. It is a story of being

[22] Ibid., 58.
[23] Ibid., 59.

both individually and communally crafted by the gift that never ends (for, we are told, even in heaven the angels will be delighted by this gastroerotic gift).

2 Manna from Heaven: Sources of Divine Sharing

I believe that Dinesen's story provides much food for thought, for imagining God as a sort of Babette, an artistic chef generously sharing divine superabundance with, and transforming creation by, such sharing. In the previous chapter, I offered some taste of God's culinary art that provides food both at the beginning of creation, and more lavishly, in the figure of Sophia – God's Wisdom – who, like Babette, is not only the cook and host of a banquet, but even more perplexingly than Babette's story, becomes the food itself. Like Babette's feast, the story of God's sharing of food is not only about aesthetics (an art, a beautiful and skillful crafting); it also implies an ethical dimension. God's sharing of food, and self-sharing *as* food, is the source of divine goodness that heals spiritual and physical hungers, but in addition urges us to share with and care for one another.

There are many instances in both the Hebrew and Christian Scriptures where we could find a pattern of God establishing community with people via food and drink, and of God's invitation to feasting. Salvador Martínez explores this trajectory within the Hebrew and Christian Scriptures, wherein a pattern of God's desire for intimacy with people is mainly expressed with and via food and drink.[24] God wants to communicate love and a desire to be near. Apart from direct communication (as in the Garden of Eden) through angels, prophets, and priestly representatives, God in the Bible also communicates with people through sacred signs, places, things, and rituals. Martínez points out that food and drink – alimentation – provide another significant channel of divine communication.

To contemplate the eucharistic mystery of God becoming nourishment for his people, we should look at it in the context of the figures of divine alimentation in the Hebrew Scriptures. There is not enough space here to cite all the instances where the figure of food appears in these sacred texts. In the next section I will therefore concentrate on the rich scriptural figure of the "manna from heaven," which, as I will argue, ties

---

[24] Salvador Martínez Ávila, "De Dios que Alimenta a su Pueblo a Dios que se Hace Alimento para su Pueblo," in Ricardo López and Daniel Landgrave (eds.), *Pan para Todos: Estudios en Torno a la Eucaristía* (Mexico City: Universidad Pontificia de México, 2004).

together a variety of food-related scriptural narratives that speak of God as a source of superabundance, a nourishing gift that shapes a *polis*, or a communal body with a vocation to sharing such a divine gift.

2.1 Manna in the Hebrew narratives

One of the most significant forms of divine nourishment in the Hebrew Scripture regarding bread in general, and God's nurturing action in particular, is manna (Exod. 16:1–36). According to this narrative, the word manna derives from the people wondering what exactly this nourishment was, hence the Hebrew term *Man-hu* – "What is it?"[25] Manna is a form of nourishment that the people of Israel ate while in the desert as they were moving towards the Promised Land. Manna is described as "a coriander seed; it was white [and powdery] and its taste was like that of wafers made of honey" (Exod. 16:31). It is a strange "bread" that "rains down from the heavens," and which people believed God sent as an answer to the people's cry while they were hungry in the wilderness.[26] The Exodus narrative relates how, in addition to the manna's miracle of provision, God also sent quails, and water from a rock to drink. This divine nourishment, the narrative tells us, sustained the people for forty years in the wilderness.

According to Martínez, the manna is "a sign of God's commitment to nourish his people; a commitment that was not only verified during the wilderness period, but which was further accomplished by God's promise to settle his people in a land that 'flows with milk and honey.'"[27] Raúl Duarte Castillo also highlights this tradition of looking at manna as being of divine origin, and recalls the sapiential texts' description as

---

[25] Walter Houston explains that this term is not totally correct, for it "is not the normal word for 'what?' (*mah*), but near enough for a Hebrew pun: it is the word for 'manna'." Walter Houston, "Exodus," in John Barton and John Muddiman (eds.), *The Oxford Bible Commentary* (Oxford: Oxford University Press, 2001), 78.

[26] Walter Houston explains that a probable source of manna was the tamarisk tree found in the Sinai peninsula, which during the months of May and June "exudes drops of a sweet substance which is gathered and eaten by the local people, who still call it *man*." Houston also points out that the belief that manna was a miraculous provision was mainly founded on the observation that "the amounts are small, and obviously the story goes beyond natural fact. It speaks of a miracle which provides enough food every day, all the year round, to sustain a whole people on the march." Ibid., 78.

[27] "El maná es el signo del compromiso de Dios para alimentar a su pueblo un compromiso que no se verificó solo durante la etapa del desierto (cf. Exod. 16:12) sino que Dios prometió y cumplió al instalar a su pueblo en la tierra que mana leche y miel." Martínez, "De Dios que Alimenta a su Pueblo," 36 (my translation).

"wheat from heaven ... bread of angels" (Ps. 78:25; Wisd. 16:20).[28] In line with these arguments, Walter Houston also points out that the main role of manna is to express God's desire to care for his people. It is an initiative that does not come directly from Moses and Aaron, who brought the people out of Egypt, but from "YHWH alone who will provide for them."[29] Manna expresses divine generosity as grace, as a divine gift of daily sustenance that even allows people to rest – mirroring God, who rests at the seventh day of Creation – on the Sabbath without too much anxiety as to what they will eat: thus it expresses the need for absolute trust in God's superabundance and generosity.

Since God is the ultimate sustainer, manna calls us to avoid the temptation of living falsely without any relationship with God or awareness of our dependence on God. In this Exodus narrative of the manna, God insists that the Israelites should only collect what is sufficient for each day's needs, without being greedy (Exod. 16:16–21). This interpretation echoes the narrative of eating the forbidden fruit in the book of Genesis, which could also be read as an occasion of sin understood as claiming total autonomy from God – and subsequently, from one another.[30] In the wilderness, God tests the faith of the people, and wants to reshape the life of the community so that it is rooted in the divine gift, rather than on a merely human enterprise devoid of God. Just as God is good and merciful to Adam and Eve after they eat the forbidden fruit in Eden, God does not allow the people of Israel to starve: the purpose of manna is life, not death. And God is not indifferent to the cries of the people. Thus, the manna is a sign of God's goodness, mercy, and compassion.

For this reason, rather than encouraging the accumulation or possession of God's gifts for private or individualistic purposes, the story of the manna is a call to share with one another and thus nurture the life of the community, particularly those who are in greatest need. This view is aligned with those biblical passages where God commands solidarity and sharing of food, particularly with the hungry, the poor, infants, widows, and foreigners.[31] However, this does not render the gift

---

[28]   Raúl Duarte Castillo, "Los Beneficios del Maná Ayer y Hoy," in López and Landgrave (eds.), *Pan para Todos*, 5.
[29]   Houston, "Exodus," 78.
[30]   For further analysis of sin and eating the forbidden fruit, see chapter 3 above.
[31]   See e.g. Deut. 10:18, 12:18, 14:28–9, 24:19–21. Hospitality to foreigners echoes Abraham's gesture toward Yahweh (in the form of three men passing by) in Gen. 18:4–6. Also, when Hagar is sent away, he is given bread and water for the journey (Gen. 21:14). Bread and drink are so important that they must be shared even with one's enemies (Prov. 25:21–2).

a unilateral gesture. As a reminder of dependence on the "other" (as bread, creation, God, and so on), manna also suggests a dimension of reciprocity, relationality, and interdependence. Not only are the needy and the "alien" dependent on those who have more, but God's people in turn depend on them as well. Wells argues that the stranger is also a gift to God's people:

> It is Melchizedek who brings out bread and wine and blesses Abraham. It is Pharaoh whose "fat cows" sustain Jacob's family in times of hardship. It is Balaam who blesses Israel in the sight of her enemy Balak. It is Ruth who demonstrates the faithfulness and imagination that Israel will need under her descendant David. It is Achish of Gath who gives a safe home to David and his followers when they are pursued by Saul. It is the Queen of Sheba who gives independent testimony to the wisdom and prosperity of Solomon. It is Cyrus who opens the way for the Jews to return from Exile. Israel depends on these strangers. Strangers are not simply a threat. They are not all characterized by the hard-hearted hostility of Moses' Pharaoh, of Goliath of Gath, of Sennacherib of Assyria, and Nebuchadnezzar of Babylon. Time and again strangers are the hands and feet of God, rescuing, restoring, and reminding Israel as elsewhere God does himself.[32]

Remember that this pattern of receiving blessings and grace by welcoming the stranger is also present in Dinesen's story. Babette is the stranger who is welcomed, and the one who will eventually nurture and help the community that welcomed her. The "alien other" is the one who becomes a gift of unity and transformation, and it does so in the context of the gift exchange. In a similar way to Babette, this strange bread, the manna from heaven, is thus a sign of interdependence, hospitality, and solidarity, for it is a material demonstration of God's ultimate compassion.

There is also a tradition of looking at manna as a metaphor and heuristic device referring to God's Word and Law, particularly from the perspective of the book of Deuteronomy 8:1–6. This text interprets the manna story by making it explicit that the main purpose of God's feeding his people was not only to satiate their physical hunger but, additionally and very importantly, to make people understand "that man does not live by bread alone but that man lives by everything that comes from the mouth of Yahweh" (Deut. 8:3–4). As a rabbinic tradition has

---

[32] Wells, *God's Companions*, 105.

it, manna is compared to the Word of God, which tastes different to each individual, expressing the human "power" to craft, in multiple ways, the same and one divine Word:

> If the manna tasted differently according to men's power, how much more the word. David said, "The voice of the Lord with power" (Ps. xxix, 4). It does not say "with His (God's) power," but "with power," that is, according to the power of each. And God says, "Not because you hear many voices are there many gods, but it is always I; I am the Lord thy God."[33]

In chapter 2 above I explored the relationship between *saber* and *sabor*, that is, the relationship between knowing and tasting or savoring. The story of the manna illustrates my earlier argument that knowing God's Word is a form of savoring, and this is a tasting that is different each time, on each occasion on which it is "ingested," and thus it is a knowledge that is crafted by human creativity and imagination. Here there is a dimension of aesthetics as an expression of *poiesis*. God's Word, that is Truth, is also dynamic, delectable, beautiful, good, and edible as well.[34] And it is a Word that includes human reception, initiative, and creativity, but always depending on God's primary source – that is, divine caritas as nourishment. God does not leave humanity empty, but satiates the hunger for God by sending God's edible Word that is ever dynamic and life-giving. Keeping the commandments and showing reverence to God are ways of right living in accordance with this divine gift-as-nourishment.

The story of the manna also recalls God's faithfulness to his chosen people, and invites us to treasure it as a memorial of divine providential care. The Exodus narrative relates how Yahweh commanded Moses and Aaron to put a full omer of manna in a jar and to keep it placed before the ark of "testimony," with the purpose of recalling God's salvific action (Exod. 16:32–4). Martínez points out that the later instructions to the Israelites to make a ritual offering of unleavened bread had a strong connection with the manna memorial (Exod. 25:30, 29:1–3, 40:23).[35] From this angle, manna and bread do not only express an ordinary understanding of food as physical sustenance, but they also move our

---

[33] Taken from C. G. Montefiore and H. Loewe (eds.), *A Rabbinic Anthology* (New York: Schocken Books, 1974), 7. I should like to express my gratitude to Fr. Richard Conrad, OP, for bringing this book to my attention.

[34] There is a biblical tradition of considering God's Word to be edible. See e.g. Deut. 8:3; Neh. 9:29; Ezek. 2:8–3; Amos 8:11; Wisd. 16:26; Jesus' temptations at Matt. 4:4; ; Rev. 10:8–10.

[35] Martínez, "De Dios que Alimenta a su Pueblo," 37.

understanding of food into a new symbolic, ritualistic, and liturgical sphere. Bread is food for the body, but it is also a symbol of divine presence, for it manifests God's nourishment of body and spirit. The manna recalls God's shaping of a chosen community to which he reveals a nourishing Word and Law. These ritual actions or performances, which involve consuming and offering food, construct a communal identity, a *polis*, within a complex temporal and spatial framework. Food rituals are used to re-enact the past by bringing it into the present while projecting it into the future – God's providential care. But not only time is involved here. Space is also imagined as the locus of the intersection of humanity with divinity. Sacred space draws a vertical line that goes down from heaven to earth: the pouring down of the divine edible gift. This line also travels up, from earth to heaven: as an offering that is an expression of gratitude; a doxological expression from the people to God. Simultaneously, space includes a horizontal line, which is the social interaction of the sharing of manna and caring for one another, and which imitates God's initial gesture of nurturing love.

Understanding the story of the manna within a ritual and symbolic context that brings together space and time also suggests a journey, a sense of pilgrimage, an existential dimension that is a dynamic *telos*. The pilgrim people of Israel advance together into the Promised Land, and are given food for their journey. The manna evokes a sense of building a historical journey together, in community, and of God walking with – while nourishing – God's people. The manna is thus a figure that evokes a certain *polis* that is crafted in and through a historical pilgrimage: a collective identity based on God's gift given as nourishment to sustain and provide a collective *telos*.

The manna is an expression of divine rescue. There is a salvific aspect to this bread as gift that is the manna. God expresses a desire to be close and bring about salvation when people most hunger. For this same reason, the manna is a reminder to the community that, in the same way that God cares for them and shows them compassion, they are also called to imitate God in their solidarity with one another. One could say that this is a call to "become bread" for one another, just as God's care and compassion are expressed in the form of bread. This sense of communal identity (between God and people, and between one another) founded upon the figure of bread continues in the New Testament, and inaugurates a new sort of community, a new *polis*, that is the ecclesia. In the Gospels, Jesus recalls, reinterprets, and reorients the manna tradition. He identifies with the divine manna understood as bread, God's Word and Law, divine superabundance and generosity. In and through Jesus, the manna becomes the new "event" that is God's incarnation, and his becoming the "bread of life eternal."

2.2 Manna in the Christian narratives

The message of God's superabundance and care expressed through the figure of food is repeated in several narratives within Gospels. A clear instance of this is Jesus' miracle of the multiplication of loaves and fishes.[36] Although this narrative is told in the four Gospels, I shall here briefly concentrate on the Johannine account because the figures of food and drink are so relevant to this Gospel's theology.[37] Martínez explains that John's account is also relevant because of the time and place in which the miracle is situated. Regarding time, the miracle occurs "shortly before the Jewish feast of Passover" (John 6:4): a feast that involves a meal that shapes a communal identity and enacts a covenantal relationship with God. In addition, this miracle echoes Jesus' first recorded miracle, – the changing of water into wine at the wedding at Cana (John 2:1–11) – which similarly takes place around the time of this important Jewish feast. Finally, the Last Supper also occurs on the eve of Passover.[38] The fact that these episodes involving food and drink all occur in the context of the Passover feast suggests the shaping of a new community, a configuration of a new sort of Israel. Secondly, regarding place, Martínez points out that, locating the miracle of the loaves and fishes by the shore of Galilee, a geographical site which has areas of both desert and vegetation, suggests a symbolic reference to some passages in the book of Exodus:

> In the same way as God directed the passing of the people through the Sea of Reeds (Exod. 15:22) so Jesus takes the people to the other side of the Sea of Galilee into a place in the wilderness (John 6:1). However, it does not seem irrelevant, but rather of great significance that the environment of that location was not total desert but was a fecund site (v. 10); that is to say that ultimately God takes his people into a land that flows with milk and honey (Josh. 24:13).[39]

This miracle makes a symbolic suggestion that Jesus is a new Moses, and thus also symbolizes a new Exodus. However, Jane S. Webster correctly

---

[36]   The Gospels of Matthew and Mark both present two miracles of the multiplication of fish and loaves (Matt. 14:13–21, 15:32–9; Mark 6:30–44, 8:1–10). Luke and John present only one (Luke 9:10–17; John 6:1–15).

[37]   For further research on the role of eating and drinking in the Gospel of John, see Jane S. Webster, *Ingesting Jesus: Eating and Drinking in the Gospel of John* (Atlanta: Society of Biblical Literature, 2003).

[38]   I revisit the Last Supper narrative below.

[39]   Martínez, "De Dios que Alimenta a su Pueblo," 41 (my translation).

argues that, while there are similarities between the two, there are also some contrasts:

> For example, instead of leading the people into the wilderness, as Moses does, Jesus goes alone (John 6:15). Instead of leading the people across the (dry) sea, Jesus abandons them on the shore (6:24). However, like Moses, Jesus does provide food for people in the wilderness (cf. Exod. 16–17). Thus, allusions to the Exodus focus on Jesus as one who provides food for the people. Jesus delivers the people by feeding them.[40]

Webster also points out that, as in the case of manna, the miracle of the multiplication shapes a new *polis*, which is symbolized by the disciples' gathering the fragments of left-over bread into twelve baskets – echoing the twelve tribes of Israel. This gesture of gathering mirrors "the 'harvest' of manna in the wilderness."[41] But in this figure of "gathering" there is also – Webster argues – an eschatological dimension to the shaping of a communal identity (as I explain below, there are some eschatological and eucharistic elements in this figure of gathering which echo some gestures of the Last Supper). Thus, this miracle of Jesus' feeding the multitude suggests a sense of shaping a communal identity expressed by the interrelated symbols of gathering and nourishing. Webster also explains that the word "gathering" describes "the action of God in bringing all of Israel back to the land, either after the exile or in the eschaton."[42] While gathering refers to the harvest of grains, it also

---

[40] Webster, *Ingesting Jesus*, 68.

[41] Webster (ibid., 71) is making explicit allusion to Exod. 16:15–21, where the text also uses "gathering" on several occasions.

[42] Ibid. Webster provides a citation from Deuteronomy: "When all these things have happened to you, the blessings and the curses that I have set before you, if you call them to mind among all the nations where the LORD your God has driven you, and return to the LORD your God, and you and your children obey him with all your heart and with all your soul, just as I am commanding your today, then the LORD your God will restore your fortunes and have compassion on you, *gathering* you again from all the peoples among whom the LORD your God has scattered you. Even if you are exiled to the ends of the world, from there the LORD your God will *gather* you, and from there he will bring you back" (Deut. 30:1–4 (emphasis added); cf. Ps. 50:3–5, 107:2–9). Webster (ibid., 72) also makes reference to Isaiah 11, "which speaks of an eschatological vision of a renewed creation in which God will *gather* all people of Israel and return them to the land" (emphasis added). In addition, regarding the eschatological dimension of this biblical notion of "gathering," Webster makes reference to the following passages: Ezek. 11:17, 28:25, 36:24; Jer. 23:2–4, 31:8, 32:37; Mic. 2:17; Zeph. 3:20; Matt. 24:31, 25:32–3.

suggests the gathering of the people by God, which John also uses to make reference to both "the harvest of grains (4:36) and to the eschatological gathering of the dispersed children of God (11:52; cf. 15:5–6)."[43]

To summarize this relationship between manna and Jesus' miracle of multiplication: in the face of people's hunger and despite the scarcity of bread and fish (five barley loaves and two fishes), Jesus' miracle of multiplication ultimately – like that of the manna in the desert – feeds the multitude and heals their hunger. There is a parallel with Babette's feast as well. Babette's culinary gifts to the community also move from scarcity to abundance, and from weakness to strength: "And they [the people in the village] soon found that from the day when Babette took over the housekeeping its cost was miraculously reduced, and the soup-pails and baskets acquired a new, mysterious power to stimulate and strengthen their poor and sick."[44] Like the manna, Jesus' feeding the multitude points to divine superabundance and rescue, a saving action expressed in the context of food sharing. Such miraculous feeding constructs a new communal identity, now gathered by Jesus Christ.

I mentioned earlier that there is a tradition of looking at manna as a symbol of God's nurturing Word, which calls us to trust in God's providential care. Jesus in the Gospels continues with this tradition of absolute trust in the nurturing Word of God. He makes this explicit in the narrative of the temptation in the wilderness (Matt. 4:1–4; Luke 4:1–4). This narrative also echoes Israel's forty days in the desert when led by Moses into the Promised Land. In the temptation narratives, Jesus is led (as he is "filled") by the Holy Spirit into the desert. As the Israelites experienced hunger in the wilderness, Jesus is also hungry, for he eats nothing during these forty days in the desert. The Gospel narratives relate that the Devil tempts Jesus by saying: "If you are the Son of God, tell this stone to turn into a loaf" (Luke 4:3). To this, Jesus replies quoting Deuteronomy 8:3: "Man does not live by bread alone but by every word that comes from the mouth of God." Dale C. Allison argues that this narrative has to do with Jesus' messiahship. But it expresses a sort of counter-politics, for it results not from obedience to earthly powers, nor to the power of Satan, but from total obedience to the Father, as he is declared the Son of God.[45] And this understanding of Jesus regarding God's politics is first manifested, in the Gospels of both Matthew and

---

[43]   Webster, *Ingesting Jesus*, 72.
[44]   Dinesen, *Babette's Feast*, 32.
[45]   See Dale C. Allison, Jr., "Matthew," in Barton and Muddiman (eds.), *The Oxford Bible Commentary*, 844–86. For a particular commentary on the pericope of Jesus' temptation in the wilderness, see p. 851.

Luke, during his temptation in the desert, which is – according to Allison – "a statement about salvation history." The same saving power of the God who cares for the people is now manifested in and through his Son, who, unlike the people in the desert, "neither murmurs nor gives in to temptation."[46] Jesus trusts in and is obedient to his Father's saving Word that is a sort of manna, a divine sustainer and giver of life.

Eric Franklin's commentary on Luke's account of the temptations in the desert also affirms a similar argument that interprets this passage as a fragment of salvation history.[47] According to Franklin, the testing of Jesus by the Devil is a test of Jesus' divine Sonship. While Adam's forbidden eating in Eden is a mark of disobedience and sin understood as severance from God, Jesus' gesture of total obedience and trust in his Father's nurturing Word suggests that Jesus is a second Adam who restores creation by initiating a new relationship with God. This new relationship, unlike the first Adam's, is not an exercise in self-assertion over and against God, but "a way of humble obedience and service" to God the Father.[48] As an echo of this notion of dependence on divine providence, Jesus teaches a new way of relating to God as *Abba*, a loving Father to whom we humbly pray to give us *our* daily bread. The Our Father is a communal prayer, not a private or individualist request, for God cares for and feeds all his children, and at the same time challenges societies to share God's generous gift that is meant to be communal rather than private. As beloved children of God, we are to trust in his plenitudinous providence, and, accordingly, set our "hearts in his kingdom" – and "these other things" (bread, clothing, and so forth) "will be given" (Luke 12:22–31).[49]

But Jesus not only provides and speaks on behalf of divine nourishment. He identifies himself with this life-giving bread. This self-identification with manna becomes more explicit in John's Gospel wherein Jesus emphasizes that the manna in the desert was, entirely, a gift from his Father, rather than from Moses. And now, in and through Jesus – the Son of God the Father – this "true bread" comes down from heaven to "give life to the world" (John 6:32–3). Jesus declares that he is the "bread of life," and acts in obedience to God sending him down to do his Father's will of giving eternal life to those who believe in Jesus (John 6:36–40). In Jesus, the manna is redefined: from being perishable to

---

46 Ibid., 851.
47 Eric Franklin, "Luke," in *The Oxford Bible Commentary*, 922–59.
48 Ibid., 932.
49 I say more about God's "kingdom" below.

offering imperishability, from leaving humanity hungry and thirsty to a promise that hunger and thirst will cease (John 6:34–5, 49–50).

There is yet a further and more radical – and perhaps more scandalizing – reorientation: the manna is now Jesus' resurrected "flesh" as "real food" to be eaten (or, more precisely, "chewed"), and his own "blood" is "real drink" to be consumed. As Graham Ward correctly points out, John's text uses the Greek term *sarx*, meaning "flesh," rather than *soma*, "body." Additionally, this particular text uses the term *trogo* for eating, which literally means chewing or gnawing.[50] Ward argues that Jesus' new definition of manna moves from an image of eating bread into a figure of gnawing flesh because the purpose is to draw attention to the image and thus to recenter it on the act of ingesting Jesus, the God-human. Christ, the Word made flesh, encounters (or abides in) the world (John 1:14) at the depth of human *pathos* that is the flesh; and this is an edible word, a manna to be eaten, so that the eaters may become one flesh with Christ.[51] For, according to John's Gospel, Jesus reveals that those who eat his body and drink his blood live in him as Jesus lives in them (John 6:56).

This more "graphic" move also takes a Hebrew tradition of ritual sacrificial offerings wherein an animal (lamb, goat, or bull) is slaughtered in the Temple and then eaten with the purpose of ritualizing God's covenant to his people. Now, though, this animal is shockingly replaced by Jesus himself (whom Christians believe in as God's incarnation). Earlier in John's Gospel, John the Baptist identifies Jesus as "the lamb of God who takes away the sins of the world" (John 1:29). This identification points to Jesus' own passion, his death on the cross, and his resurrection, which are believed to be God's own redeeming act. The book of Revelation also uses the same image of Jesus as the lamb; this lamb is given in "marriage" in a heavenly and final messianic banquet at the end of the world, yet this banquet starts to take place (it "has come") in and through Jesus' life, death, and resurrection (Rev. 19:7–9).

To this perplexing image of a divine–human self-sacrifice, one also needs to add the scandalizing image of drinking Jesus' blood, a practice that contradicts God's law (Lev. 3:17; Deut. 12:23). How is this possible? Or, more precisely, what does this extravagant feeding mean?

---

[50] Ward, *Christ and Culture*, esp. 104–5. On the subject of eating and drinking Jesus' flesh and blood, see Webster, *Ingesting Jesus*.

[51] For a view of flesh as human pathos, see Michel Henry, *Encarnación: Una Filosofía de la Carne*, trans. from the French original, *Incarnation: Une philosophie de la chair*, by Javier Teira, Gorka Fernández, and Roberto Ranz (Salamanca: Ediciones Sígueme, 2001).

Ward explains that the Johannine "bread of life" discourse contains a eucharistic notion, which opens up a dimension of a reciprocal relation or "co-abiding" between Christ and humanity, which constitutes the ecclesia:

> if we interpret the "How" of the Jewish question – "How can this man give us his flesh to eat" – not as a technical question ("in what way") but a hermeneutical question ("in what manner do we understand the offer of his flesh to eat"), we can further appreciate how the materiality of what Jesus is saying offends cultic rationality. What is suggested by this corporeal feeding is not simply absorption, and this is significant. There is an "abiding" *in* Christ, but there is also an abiding *of* Christ (in the one who eats). This co-abiding is complex and richly suggestive. It is, I suggest, the chiasmic heart of an *ekklesia* performed and constituted through the eucharist. Why chiasmic? Because observe the curious manner of the reciprocal relation. I eat the flesh of Christ. I take his body into my own. Yet in this act I place myself *in* Christ – rather than simply placing Christ within me. I consume but do not absorb Christ without being absorbed into Christ.[52]

Eating and drinking this divine manna – Christ's body and blood – is a sign of participation in God's life, as it is a sign of God's participation in human life, at the core of materiality, at the heart of the flesh. In God's identification and assumption of the deepest dimension of human life there is also a reversal, that is, a participation of humanity in divine life: "Something of what it is to be fully human comes about by an identification with that which is divine; so there is something of what it is to be God that comes about by an identification with what is human."[53] Incarnation is, then, fully realized in this divine self-offering as flesh and blood that is true nourishment, for it is an excessive, intimate form of the "participation of God in human life and the participation of human life in God."[54] In Christian thought, the enactment of this mutual participation is the Eucharist, which shapes a new *polis*, which is the Church: the mystical Body of Christ – *corpus mysticum*.[55]

[52] Ward, *Christ and Culture*, 105.
[53] Ibid., 105–6.
[54] Ibid., 106.
[55] See Henri Lubac, *Corpus Mysticum: L'Eucharistie et l'Eglise au Moyen Age*, 2nd edn. (Paris: Aubier, 1949). See also Michel de Certeau, *The Mystic Fable* (Chicago: University of Chicago Press, 1992). I say more about the Body of Christ below.

The notion of God's self-offering is also depicted in the Last Supper narratives where, again, the elements of bread and wine become central for emphasizing – in the words of John Koenig – "God's covenantal redemption of the world."[56] In the Last Supper, Jesus identifies with bread and wine as his own body and blood. Although the synoptic Gospels use the term "body," instead of the Johannine "flesh," the message is the same: the sacrificial offering of an animal is now replaced by the offering of Christ as a sign of a covenantal relationship between God and humanity. Koenig remarks that, even though the Last Supper "was not a Passover seder as such," nevertheless, it is said to occur on the eve of the Jewish Passover celebration, and thus makes concrete the idea that this meal is symbolic of a "new covenant" – particularly signified by the wine, which Jesus identifies as his own blood.[57] Again, the notions of God's faithfulness for his people found in the figure of manna are now intensified in the Last Supper, where God not only provides food but becomes nourishment itself. While the feast of Passover commemorates God's liberation (an "exodus") of the chosen people from being enslaved in Egypt (which also echoes the message of the manna), Christianity would read Jesus' Last Supper as a new "paschal banquet" that commemorates the passing over from sin into forgiveness, death into eternal life.

Since the Last Supper prefigures both Jesus' death on the cross and his resurrection from the dead, his mentioning (in the synoptic Gospels) a future "kingdom banquet" could be read as a promise of God's faithfulness to humanity – despite Jesus being rejected by the people and being abandoned by most of his disciples, and even in the face of imminent death. Howard Marshall puts it as follows:

> the way in which Jesus performed this act [the Last Supper] before his death implies that he was giving his disciples a way of remembering him and enjoying some kind of association with him after

---

[56] John Koenig, *The Feast of the World's Redemption: Eucharistic Origins and Christian Mission* (Pennsylvania: Trinity Press International, 2000), 43. The Last Supper narratives are found in the synoptic Gospels (Matt. 26:26–9; Mark 14:22–5; and Luke 22:17–20) and 1 Cor. 11:23–5.

[57] Koenig, *The Feast of the World's Redemption*, 32. Notice that Matthew and Mark do not use the term "new" covenant. Also, in John's Gospel, and unlike the synoptic Gospels, there is no account of what is called the "words of institution" (referring to later eucharistic readings of the Last Supper). However, as Howard Marshall explains, the eucharistic elements (bread and wine as Jesus' body/flesh and blood) are recorded in Jesus' teaching about eating his flesh and drinking his blood (John 6:53). See Howard Marshal, "The Lord's Supper," in Metzger and Coogan (eds.), *The Oxford Companion to the Bible*, 465–7.

his death and during the period before they would share together in the kingdom of God. Hence, the meal that his disciples were to celebrate could be regarded as in some sense an anticipation of the meal the Messiah would celebrate with his disciples in the new age (cf. Matt. 8:11; Luke 14:15). Such a meal would not be merely a symbol or picture of the future meal but would be a real anticipation of it.[58]

Along the same lines as Marshall's interpretation, John Koenig correctly observes that, in the Gospels, there "is a striking fact that a great number of images in Jesus' talk about the kingdom have to do with eating and drinking."[59] Koenig provides the following examples, from the Gospels, where there is a close connection between the figure of God's kingdom and a meal:

- Blessed are you poor, for yours is the kingdom of God. Blessed are you who are hungry now, for you will be filled [in the kingdom] (Luke 6:20).
- Your kingdom come. Give us this day our daily bread (Luke 11:2).
- Many will come from east and west and will eat with Abraham, Isaac and Jacob in the kingdom of heaven (Matt. 8:11; see also Luke 13:28).
- The kingdom of heaven may be compared to a king who gave a wedding banquet for his son (Matt. 22:2).
- Then the kingdom of heaven will be like this. Ten bridesmaids took their lamps and went to meet the bridegroom [for the wedding feast] (Matt. 25:1; and see v. 10).[60]

It is therefore not uncharacteristic of Jesus to celebrate a last supper with his disciples with the purpose of bringing to a close his ministry on earth (and yet this eating and drinking will also become a *beginning* in the post-resurrection life of the church).

---

[58] Marshall, "The Lord's Supper," 467.
[59] Koenig, *The Feast of the World's Redemption*, 15.
[60] Ibid. To this set of examples, Koenig also adds other texts in which the Gospels indirectly imply this notion of the Kingdom as related to a feast: "One of these is the parable of the prodigal son (Luke 15:11–31); another is Jesus' ironic complaint that when he, the Son of Man, came eating and drinking in the communal meals of his ministry, certain righteous people took great offense at his behavior: 'They say, Look, a glutton and drunkard, a friend of tax collectors and sinners!' (Matt. 11:19)." Ibid., 16.

John's account of the Last Supper (John 14–17) does not use the words of institution, but his earlier identification with bread and wine (as in the "bread of life discourses"), hints at a co-relation. What is interesting in John's account of the Last Supper, and something that is not reported in the synoptic Gospels, is Jesus' gesture of washing his disciples' feet – a gesture of humility and service. This gesture is to be imitated by the disciples, for it is a way of echoing God's love. In loving one another they not only become friends of God, but they co-abide with Jesus as the Son abides with the Father. The sacrificial offering of Jesus' own life is an expression of the Father's gift of love, peace, and forgiveness. In the same way as the Father does not abandon his Son when he dies, but offers him the gift of resurrection, so God promises eternal life to his beloved ones. Thus, death and sacrifice are not final but, rather, eternal life and God's providential care (as also is the promise of the sending the gift of the Holy Spirit: John 16:5–15). A retrospective look at Jesus' crucifixion, both from the perspective of the resurrection and Pentecost, also intimates the paradoxical power of the cross: just as food needs to be "consumed" in order to sustain life. Therefore, regarding our previous reflection on God's kingdom, one could say – from a Johannine perspective – that the kingdom of God is founded on radical love that is to be shared among one another, and in loving one another, serving one another, we more fully participate in the powerful divine language of love that even surpasses death.

Not only could the Last Supper narratives be read in relation to John's "bread of life" discourses which, as I earlier argued, echo the manna tradition, but they could also be read in light of the manna symbolism found in the narratives of Jesus' miraculous feeding. Although not all the synoptic texts coincide in their accounts, some gestures are repeated in these narratives: the blessing of food, the breaking of bread, giving thanks, and sharing. Marshall points out that these analogies (between the Last Supper narratives and the miraculous feeding) suggest that "the evangelists saw a parallel between Jesus' feeding the people with bread and his spiritual nourishment of the church."[61] Also, as Koenig points out, these same gestures would then be repeated in early Christian eucharistic meals – communal "meals of gratitude" (from the Greek verb *eucharisteo*, "to give thanks.").[62] Again, the message in both the miraculous feeding and the Last Supper echoes the message of the manna tradition: God's superabundance and a generous sharing that nourishes communities and invites them to repeat this same gesture among one another.

---

[61] Marshall, "The Lord's Supper," 467.
[62] Koening, *The Feast of the World's Redemption*, 95.

The Last Supper prefigures Christ's death on the cross, and at the same time it can be read retrospectively, from the perspective of the resurrection. Here again, the message of the Last Supper blends with the manna tradition, that is, God's saving action expressed as life-giving nourishment, generosity, and a call to share. This is particularly the case in the post-resurrection Gospel narratives, in which the risen Christ shows companionship by eating and drinking with his disciples.[63] For instance, the post-resurrection narrative of Jesus' appearing to his disciples on the road to Emmaus presents some of these gestures of the blessing, breaking, and distributing of bread (Luke 24:30–5). The two disciples walking on the road to Emmaus do not recognize the resurrected Christ on the road. After inviting Jesus to stay overnight and eat with them, their "eyes were opened" as Jesus performs these familiar gestures of taking bread, blessing, breaking, and passing it to them. Later in this same Gospel, the risen Christ appears once again to a group of disciples, whom Jesus asks for something to eat. In reply, the disciples "offered him a piece of grilled fish, which he took and ate before their eyes" (Luke 24:42–3). Mark's Gospel reports that the risen Christ appears to his disciples "while they were at the table" (Mark 16:14). Finally, the Gospel of John tells of a "resurrection breakfast" that follows a miraculous catch of fish (John 21:1–25).[64] John's account is particularly telling, for his narrative mirrors the patterns of the miraculous feeding stories, and suggests the same message of God's superabundance, table fellowship, and a call to share.[65] In the context of the resurrection, the message also regards God's redemption, for God is faithful to his promises of life eternal through the risen Lord. Samuel Wells argues that eating together with the risen Christ is a sign that God wants to "share companionship with his people." And, Wells continues,

This companionship is expressed definitively in eating together. At this resurrection meal [Wells refers here to the meal at Emmaus in

[63] Mark is the only Gospel that does not report Jesus eating and drinking with his disciples in the post-resurrection accounts.

[64] See the chapter entitled "Resurrection Breakfast" in Webster, *Ingesting Jesus*, 133–46.

[65] The message of divine sharing as nourishment is particularly explicit in Jesus' dialogue with Simon Peter (John 21:15–18). As a mirror to Peter's denying Jesus three times when Jesus is arrested (John 18:17, 25, 27), this dialogue, which occurs after the meal, is where Jesus asks Peter three times: "Do you love me?" Three times Peter answers positively: "Yes Lord, you know I love you" (the third time is more emphatic: "Lord, you know everything; you know I love you"). Twice Jesus responds to Peter: "Feed my sheep" (the third reply is "Look after my sheep"). Peter's role as a shepherd (a role of leadership) is a call to imitate God's caring for and nourishing of his people.

Luke's Gospel] disciples rediscover that in Jesus, God has given them everything they need to follow him, and that following him means to worship, to be his friends, and to eat with him.[66]

As the manna is nourishment that strengthens the body and spirit of Israel in the desert, and as Jesus nourishes the crowds with a miraculous feeding, eating and drinking with the risen Lord means to participate in God's saving actions – to be one with God at the same table.

The sense of God's desire to accompany people and his invitation to participate in God's sharing does not stop after Christ ascends into heaven. For the Holy Spirit comes down from heaven as a "gift" from God – like the manna in the desert – to take the role of divine companionship, to fill "with gladness" the hearts of those who hunger for God, to nurture and strengthen those who once were afraid of publicly proclaiming the lordship Christ achieved in his resurrection and heavenly ascension, where he is "at the right hand of the Father" (see Acts 2:1–18). The early Christian communities believed that God had not abandoned them, nor had he left them malnourished: God's saving actions (both as Father and Son) continue in and through the Holy Spirit, who shapes a new sense of being "one Body" with one another and with God.[67] The gift of the Holy Spirit provides a new pneumatological dimension to divine sharing as alimentation and the building of this new *polis* that is the ecclesial body.

That is why table companionship, gestures of the breaking of bread, thanksgiving, and sharing in a communal meal become very important in the shaping of the early Christian communities, and in their development of liturgies (Acts 2:42, 46, 20:7, 11). The Greek term *koinonia* refers to this early Christian self-understanding as a divine–human community that has to do with being nourished and with communal sharing. Thus, Koenig correctly argues that it is very revealing to explore how this term developed into a later notion of "holy communion" which was closely related to these communal gatherings,

> some of which surely involved ritual meals (Acts 2:42); and Paul uses the word to describe a deep participation in Christ's body and blood that believers experience during the Lord's Supper, as well as

---

[66] Wells, *God's Companions*, 28.

[67] For further research on the role of the Holy Spirit, its indivisible Trinitarian action, and the incorporation into the Trinitarian life – via the Holy Spirit – of creation in general and humanity in particular, see Eugene F. Rogers, Jr., *After the Spirit: A Constructive Pneumatology from Resources Outside the Modern West* (Michigan: SCM Press, 2005).

the spiritual uniting into one body of worshipers (1 Cor. 10:16f.). Moreover, early in 1 Corinthians the apostle mentions "a *koinonia* of [or with] God's Son, Jesus Christ our Lord" into which believers are called (1:9). Given Paul's belief that such *koinonia* represents a bonding between the individual believer and Christ that excludes all comparable relationships with other deities and expresses itself physically at the table of the Lord (1 Cor. 10:18–22), we can understand how the phrase "holy communion" evolved into a favorite name for the chief ritual meal of the church.[68]

This "chief ritual meal of the church" that Koenig points to is an early precursor of the eucharistic meal, which also contains elements of the Last Supper's "words of institution" over the elements of bread and wine. This meal also integrates liturgical gestures of giving thanks, blessing, breaking, and sharing of bread and wine. The breaking and sharing of bread is central in the shaping of the Christian communities, for it is not an ordinary meal, but a re-enactment of Jesus' preaching of God's kingdom: giving life to others, shaping a "responsible body" based on sharing and mutual caring, building a communal "resistance to hunger."[69] This is why Paul's reflections on the Last Supper insist on the communal dimension of this memorial meal (1 Cor. 11:17–34). When one part of this body suffers, the entire body also suffers, and when there is division, greed, and carelessness, the community is malnourished, and even runs the risk of suffering starvation. This eucharistic meal shapes a eucharistic community. Herein, at the core of the eucharistic community gathered by the Holy Spirit, where Christ becomes present in the bread and wine, the ecclesia ultimately finds its meaning, orientation, and source of nourishment.

In Pauline terms, this new community is united by one Body that is Christ (1 Cor. 12:12–30). As the figure of manna unifies and shapes a communal identity, the Body of Christ given to eat and drink constructs a new *polis* rooted in participation and reciprocity – a politics of co-abiding. I mentioned earlier that the Johannine account of Jesus' "living bread" discourses suggests that the communal eating and drinking of this divine manna is a performance of a corporeal union between God and humanity. The politics of the Body of Christ is – in Ward's terms – a "transcorporeal" performance of complex dimensions of co-abiding: the three persons of the Trinity abiding in one another, and

---

[68] Koenig, *The Feast of the World's Redemption*, 93.
[69] See Whelan, "The Responsible Body."

further abiding in creation; Christ abiding in the elements of bread and wine as well as in the partakers; the partakers abiding in Christ and in one another. Thus, the politics of this Body of Christ is a feast of loving relationships, a love union, a "holy communion." Ward makes an interesting suggestion when he recalls the Pauline images of betrothal, which evoke a loving union: particularly in "the way St. Paul parallels the cup of blessing of the covenant participation with the wedding contract (1 Cor. 10:14–22 with 2 Cor. 11:1–2)."[70] Koenig remarks that some of these early Christian ritual meals were given the Greek term *agape* ("love feast"), for they were about celebrating a love union between Christ and the faithful, which further built agapeic communities founded on the practice of nurturing caritas.[71] Ward calls these practices the "erotic politics" of the ecclesial body.[72] This is to say that, in the eucharistic sharing, a new community is constructed by the ecstatic union of divine and human desires. And its rituals of eating and drinking would be a communal bodily performance for the re-enactment of Christ's abiding in the partakers as well as the partakers abiding in one another and in Christ.

Moreover, in this erotic/agapeic eucharistic practice, the politics of the body of the church is not static or fixed, for it constantly reconfigures its boundaries.[73] Identities such as national, ethnic, gender, social class, and so forth are reconfigured by a new and ever dynamic identity that is Christ's Body. Because the source of this ecclesial body is divine superabundance, its location is "liminality; a co-relation that lives always on the edge of both itself and what is other."[74] Self and other, the human and divine, spiritual and material, the individual parts and the whole, do not collapse into one another, but, rather, they coexist or mutually indwell in and through this *metaxu*, the in-betweenness that is the Body of Christ. Difference is not eliminated, but it is brought into a new harmonious and excessive unity (Christ's Body) that opens up an infinite space for relations of affinity, mutual care (mutual nurturing), and reciprocity.

---

[70] Ward, *Christ and Culture*, 108.
[71] See Koenig, *The Feast of the World's Redemption*, 93–4. Also, for a further historical research on the development of agapeic banquets in the early church, see Dennis E. Smith, *From Symposium to Eucharist: The Banquet in the Early Christian World* (Minneapolis: Fortress Press, 2003).
[72] See Ward, "The Body of the Church and its Erotic Politics," in *Christ and Culture*, 92–110.
[73] As I argued in chapter 3 above, the erotic and the agapeic constitute one another rather than the erotic being surpassed by the agapeic.
[74] Ward, "The Body of the Church," 107.

I said earlier that the manna of the Hebrews is a symbol of a vertical and horizontal intersection between heaven and earth, God and humanity. As it comes down from heaven to nourish humanity (a vertical line), it is to be shared among others (a horizontal line), particularly those who are in greatest need. The eucharistic sharing of Christ's flesh and blood, this new manna, is also a symbol of liminality wherein divinity and humanity intersect. Christ, the Word made flesh, becomes food and drink, and so abides in the world: the extraordinary becomes ordinary, and this kenotic movement makes the ordinary extraordinary, from within the everyday nature of bread. God shares divinity in this meal, and so challenges the partakers to become nourishment for one another. Here too, a vertical and horizontal line intersect in one divine feast. Space is, then, complex, for, as Ward remarks, it is the space of an infinite Body that constantly "over-reaches itself."[75]

A reading of the manna tradition could also suggest a complex construction of temporality. The manna evokes a sense of being in a communal pilgrimage, collectively moving toward a future divine promise. In this journey God strengthens people with divine sustenance. In Christian thought, this divine promise is the eschaton – the final culmination of history, the consummation of God's kingdom. The ecclesial body is on the road, walking – by the guidance of the Holy Spirit – toward this promised future. There is here a complex temporality, wherein past, present, and future intersect at a point that is a redeeming narrative: the *telos* that is also a *pathos* of salvation history. Throughout this historical interim, the ecclesial body is nurtured by the eucharistic sharing of God's divinity in the form of food and drink. In feasting today as a memorial and enactment of yesterday's celebration, there is a public proclamation that, at the end, there will be a collective feast as well. It is therefore remarkable, but perhaps not too surprising, to observe how both the Hebrew and Christian Scriptures give expression of a future divine promise with allegories of a lavish banquet, where hunger will be no more.[76] As I have mentioned, the book of Revelation (19:5–10) alludes to an eschatological wedding feast that will celebrate a final consummation of the loving union between God and humanity. But this loving union has already started in Christ's self-giving; and so it is performed day by day, in every eucharistic sharing. Thus, eucharistic celebrations within the daily pilgrimage of history become an erotic/agapeic

---

[75] Ibid., 107.
[76] See e.g. Isa. 25:6–10, 55:1–4; Amos 9:11–15; Jer. 31:10–14; Matt. 8:11; Mark 2:11; Luke 6:21, 12:35–48, 13:28–30, 14:7–24, 22:28–30; Rev. 19:5–10.

anticipation and enactment of a future eschatological banquet – the final consummation of this divine–human loving union.

At a high point in *Babette's Feast* the general offers a toast, and recalls the famous French cook who used to turn her culinary art "into a kind of love affair – into a love affair of the noble and romantic category in which one no longer distinguishes between bodily and spiritual appetite or satiety!"[77] I believe that such a fictional image is evocative of the "strange" manna that comes from heaven, which in Christian terms is God's love becoming alimentation. In the Eucharist, God's culinary art turns into a communal erotic/agapeic performance where the partakers no longer distinguish "between bodily and spiritual appetite or satiety." As Babette's feast transfigures what was broken into a harmonious shape, and heals that which was wounded, the eucharistic feast is meant to transfigure the atomized, broken, and wounded members into a communal, harmonious unity-in-difference that is the Body of Christ.

3 Sharing in the Divine *Edible* Gift, Becoming Nourishment

Following on from the above discussion, I will briefly explore the notion of the gift, particularly as it regards the practice of alimentation, which is an analogy common to both Babette's and God's feasts. The strange manna is said to be a "gift from heaven," which, as Babette's culinary gift, brings about communal nourishment and transformation. In this section, I will argue that this relationship between gift, alimentation, and self–other transformation sheds light on the meaning of the eucharistic sharing, and will, I hope, serve as a basis for better understanding what is meant by the theopolitics of sharing in the Body of Christ.

This correlation between alimentation and gift is by no means a novel discovery. Lewis Hyde correctly points out that several anthropological, social, and cultural studies on the gift make direct reference to food practices that reflect both a metaphorical expression and a material performance of the gift and gift-exchange social systems.[78] The now classic work by Marcel Mauss, *Essai sur le Don*, reflects on "archaic" societies wherein a system of gift exchange is frequently centered on food, or where durable goods are treated as food.[79] The practice of "potlatch" by

---

[77] Dinesen, *Babette's Feast*, 51.
[78] Lewis Hyde, *The Gift: Imagination and the Erotic Life of Property* (New York: Vintage Books, 1983).
[79] Marcel Mauss, *Essai sur le Don* (Paris: Presses Universitaires de France, 1950); trans. W. D. Halls as *The Gift: The Form and Reason for Exchange in Archaic Societies* (London: W. W. Norton, 1990).

northwest American tribal groups, for instance, is frequently translated by Mauss as "nourishing", or "consuming" – if it is used as a verb – or "feeder" or "place of being satiated" – if it is used as a noun.[80] Potlatch is a complex gift-exchange system that creates social bonds in these groups. But the gift is never static, for it is enacted in its being received, or consumed. Thus, regarding this aspect of the edibility of the gift, Hyde reflects:

> Another way to describe the motion of the gift is to say that a gift must always be used up, consumed, eaten. *The gift is property that perishes* ... food is one of the most common images for the gift because it is so obviously consumed. Even when the gift is not food, when it is something we would think of as a durable good, it is often referred to as a thing to be eaten.[81]

The notion of the edible gift thus displays a dimension of giving and receiving that constitutes social relations. In pre-industrial agricultural societies food is also meant to be a gift given not only by other people, but also by the earth or nature, and often by spiritual beings, gods, and goddesses. Food as gift, and gift as food, show a dimension of interdependence between social groups, and of humanity with the earth and with divine agency. But the gift is fully performed in the act of receiving, eating, and consuming it. In this act of reception, there is a sense of being nourished by the gift that is shared by other people, nature, and supernatural entities.

Alimentation is conceived as it is received, as it is eaten. Likewise, we speak of the gift in the midst of its giving, when it is already somehow altered by our reception, which here – following Mauss and Hyde – I call "consumption." In chapter 2 I explored the dimension of *poiesis* (crafting) that is involved in tasting and eating. There is always a mediatory or "digestive" process in the reception of otherness (whether this is a piece of bread or another person). The giving of the gift does not annul or inhibit the recipient's creativity and innovativeness, which are displayed in the process of receiving or digesting the gift. The other is a gift, an edible gift. Thus, I emphasize the element of the gift's consumption because there is an aspect of kenosis that the gift must undergo in order to be received. In the gift there is a risk, a kenotic performance, but in the most fleshy and extremely intimate sense of proximity, to the extent

---

[80] Ibid., 6, see also 86 n. 13.
[81] Hyde, *The Gift*, 8 (emphasis in original).

that it is broken apart and consumed until it enters our very flesh, and further transforms itself into energy, words, and deeds. Thus, regarding the Eucharist, since one of the most primal forms of sharing is alimentation, one could state that it is suitable or "convenient" (in Aquinas' senses of *convenientia*) that Christ's donation is, par excellence, precisely given as food and drink.[82] The kenosis of the eucharistic gift is a self-immersion of Christ with the Holy Spirit into finite humanity and materiality.[83] In the Eucharist, divinity takes the risk of becoming food because of a desire to indwell (or abide) in the beloved, just as food becomes a part of the eater. But in this kenotic giving there is not only a self-immersion of the supernatural in the natural. This *convenientia* of the Incarnation as well as the eucharistic feeding allows the elevation of the human condition to the supernatural: a tendency or forward direction toward a deeper reality of intimacy with God as in the beatific vision and the final destination at the eschaton.

In this kenotic act, desire and self-expression, though consumed or digested by the recipient, are never suppressed or annihilated by the act of reception.[84] In the last chapter I explored this characteristic of

[82]   There is also a dimension of "aesthetics" in Christ becoming, precisely, bread and wine: for instance, bread can be used to stand for food in general, and wine is an intoxicating drink that lifts the spirits. It is also fitting that, just as sin is brought into the world through eating the forbidden fruit, now the eating and drinking of the eucharistic meal is a practice of salvation and deification. Redemption is prompted by sensual experience – particularly through the most intense and penetrating senses such as touch and taste – which in the Eucharist give guidance to both the intellect and the soul. Since God is always in excess, this (aesthetic) manifestation is only an *analogical* dimension of his Beauty, which also includes divine Truth and Goodness. Nevertheless, the fittingness of God becoming incarnate as human, and becoming eucharistic nourishment allows us to conjecture on the dimension of "co-belonging" (which is also a form of ontological affinity) between God and his creatures. This divine–human co-belonging is made possible by God's self-sharing, precisely in ways that appropriate to the human capacity to receive the divine gift (as food and drink in the Eucharist, for instance). See Thomas Aquinas, *De Veritate*, in *Disputed Questions on Truth*, trans., V. J. Bourke (Chicago: Chicago University Press, 1987). On this issue of Aquinas' *convenientia*, see Gilbert Narcisse, OP, *Les Raisons de Dieu: Arguments de convenance et esthétique théologie selon St. Thomas d'Aquin et Hans Urs von Balthasar* (Fribourg: Editions Universitaires Fribourg Swisse, 1997), and John Milbank and Catherine Pickstock, *Truth in Aquinas* (London: Routledge, 2001).
[83]   In a way, there is here a paradigm of what John Milbank calls the "double descent" of the divine gift given by the Son with the Spirit. See Milbank's foreword to Smith, *Introducing Radical Orthodoxy*, 20.
[84]   This is one of the major arguments in John Milbank's essay "Can a Gift be Given? Prolegomenon to a Future Trinitarian Metaphysics," *Modern Theology*, 11/1 (Jan. 1995). See also John Milbank, *Being Reconciled: Ontology and Pardon* (London: Routledge, 2003). My discussion here on the concept of gift is greatly influenced by Milbank's work.

inventiveness, desire, and self-expression that presents Sophia as a culinary artist and as food itself. Manna is also a gift that expresses God's desire to be near to and redeem and nurture his people. This is also the case with the eucharistic sharing, in which God's desire and self-expression are given as food and drink: in a fashion parallel to the way in which Tita in Laura Esquivel's *Like Water for Chocolate* (see chapter 2) makes food an extension of her desire and self-expression, and as Babette's feast is an expression of her own self. There is a delight in the giving of the gift which, *pace* Mauss, Hyde, et al., is imperishable despite its being consumed. And in God, desire and self-expression constitute one and the same divine gift, for the divine gift is God's language of love that nourishes the life of the Trinity. Such a divine alimentation (the substance, *ousia*, that is intra-divine love) is further shared, perpetually, and despite our refusal, in the eucharistic banquet.

From a Trinitarian perspective, the threefold aspects of the gift that are the giver, the given, and the giving infinitely coincide in this perpetually ecstatic exchange.[85] Or, if I am permitted to use an "alimentary" analogy, one could say that in God's ecstatic exchange there is a coincidence and dynamic interplay between the cook, the meal, and banqueting. That is why the divine gift allows a conjecture on the coincidence between agape and eros (it is agapeic/erotic at once, as I argued in chapter 3).[86] For the desire *of* the other is as intense as the desire to give *to* the other (this giving is an initial self-giving to the other as much as it is a return as thanksgiving to the giver). Such is the superabundance and infinite dynamism of the divine gift, which David Bentley Hart articulates as follows:

> The Father gives himself to the Son, and again to the Spirit, and the Son offers everything up to the Father in the Spirit, and the Spirit returns all to the Father through the Son, eternally. Love of, the gift to, and delight in the other is one infinite dynamism of giving and receiving, in which desire at once beholds and donates the other.[87]

The divine gift, which is God's desire and self-expression, is not only imperishable, but allows the transformation of the recipient. In fact, the

---

[85] See e.g. Stephen H. Webb, *Gifting God: A Trinitarian Ethics of Excess* (Oxford: Oxford University Press, 1996).

[86] Again, as I argued in chapter 3, this notion of the agapeic/erotic attempts to move beyond a reduction of agape to eros, and of eros to agape. Herein (within Trinitarian ekstasis) is envisioned a complementarity and mutual constitution of eros and agape.

[87] David Bentley Hart, *The Beauty of the Infinite: The Aesthetics of Christian Truth* (Grand Rapids, MI: Eerdmans, 2003), 268.

recipient becomes fully himself or herself in this act of reception. For this reason, reception is also an expression of gratitude (*eucharistos*) for this divine gift. In the eucharistic sharing, while Christ abides in the one who partakes of his flesh and blood, the partaker is also transformed in the reverse direction and incorporated into the body of Christ. The partaker becomes eucharistic. The self is a joyful expression of thanksgiving for becoming the recipient of such a divine gift. In the words of Hart, "One becomes a 'person,' one might say, analogous to the divine persons, only insofar as one is the determinate recipient of a gift; one is a person always in the evocation of a response."[88]

From a communal perspective, the Body of Christ is his self-expression, his desire as self-giving that is repeated non-identically by the further communal sharing of such a divine gift. Therefore, the message of the Eucharist is that the communal Body of Christ is a dynamic in-betweenness of the giving, receiving, and charitable sharing of God's gift. Divine and human desires enter into a deep sense of intimacy and reciprocity in this agapeic/erotic "holy communion" that is the eucharistic ecclesial performance.

From a Christian perspective, the paradigm of kenosis of the gift given to be consumed intimates dispossession as an act that does not make self-sacrifice an end in itself, but – in the context of the resurrection – it becomes a practice of hope, gratitude, and trust for a return in God's superabundant love and fidelity. Still prior to the resurrection, the divine gift is an expression of the superabundant "charity and joy that is perfect in the shared life of the Trinity, and in him desire and selfless charity are one and the same."[89] Accordingly, there is a paradox in the gift: while being superabundant, it cannot be fully possessed; it moves beyond itself in giving itself away. There will be no fear in giving away or in letting go. This paradox is comparable to the Gospels' discourse on the Beatitudes, where the gift is both kenosis and plenitude as it reveals the essential character of blessedness in the practice of being fulfilled by way of dispossession.[90] The paradoxical message of the Beatitudes is rooted in communion with and commitment to one another, and is never a merely individual "devotional" practice or one seeking "personal" salvation. Martyrdom is understood in this dimension of the paradox of kenosis, a commitment to life, even when there might be death involved. Such, for instance, is the understanding of many martyrs in Latin America. As the

---

[88]   Ibid., 263.
[89]   Ibid.
[90]   See Matt. 5:1–10; Luke 6:20–30.

General of the Jesuits, Father Piet Hans Kovenbach, expressed it in 1983: "For reflection on the Beatitudes to be authentic, it has to be founded on a communion of life and death, as shown by our Lord, with the poor and those who weep, with victims of injustice and those who hunger."[91] Giving is also learning to let go, for in generous giving there is an implicit return, even when this return is never identical, even when there is a delay in returning; for if there is generosity and gratitude at all, the gift surpasses exact calculations of time and quantity. But this only shows that delay, non-identical repetition, and perpetual giving are the life of the true gift. The paradoxical beatific dimension of the gift also recalls Babette's own letting go of all her fortune for the making of a lavish meal that she offers to the community, knowing that her kenotic gesture will not end in absolute scarcity, for her gift is already an expression of the superabundance of art: "an artist is never poor."

In Isak Dinesen's story, Babette "interrupts" the narrative of the village people, and brings a gift that allows the community to enter into a new self and communal realization: a harmonious unity between the spiritual and the bodily, a deeper and more intense form of relationality with one another, and with God. At first sight, one could argue that the (Hebrew and Christian) manna is also an interruption. Manna is a gift that interrupts a community that hungers and is near to losing hope, and opens up a new collective realization of being loved by God who nourishes his people and gives hope for a promised collective future. From a Christian perspective, one could also say that God interrupts historicity by becoming incarnate and further becoming food and drink as an act of self-sharing, as well as an invitation to share with one another this divine gift. An initial reflection could lead one to argue that the eucharistic performance is, thus, interruptive.

Yet, from a Christian angle, there is "more" in the eucharistic gift than mere interruption. The bread of eternal life that is Christ is not a merely extrinsic and unilateral intervention. Undoubtedly it is an instance of a freely giving love and grace initiated from a prior intra-Trinitarian reciprocal love, which is further shared, *ex nihilo*, with creation. But for this same reason the divine gift is already both reciprocal and *intrinsic* or inherent in creation. All creation is a gift: its "isness" is as much a gift as it is gratitude. As I argued in chapter 3, Being is already a gift from the Creator, and participates in divinity. The sophianicity of Being is the gift-character of all that "is" by virtue of being nourished by God's Wisdom

---

[91]   Cited in Enrique Dussel, "From the Second Vatican Council to the Present Day," in id. (ed.), *The Church in Latin America 1492–1992* (New York: Orbis Books, 1992), 168. Dussel cites a homily given in Rome, Oct. 1983, in *Servir*, 28 (1983), 1.

and Love. The same goes for creatures who, as Milbank correctly explains following de Lubac, are not mere recipients of the divine gift, since they are already themselves "this gift."[92] The capacity to receive is already a gift (a gift to a gift). Incarnation and the Eucharist enter into the heart of the flesh of human *pathos* in order to recover and reorient what is somehow already "there," and yet it becomes "more itself" through God's plenitudinous sharing that is the incarnate Logos. One could say, then, that, more than a mere interruption, the eucharistic gift is a *completion* of both creation and humanity. The divine gift sets in motion the possibility of accomplishment or fulfillment of such a deifying process. The Eucharist intensifies this intrinsic gift-character of creation and further performs a rich mixture of gift exchanges that go from the inner Trinitarian exchange to an exchange of divinity with both materiality and humanity, and which is then presented as a doxological return of the gift to God in Christ's perfect self-offering at the altar, and within concrete communities gathered in the presence of the Holy Spirit. The eucharistic sharing reorients space and time by reawakening a memorial of God's self-sharing with all that already "is" while envisioning a more plenitudinous sphere of this "isness" that is allegorized as a collective future eschatological wedding banquet – that final feast yet to come. Babette turns her culinary gift into a "love affair" that satiates both physical and spiritual hungers. Similarly, the Eucharist tells of God as an edible gift freely given out of a reciprocal intra-Trinitarian love that feeds humanity's longings by making them intimate (beloved) companions at this delightful banquet of love; and this sharing brings about transformation (deification, which is not suppression) by providing physical and spiritual nourishment. And, simultaneously, because it is excessive, it promises yet more to taste. Praying to *Abba* to give us today our daily bread means to be constantly, daily nourished while being constantly renewed by the desire – appetite – for yet more to be given.

While there is transformation, Being and the created order are not at all "surpassed" or canceled in this receiving and sharing of the divine gift. The eucharistic gift reaffirms the materiality of bread and wine, the body and the senses; it affirms humanity and expresses a radical solidarity toward those who hunger and are outcasts (Matt. 25). There is a highly flavored sense of mutuality in play here, for divine agency through the Incarnation takes place within a gesture of hospitality offered by humanity: for instance, Mary's *Fiat* becomes, in the midst of grace, the welcoming

---

[92]   John Milbank, *The Suspended Middle: Henri de Lubac and the Debate Concerning the Supernatural* (Grand Rapids: Eerdmans, 2005), 43.

receptivity of humanity to the divine gift sent by the Holy Spirit. This is parallel to Babette, the stranger who is welcomed, and whose gift therefore expresses itself already in the midst of hospitality. One could say that the paradigm in *Babette's Feast* displays the gift as already taking place on some level of exchange rather than being merely the reception of a unilateral gift. And regarding the eucharistic gift, the fact that there is a specific historical narrative, embodiment, bread and wine, a gathered community, a liturgical and sacramental space and time, and so on, expresses the complex system of gift exchange that is staged or performed in the eucharistic sharing.[93] As I have argued, the eucharistic sharing is a performance of relationality wherein self and other are mutually complementing and constituting. This reciprocal dimension of the eucharistic gift sharply displays what I have called the complex entanglement of the "in-betweenness" of Being: immanent–transcendent, human–divine, material–spiritual, nature–grace, and so forth.[94] The eucharistic gift, which is always expressed as a dynamic sharing, deconstructs and moves beyond antagonizing dichotomies. This dynamic sharing is enacted at the heart of situatedness: that which is the locus wherein the in-betweenness coincides. If we use a visual image, we could paraphrase James K. A. Smith by saying that the eucharistic sharing is a performance on the "stage of the world" wherein "the invisible is seen *in* the visible, such that seeing the visible is to see more than the visible. This zone of immanence is where transcendence plays itself out, unfolding itself in a way that is staged by the Creator."[95] But, as I argued before, this eucharistic performance is much more than a visual and audible experience, for this form of divine alimentation also involves higher and deeper levels of agapeic/erotic intimacy such as touching, tasting, eating, and drinking.

4   Sharing in the Body of Christ: The Theopolitics of Superabundance

The Trinitarian intrinsic sharing of the superabundant divine gift is further shared with humanity as Christ's own body and blood. This divine self-sharing as food and drink, this sacred banquet, reminds us that God is attentive to the most primary needs of his people, for he not only

[93]   This is one of the main arguments in Catherine Pickstock, *After Writing: On the Liturgical Consummation of Philosophy* (Oxford: Blackwell, 1998).
[94]   This complex entanglement is what John Milbank calls, after de Lubac, the "suspended middle." See Milbank, *The Suspended Middle*.
[95]   Smith, *Introducing Radical Orthodoxy*, 222–3.

brings about physical and spiritual nourishment but also incorporates the partakers into his own Trinitarian community. As God becomes bread from heaven in order to nourish and constitute his own Body, so the members of the ecclesial community are called to nourish one another. From an ecclesial perspective (founded upon the Eucharist) the public communal and celebratory circulation of the gift shapes the life of the *polis*.

In view of this sharing in the same divine Body, the eucharistic practice presents a great challenge both to the church and to the entire world. Érico João Hammes puts it succinctly:

> Sharing at Jesus' table means extending it for more people, making space for others to eat, finding fulfillment in setting the table for those who are hungry. The table extended in this way becomes a feast, a banquet at which humankind and divine mystery mingle in mutual fellowship.[96]

In the current increasingly globalized world, superabundance becomes paradoxical, if not scandalous. Few people live in opulence, yet a great number live in extreme poverty.[97] As Marion Nestle and Samuel Wells argue, the problem is not so much a lack of resources; the real problem is the human refusal to share and care for one another, particularly those who are in most need in our midst.[98] Clear examples of this are the realities of world hunger and malnutrition, which are as pervasive as extreme poverty: more than 1 billion people subsist on less than one dollar a day,

---

[96]   Érico João Hammes, "Stones into Bread: Why Not? Eucharist-Koinonia-Diaconate," trans. Paul Burns, *Concilium*, 2 (2005), 32.

[97]   For a study of this paradox, see H. Levenstein, *Paradox of Plenty: A Social History of Eating in Modern America* (Oxford: Oxford University Press, 1993). In the US this paradox of plenty is creating a greater gap between the rich and the poor. A recent article in the London *Observer* – Paul Harris, "Wake Up: The American Dream is Over" (June 2006) – reveals the following US reality: "This [economic gap between rich and poor] has lead to an economy hugely warped in favour of a small slice of very rich Americans. The wealthiest one percent of households now control a third of the national wealth. The wealthiest 10 percent control two-thirds of it. This is a society that is splitting down the middle and it has taken place against a backdrop of economic growth. Between 1980 and 2004 America's GDP went up by almost two-thirds. But instead of making everyone better off, it has made only a part of the country wealthier, as another part slips ever more into the black hole of the working poor. There are now 37 million Americans living in poverty, and at 12.7 percent of the population, it is the highest percentage in the developed world." <www.observer.guardian.co.uk/columnists/story/0,,1792399,00.html>.

[98]   See Nestle, *Food Politics*; Wells, *God's Companions*.

and more than 800 million people have too little to eat to meet their daily energy needs.[99]

I agree with Frei Betto, who points out that alleviating hunger is not just about giving food to people or making donations, but also requires more holistic action that targets structural change:

> The aim is to mobilize world resources, under UN supervision, in order to finance entrepreneurial schemes, co-operative movements, and sustainable development in the poorest regions. Hunger cannot be fought just through donations, or even by transfer of funds. These need to be complemented by effective policies of structural change, such as agrarian and fiscal reforms that are capable of lessening the concentration of income from land and financial dealings. And all this has to be guaranteed by a daring policy of loans and credit offered to the beneficiary families, who must become the target of an intense educational programme, so that they can become socio-economic units and active agents in political and historical processes.[100]

Alleviating hunger also requires a theopolitical vision rooted in eucharistic sharing to promote the sort of structural changes that Frei Betto advocates. For prior – and even counter – to the hegemony of the policy of the secular state, which emphasizes proprietary rights and runs the risk of treating humans as merely individual parties to a contract, the eucharistic envisioning of co-abiding with a Trinitarian God ensures that people are embraced as integral members of the same divine Body – a divine gift that cannot be privately possessed by anyone since, as I have argued, it is already a communally shared reality. This eucharistic envisioning of the edible gift claims that "food matters" (see chapter 3), precisely because at the heart of the material – that is an entanglement of social, economic, cultural, and political realities – there is a theological realm, which is the co-abiding of divinity with humanity.

The body politic of the church is, then, centered on a practice of table fellowship: where sharing is an enactment of participation or co-belonging with one another, humanity with creation, and the whole of creation with God. In this body, and at this table, all members are interdependent.

---

[99]   This information is taken from the Food and Agriculture Organization, <www.fao.org/faostat/foodsecurity/MDG/MDG-Goal1_en.pdf>. See also Nestle, *Food Politics*; Wells, *God's Companions*.

[100]   Frei Betto, "Zero Hunger: An Ethical-Political Project," *Concilium*, 2 (2005), 11–23: 13.

The interdependence, which is the catholicity of Christ's Body, configures a complex sense of spatiality where the universal and the local, the living and the dead, transcendence and immanence belong together, yet without annihilating each other, but instead celebrating harmonious difference. In addition, the catholicity of this body also configures a complex sense of temporality wherein past, present, and future, *chronos* and *kairos*, also belong together without annulling one another. The complex spatiality and temporality of the ecclesial body enables us to reach beyond secular boundaries wherein the private and public, the political and the religious, are often mutually antagonistic. By embodying a participatory politics of God's kingdom the ecclesial body can open up a space where everyone (particularly the outcast) is spiritually and physically nourished. And this reaching out to the outcast also challenges borders set up by Christendom, for by virtue of divine participation, God's kingdom is always in excess of institutional margins (as Jesus' parable of the Good Samaritan continues to teach and challenge us all – a particular challenge to Christians).

The paradox of plenty also reflects a problem of the disparity between quality and quantity, particularly when the issue is food. For instance, Marion Nestle explains that in the US, where there is an overabundance of food, there is also an increase in chronic health-related problems because of poor diet choices such as an intake of foods that are higher in calories, fat, meat, sugar, and so on. Nestle points out that obesity (particularly among children) ranks as the most serious health problem in the US:

> Rates of obesity are now so high among American children that many exhibit metabolic abnormalities formerly seen only in adults. The high blood sugar due to "adult-onset" (insulin-resistant type 2) diabetes, the high blood cholesterol, and the high blood pressure now observed in younger and younger children constitute a national scandal. Such conditions increase the risk of coronary heart disease, cancer, stroke, and diabetes later in life. From the late 1970s to the early 1990s, the prevalence of *overweight* nearly doubled – from 8% to 14% among children aged 6–11 and from 6% to 12% among adolescents. The proportion of overweight adults rose from 25% to 35% in those years. Just between 1991 and 1998, the rate of adult *obesity* increased from 12% to nearly 18%. Obesity contributes to increased health care costs, thereby becoming an issue for everyone, overweight or not.[101]

---

[101] Nestle, *Food Politics*, 8 (emphasis in original).

Nestle argues that, in countries such as the US, diet choices most often have to do with education, social attitudes regarding food, income, etc. But, according to Nestle, the problem mainly derives from the invasive and powerful influence (or "manipulation") of the food industry over American eating habits. "Eat more" – that is the slogan that most food companies advertise in the US:

> In a competitive food marketplace, food companies must satisfy stockholders by encouraging more people to eat more of their products. They seek new audiences among children, among members of minority groups, or internationally. They expand sales to existing as well as new audiences through advertising but also by developing new products designed to respond to consumer "demands." In recent years, they have embraced a new strategy: increasing the sizes of food portions. Advertising, new products, and larger portions all contribute to a food environment that promotes eating more, not less.[102]

It is not too surprising that one of the most profitable businesses in the US is precisely the food industry. In capitalist societies the notion of overabundance is used as a tool to manipulate human desires (eros). In this configuration of eros, desire is always a lack, thus a need for "more" since not only can nothing fully satisfy, but also desire itself generates more desire in a perpetual and obsessive cycle. Octavio Paz points at the irony of the liberal market of post-industrial capitalism that "has brought about [over] abundance, but ... has converted Eros into one of its employees."[103]

This capitalist practice of overabundance corrupts desire by, on the one hand, putting it in the context of perpetually unsatisfied desire for an empty (because perpetually lacking) sign searching for "more." Yet, on the other hand, this practice also claims total ownership over acquired goods. In doing so, it promotes competition and rivalry, which further ruptures the sociality (a sense of co-belonging and sharing) of desire.

Moreover, in the current era of capitalist globalization, the connection between what we put into our mouths and the human labor implied in producing it, as well as the connection between what we eat with the ecological dimension of its production, is rapidly disappearing. And,

---

[102] Ibid., 21. Also, for a parallel description of the problem of the influence of food companies over the public's eating habits, see the documentary *Super Size Me*, written and directed by Morgan Spurlock.

[103] Octavio Paz, "Eroticism and Gastrosophy," *Daedalus* (Fall 1972), 67–85: 85.

needless to say, the awareness of the relation between our food at the table and God's gracious sharing is virtually lost.

The eucharistic meal exposes these broken realities of our own eating practices, massive food waste, labor exploitation, and lack of an effective practice of sharing food with our neighbor. For we must not forget that divine superabundance equals God's generosity and hospitality, and as such it presents a challenge to the greediness of capitalist consumerism. Thus, the erotic/agapeic eucharistic gift (a superabundant gift of alimentation) could serve as a counter-practice to this capitalist crafting of desire. The theopolitical practice of the eucharistic ecclesia orients and disciplines desires toward God, and toward making communion with one another.

Moreover, a public practice of feasting can also orient and discipline individual and social desire. From a eucharistic context, feasting is a collective celebration of God's presence among us given as bread. Feasting is a collective expression of gratitude for this superabundant divine edible gift. But it is also a call to incorporate (by sharing with one another) the whole community into this expression of thanksgiving.

Fasting is also another practice for a discipline and orientation of desire, for it reminds humanity ultimately to trust in God's providential care. It reminds humanity that one does not live "by bread alone" but "by every word that comes from the mouth of God" (Deut. 8:3). Fasting could also be a public expression of protest on behalf of those who hunger in the world, for the exploitation of human labor, the devastation of the planet, and so forth. From a Catholic perspective, fasting is, then, intrinsically an ecclesial performance – beyond private devotional practices – that embraces the reality that sharing food is indeed political.

In a eucharistic context, then, both practices of feasting and fasting are indispensable for rooting appetite in the interdependence of divine–human desire, keeping a hunger that is not an ultimate lacking but an immersion in plenitude and sharing.

Conclusion

Alimentation is the gift that heals hunger, a gift that nourishes our basic hunger for an-other. Alimentation as gift, and gift as alimentation, display a political dimension of interdependence, which takes place in a complex dynamics of gift exchange. At the heart of the cosmos there is an intimate metabolic exchange of nourishing and being nourished: a "cosmic banquet," to recall Bulgakov's notion (see chapter 3). But, as I have already argued, from a Trinitarian, sophianic, and eucharistic perspective, the gift, hunger or appetite (which is ultimately a desire for God) is not a mark of mere lack or privation. Instead, and by virtue of God's superabundance, desire is a mark of excess, plenitude, and sharing.[104] In this giving and sharing of divine desire in the form of food and drink, Christianity proclaims a being incorporated into the Body of Christ, which already shares in the eternal gift of the Trinity. Gerard Loughlin puts it as follows:

> Gift and given, Christ and the donees who receive him, are one. To receive the gift of God is to be incorporated into the triune life, into the eternity of donation, of giving and receiving back again. Indeed, the unity of the body of Christ is the unity of giver, gift and given – of teller, story and listener; of playwright, play and player; of *host, meal and guest* – and the unity of the Body is the presence given in the present of the Eucharist.[105]

The excess and delight in sharing the edible gift that is God's becoming nourishment is, like Babette's feast, transformative. It constitutes the theopolitics of an agapeic/erotic community of mutual givers that is the Body of Christ – that which *makes* the ecclesial community. To receive the divine edible gift, is thus both an individual and a communal vocation to also becoming (by *imitatio Trinitatis*) nourishment. Beyond mere abstraction and speculation, this alimentary participation in the Body of Christ leads to a practice – because it is already inaugurated by a Trinitarian divine practice – that shapes and gives meaning to the theopolitics of the church.

On more than one occasion in this book I have insisted that, without caritas, we starve to death. Thus, my argument here is not only about participation, but, and to a far greater extent, about the *performance* of caritas. The performance of caritas implies, as Pope Benedict XVI remarks in his first encyclical letter *Deus Caritas Est*, entering into the very dynamic of divine self-giving, which is God's nourishing love:

> The ancient world had dimly perceived that man's real food – what truly nourishes him as man – is ultimately the *Logos*, eternal wisdom: this same *Logos* now truly becomes food for us – as love.

---

[104] Webb puts it as follows: "God gives abundantly, in order to create more giving, the goal of which is a mutuality born of excess but directed toward equality and justice. Christianity affirms both excess and mutuality by taking them to the extreme point – located through hope on an eschatological horizon – where they meet, one leading the other." *The Gifting God*, 9.

[105] Gerard Loughlin, *Telling God's Story: Bible, Church and Narrative Theology* (Cambridge: Cambridge University Press, 1996), 242 (emphasis added).

The Eucharist draws us into Jesus' act of self-oblation. More than just statically receiving the incarnate *Logos*, we enter into the very dynamic of his self-giving.[106]

The eucharistic feasting is participation in and performance of (within a complex dimension of space and time) divine caritas. It calls for creating concrete communities where communal sharing is as much a vocation as it is a challenge to our own global economies of scarcity and greed – at that precise wounded spot where superabundance is devoid of divine sharing. As an alternative to a model of political practice founded upon the atomization of communities in contractual relations, this entire book, and this chapter in particular, propose envisioning and enacting a holy (eucharistic) communion with one another, and with a God who shares divinity by becoming manna, alimentation. You could not get a more complete act of feeding than that.

---

[106] Benedict XVI, *Deus Caritas Est*, part I, 13: <www.vatican.va/holy_father/benedict_xvi/encyclicals/documents/hf_ben-xvi_enc_20051225_deus-caritas-est_en.html>.

Conclusion

Food Notes: Prolegomenon to a Eucharistic Discourse

As I have outlined in this book, I first shared Doña Soledad's *mole* recipe among friends in Mexico City at a farewell party before moving to Cambridge to start writing my thesis. Throughout the process of writing, from start to finish, this Mexican dish has nurtured my imagination and been a source of inspiration for articulating what I have called alimentary theology. Therefore, just as I began this book with a taste of *molli*, I believe it is equally appropriate to wrap it up with a further tasting of it – "food for thought" – as I list four main points that highlight some suggestive conclusions.

First, there is an aspect of "performativity" that the making of *molli* so strongly evokes. One learns how to make *molli* by enacting the recipe: from gathering the ingredients to preparing, grinding, cooking, and eating the dish. The Mexican baroque stories of *molli* also start in the midst of "action": the cooking of Sor Andrea de la Asunción and Fray Pascual Bailón. This is a making that is anticipated by the earlier pre-Colombian origins of *molli*, which was then hybridized by an intercontinental baroque cuisine. The process of writing this book on food matters has also situated me within performance. It was not enough to submerge myself in the interdisciplinary material surrounding the complex subject of food; I also sought to approach all the meals that I ate, and most particularly all the meals that I cooked – usually for Dominican communities, friends, and family – as fields of investigation for my writing.

Writing this book has been similar to the process of making *molli*: a discerning of overlapping ingredients, and searching for alchemical processes to bring about some form of personal, and I hope communal, nourishment. In the process I have learned that theology is indeed an art that one learns in the actual making of it. Cooking and researching were also blended with other actions that equally informed my theological arguments. Some of these actions included daily prayers at communal liturgies, daily partaking of the eucharistic banquet, leading group reflections on the interrelated subjects of food and theology, and engaging in dialogue with different people and from different backgrounds on subjects related to food matters.

In this performative alimentary theology there must be a process of digestion, which is a form of interpretation, and of hermeneutical discernment. Theology forever performs an "alimentary hermeneutics." In this hermeneutical process the theologian is somehow transformed by what she or he "eats." Some of these edible signs are already supplied by the theologian's particular milieu: culture, language, doctrine, traditions, and so forth. This theological ingestion is also nurtured by a constant process of listening, observing, and letting oneself be led by imagination and inspiration. Hence the general analogy between theology and food: food becomes part of our bodies, just as actions and contexts become part of a body of theological practice. But the theologian may also become an agent for both personal transformation and for communal practices. Here one could also point out an analogy between *molli* and theology, which recalls that the main purpose of making *molli* is to share something, and to transform spaces and temporality into "festivity," just as theology is to be shared among communities, healing hungers and thus recovering the sense of a communal (human–divine) banqueting. Thus, as a first conclusion I want to reiterate the relevance of acknowledging that theology in general, and alimentary theology in particular, is best learned in the actual making and sharing, in the midst of an action that is already a hybrid of many more actions and practices. And here action is intimately related to contemplation, just as Word and Silence mutually constitute each other.

A second point I would like to emphasize is the fact that the writing of this book has led me to enter the world of cuisine in general, and of cooking *molli* in particular. Cuisine is about transforming ingredients into dishes made with the purpose of nurturing and – hopefully – providing joy to body and soul. Cuisine translates culinary signs such as recipes, traditions, and substances, and presents them in a transfigured alimentary form.[1] Cuisine is also about creating alchemical mixtures between ingredients, traditions, peoples, time, and space. Theology is analogous to cuisine in that it sets us in the midst of a complex mixture of ingredients such as traditions, doctrines, beliefs, personal and communal experiences of sharing, and the intermediate space between humanity

[1] For more on "culinary signs," see Louis Marin, *Food for Thought*, trans. Mette Hjort (Baltimore: Johns Hopkins University Press, 1989).

and God. In chapter 3 I remarked that this space of the "in between" is called by William Desmond the "metaxogical," a notion that echoes Plato's *Symposium*, which is set in the context of a banquet, or a post-banqueting convivial reflection on the satiation of desires. Theology, like cuisine and the making of *molli*, is a performance of the *metaxu* where God and humanity blend desires without annulling difference.

Thus, theology – and here I call it "alimentary" – is about the mixing of many ingredients and transforming signs for the purpose of creating a nurturing product that can also and hopefully bring about delight. Like cuisine, and like the making of *molli*, theology should be a refined crafting, a making that is both aesthetic and brings about communal goodness, so that people can genuinely utter the Psalmist's expression of gratitude, "O taste and see how good is the Lord."

Thirdly, as a Catholic – a particular form of enacting Christian doctrines and practices – I have argued that matters of food are closely related to the Eucharist. As Claude Fischler remarks, the vitality and intimacy of eating food is ever intensified by the act of performing-via-eating at the eucharistic table. The Eucharist is primarily a vital and intimate alimentary action: God's kenotic sharing as bread, humanity's alleviating hunger by participating in God via food and drink, a communal re-enactment of early Christian narratives of Christ's Last Supper, a sacramental celebration of thanksgiving to God performed by a community – Christ's Body – gathered in the presence of the Holy Spirit, and so on. From this "alimentary" perspective, the Eucharist is the culinary sign-as-gift par excellence, for it is an action that transfigures hunger into satiety and individualism into a communal feasting, and that deifies humanity along with all creation by enacting a cosmic-divine banquet. Being paradigmatic of a culinary sign, the Eucharist enacts multiple translations that transit from one sign to another, such that Christ's absence is translated into presence in the edible signs of bread and wine that further signal Christ's body and blood, which then signify the ecclesial Body. Here, sign and body co-arise, rendering meaning and signification as, effectively, a doxological and alimentary event.

In this sense, then, the Eucharist is also intrinsically metaxological, for it is an ecstatic enactment of the in-betweenness of God and creation, transcendence and immanence, word and action, desire and satiation, eros and agape, self and other. A reflection on food matters can highlight a dimension of interdependence in all living organisms, and so increase the awareness of what ultimately takes place in the eucharistic performance, which is the enactment of multiple interdependencies and the *metaxu*.

My fourth and final point is that food and alimentation describe something fundamental about what takes place in the Eucharist, but that the converse is also true. I have argued that paying closer attention to the message of the Eucharist poses a challenge to us to reorient our own daily exchanges of God's gift-as-bread. The eucharistic banquet makes it more evident that food should not be a fetish, but should primarily be offered to provide physical and spiritual nourishment. The Eucharist tells a story of "what's cooking" by virtue of divine caritas, which is a lavish banquet inviting us to bring about true nourishment, and so allowing us to become more who we are called to be.

To nourish implies a movement beyond the self in order to respond to the other's hunger, and in this act create a space of true *convivium* that reveals new meanings of the self as being constituted by the other. The Spanish term for *convivium* is *convivir*, which is a twofold notion: to *live*, and *with*. It means to create a communal space, which is inaugurated by a gesture of hospitality that offers nourishment to the other.[2] In creating a space of *convivencia*, alimentation enacts a dynamic of gift exchange: it is giving, receiving, and returning the gift in gratitude and friendship. If all these things are possible because of alimentation, this is even more true in the case of the eucharistic sharing that reveals Being as intrinsically relational. The Eucharist is believed to be a *sacrum convivium*: God offering hospitality by becoming food and co-abiding with the other. Such divine–human eucharistic action opens up a time and space of fellowship wherein physical and spiritual hunger will be no more.

When I look at Catholic liturgies, and the actual life of Catholics, I painfully realize how far we are from the vision I have outlined in this book. I feel a similar disappointment when I look at our daily exchanges of food, both at local and global levels, including our devastating treatment of our ecological resources. But I am also aware that somehow all action, and most particularly eucharistic action, contains within itself a surplus of meaning that overflows all possible calculations. In faith, I believe that God's self-giving over and over again, despite our rejection and indifference, still brings about some form of nourishment, telling a story of hope in divine caritas that is meant to be embraced in our daily life. Since the Eucharist also narrates an eschatological banquet it is forever open to mystery. Faith tells me that there is yet more to taste of and to be nourished by God. I thus acknowledge that this book is only a prolegomenon to a eucharistic, open-ended discourse, a prayer to God to give us today our daily bread.

---

[2] For a further exploration on the notion of *convivencia* as a precondition to discussions and practices of interculturality and theology, see Orlando O. Espín, "Toward the Construction of an Intercultural Theology of Tradition," *Journal of Hispanic/Latino Theology*, 9/3 (Feb. 2002), 22–59.

Index

Manufactured by Amazon.ca
Bolton, ON